A Shirt Box F...

The Autob...

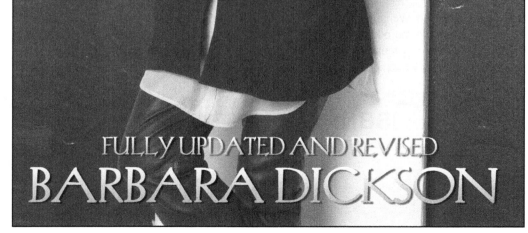

FULLY UPDATED AND REVISED

BARBARA DICKSON

Typeset by Jonathan Downes, edited by Corinna Downes, scanned by Andrea Rider
Cover and Layout by SPiderKaT for CFZ Communications, Chloe Gray
Using Microsoft Word 2000, Microsoft Publisher 2000, Adobe Photoshop CS.

First published in Great Britain by Gonzo Multimedia

c/o Brooks City,
6th Floor New Baltic House
65 Fenchurch Street,
London EC3M 4BE
Fax: +44 (0)191 5121104
Tel: +44 (0) 191 5849144
International Numbers:
Germany: Freephone 08000 825 699
USA: Freephone 18666 747 289

© Gonzo Multimedia MMXI

ISBN: 978-1-908728-68-5

To: Oliver, Colm, Gabriel, and Archie.
The Men in my Life.

C⊕NTENTS

ACKN⊕WLEDGEMENTS

With thanks to: Willy Russell for being such a good friend and a great talent in whose light I've basked throughout my career; and my brother, Alastair, for being a huge influence on me for the good, and an inspiration artistically.

So much of what I've written here would have been impossible without help: many details had disappeared in the mists of time. The following have better memories than me and have helped enormously with fine tuning (and in the case of Ian, some funny stories I'd forgotten). So, I'd like to salute Ian McCalman, Rab Noakes, Dick Gaughan, Dave Emery, Jack Beck, John and Cathy Watt, Hilda Lynch, Alan Clyde and Sheila Caldwell in particular for filling in those gaps.

Alan Clyde for help and sorting.

Wendy McCance and Bob McDevitt at Hachette Scotland for all the guidance.

Finally, without John KV Eunson, I'd have been lost at sea! His 'guid and true' Shetland seamanship has steered the boat; it seems like millions of years ago that we sat having a cup of tea in Lincoln Cathedral tea shop with me vacillating about whether to do this at all. Look, you have the evidence of his powers of persuasion in your hands. It's been a long voyage.

Sadly, in April 2009, my mother Ruth died and I've had time to reflect on what a great influence she has been on me. As Elaine Paige kindly pointed out, I was very lucky to have my mother alive until I reached sixty-one years of age. I think this means that I have to be a real grown-up now so here goes.

FOREWORD BY WILLY RUSSELL

Perhaps we should begin by giving thanks to that civil servant who once refused to allow a young member of his staff to go off and sing in Scandinavia.

One day someone might raise a statue to this particular stickler for it was he and his refusal to allow her to take unpaid leave that got the goat of a gangling girl, giving her the kick she needed to get the hell out of the civil service and do what she was born to do - sing. It really isn't too far-fetched to imagine that had it not been for such a kick we may well never have heard of Barbara Dickson, singer and actress: she has never chased celebrity or stardom, never needed fame, never for one second lived anywhere near Planet Barbara. In an age where we - the once proudly reserved and restrained Brits - now appear to chase fame and flaunt naked ambition with the same wanton abandon as the American cousins we once mocked for doing so, it is genuinely refreshing to be reminded that, for Barbara, it has always been work that comes first. Everything else, all the nonsense of celebrity, fame and stardom is not what Barbara does - merely a result of it. Never aloof or remote from the attentions of her fans and admirers, she accepts such attention and affirmation as enthusiasm not for what she is but for what she does.

A few years ago I asked Barbara if she'd contribute some backing vocals to an album of songs I'd recorded. How preposterous is that sentence! *I* asked Barbara Dickson to sing *backing vocals*! Given the limited quality of my singing voice (truly, an acquired taste), for me to ask Ms Dickson to sing mere *backing* is about the equivalent of Bob The Builder asking Sir Christopher Wren to go on the hod! Of course, Barbara being Barbara, she didn't hesitate to say yes and so we arranged to do the recording in a small studio close to Barbara's Lincolnshire village. Having set aside a couple of days for this, we then did little but watch and marvel as Barbara proceeded to nail everything quite beautifully in considerably less than a couple of hours, leaving plenty of time for me to then accompany her on the real business at hand - a shopping tour of the town where, from fishmongers to greengrocers, wine-merchants to grocers she was uniformly greeted not as 'Barbara' or 'Ms Dickson', but as 'Mrs Cookson'. I'd always known Barbara to be one of the rare ones who somehow managed to achieve the right kind of balance between being known and being oneself. But, more than ever, that shopping trip forcefully brought home to me how this woman, who has admirably earned the right to some significant pride in her achievements as both singer and actress, has every bit as much genuine pride in being the woman, the wife and the mother.

I don't doubt for a second that Barbara would have lived a rich, fulfilled and varied life even if the headlights of fame and success had not been shone on her. That, though, would have been our loss. And along with giving thanks to that civil servant, perhaps we should also give great thanks that Mrs Cookson will sometimes take a night off, put up her feet and take a well-earned rest - leaving it to Barbara Dickson to do the business.

Willy Russell.

CHAPTER ONE
BUTTONS AND BOWS

ne fine summer's day in 1949, in Dunfermline in Fife, a postman on his round in Chalmers Street, just off the High Street, heard singing drifting on the breeze. As he listened he recognised the tune - it was the song 'Buttons And Bows' from the film *The Paleface*, a popular comedy western starring Jane Russell and Bob Hope released the year before. As he kept walking he realised it was coming from Mrs Jessie Dickson's house. It didn't sound to him like the radio or a record and, strangely, though he could clearly hear the melody, he couldn't make out any of the words.

Finally, the postman traced the source: to his astonishment, the music was not coming from the house at all, but from a pram in the garden, where the bairn strapped inside was happily singing away. This, according to family legend, is how baby Barbara Ruth Dickson, not quite two, made her public singing debut. By all accounts, though I did not know any of the words, I was, reassuringly, pretty much in tune.

I have always wondered if the story might be ever so slightly of the shaggy dog variety, but my mother always insisted that this was exactly what happened and that, from the very beginning, I loved music and loved to sing. Although I do have to point out that it was also my mother who claimed that I was a very calm and sweet child and absolutely no trouble at all. Which, considering that for the rest of my life 'calm' and 'sweet' are probably the last two adjectives you would use to describe me, does give you pause for thought.

I had arrived on 27 September 1947 in Dunfermline Maternity Hospital - which, sadly, no longer exists - one of the many millions of baby-boomers born immediately after the war and in the same year as a host of wonderful fellow singers and musicians including David Bowie, Gerry Rafferty, Emmylou Harris and Sandy Denny. Not a bad vintage, 1947. And on the very day I used my vocal cords for the first time, two other well-known entertainers also made their first appearances: across the Atlantic in America, the shy and retiring Meat Loaf, best known for *Bat Out Of Hell*; and, closer to home, in the town of Crieff in Perthshire, one of our most popular actors and star of *Local Hero*, Denis Lawson. Coincidentally, thirty-seven years later, when I won the 1984 Society of West End Theatre award for Best Actress in a Musical for the role of Mrs Johnstone in *Blood Brothers*, it was Denis who was named Best Actor in a Musical for *Mr Cinders*. We even had our picture taken together for the first time.

In 1947, a world away from the West End stage, my parents and I were living with Jessie Dickson, my granny, and Uncle Bob, my dad's unmarried brother, in Chalmers Street. Granny had been born Jessie Forgie, into a farming family from Bannockburn near Stirling - scene of the famous battle in 1314 involving Robert the Bruce and the English king Edward II, who ended up going home to think again. Granny Jessie and her husband, James Dickson from Penicuik in Midlothian, just south of Edinburgh, had nine children: David, Willie, Bob, Ella, Jim; twins Douglas and Mabel; Alastair, my father, and Muriel. My dad remembered a family visit, as a young boy, to a sister of Granny Jessie's who had moved to California and married a coalmine owner. It was not as epic a journey as you might imagine since this was not California, USA but California the mining village in Stirlingshire. If my father had hoped for a taste of American opulence he wasn't completely disappointed: the family was met at the station by his aunt's clan, who came to pick them up in an impressive Model T Ford. My granny was transported to her sister's home in style, but as there wasn't enough room for anyone else my father and his brothers and sisters could only watch the car gliding off into the distance and follow on foot.

Grandpa James worked for Prudential Assurance and he and Jessie had lived in Elgin in the north-east of Scotland for a while before settling in Dunfermline where Grandpa had been promoted to superintendent. The Dicksons occupied the large flat in Chalmers Street where I spent the first months of my life. Despite my grandfather's position at the Pru, they were not what you would call well-to-do - even in those days nine kids was a lot of mouths to feed - but they were certainly not poor. Just ordinary, hard-working Scottish folk.

When my father was born in 1915, his eldest sister, Ella, who was no more than eight herself, was often given the task of looking after the new baby. This would cause my dad great embarrassment in later life since his second sister, Mabel, who always liked a laugh, took great pleasure in bringing up the family story of my dad, as a wee boy, calling out from the bathroom: 'Ee-ya, vipe my bum!' David, the eldest, was fifteen. A year later, still two years under the official age, he lied about how old he was and joined the Gordon Highlanders to fight in the Great War. His was the famous regiment immortalised in the music-hall song:

A Gordon for me, a Gordon for me
If you' re nae a Gordon, you' re nae use tae me.

A photograph of Uncle David, resplendent in his uniform, kilt and Glengarry bonnet, took pride of place in the 'best room'.

Only a few months afterwards, at the Battle of the Somme, he was shot in the stomach and died of his wounds. He hadn't even made it to seventeen. My granny received letters from the chaplain and from one of David's officers at the Front, moving memorials of a young life tragically cut short. My cousin Bob has the originals to this day. The picture of David in his uniform remained in the best room, which was only ever used for special occasions, high days and holidays, or when people came to visit. The photograph was in a copper frame made by my Uncle Willie, when he was an apprentice at Rosyth Dockyard, the Royal Navy base a few miles from Dunfermline, in remembrance of his older brother.

I can still picture the best room, which always seemed sad and dark and lonely to me as a child. It had the formal atmosphere of an Edwardian parlour with its heavy, wooden upholstered chairs - one for the lady and one for the gentleman - and an upright settee in the same style. You always felt obliged to perch stiffly on the edge of your seat, on your best behaviour, carefully holding your cup of tea, served in the best china. There was also a piano with candlesticks attached to the front. Aunty Ella was the pianist of the family but when I was a little older and had started piano lessons, I would sneak in to play it whenever I got the chance, even though it was so neglected that it was always badly out of tune.

In another room in Granny's house stood Grandpa's wooden desk. Grandpa Dickson had died in 1945, two years before I was born, but his desk had remained in the house. It was made of oak and the drawer handles were carved with the heads of oriental beasts. I was fascinated by Grandpa's desk and my earliest memory, from when I was about three, is of crawling underneath it and hiding there. It was such a safe and reassuring place. At some point the desk was sawn in half, for some reason, but the two pieces were never thrown out, and many years later I rescued them and put the desk back together. It now resides at my Lincolnshire home, though my days of seeking sanctuary there are long behind me now.

My dad, Alastair, left school at fourteen in 1929 and found work as an apprentice grocer in Dunfermline in what was then rather grandly known as a grocer's emporium. After a few years he realised that selling coffee and tea for the rest of his life was not for him. He was young and keen to see a little of the world, or at least some of the world beyond Dunfermline. He had set his heart on joining the police force but in those days, incredible as it sounds - especially in a country full of short-arses - you had to be six foot tall to be eligible for the Scottish police force. My father was of above average height for the time; indeed, at five foot ten he would have been generally considered a tall man. But even pushing his shoulders back and standing as straight as possible he was still two inches too short. It was a bitter disappointment to him, but he refused to let go of his dream. In England, he discovered, although the average height of Englishmen was not noticeably different from that of Scotsmen, the minimum requirement was far more reasonable. To be accepted by the Metropolitan Police, for example, you only had to be five foot eight. But according to Dad's friend Danny Birrell, the place to be was Liverpool (five foot ten), and they had the best police cars in the country.

So, at the age of twenty-two, my father and Danny, who would later marry Aunty Muriel and become his brother-in-law, travelled down to Liverpool and started new lives as Merseyside policemen. Although it turned out to be a short-lived career for my father, he spoke often of how much he loved his job with the police and remembered those early days in England as the happiest time of his working life.

A year later, in 1939, war was declared and my father was seconded to the Liverpool Fire Service, at the Liverpool docks, to work as a fireman. It was while working here that he met Ruth Malley, a local telephonist, who had also been conscripted into the service.

While the Dicksons were a fairly typical Scottish family, the Malleys were much more complicated. My mother, Ruth, was born in a Liverpool pub called the Dart Hotel in December 1918, one month after the end of the First World War. As I'm sure anybody who knows me well would be surprised to learn, Ruth came from a long line of very forceful women. Her mother, Margaret Malley, had been married twice: first to a Mr Wilkinson from Liverpool, a union that produced four children, and then, after he died, to James Malley, also from Liverpool, with whom she had two further daughters - my Aunty Ivy in 1912 and my mother six years later.

James Malley might have had an Irish surname, but it seems doubtful that he had any Irish roots. Very little is known of his background at all as he told my Aunty Ivy that he had been adopted as a baby and we have never been able to find his original birth certificate to verify that claim. Family legend has it that he might have been the illegitimate son of a cotton broker from Greenock in the West of Scotland and adopted by a contact of his biological father's, a rope-works manager in Liverpool by the name of Malley. Whatever the truth, Grandfather James was certainly brought up in Liverpool and was a Scouser through and through, with very refined manners.

If James's background was nebulous, Margaret's was just as much of a mystery. Granny Malley's maiden name was Howarth but she never spoke about her childhood or her family or where the Howarths had come from and when she died, we could find absolutely no trace of her birth certificate, either. A longstanding family story had it that Granny Margaret's mother, Great-Granny Howarth (I hope you are keeping up), was not actually of English stock but the daughter of a Jewish Polish cavalry officer called Wolki who had sent his family to Liverpool for safekeeping when she was a child. It was in Liverpool that my great-grandmother then met and married a Mr Howarth and where Margaret, Granny Malley, was born in 1874.

For years my mother's side of the family accepted as gospel that they were of East European Jewish descent and I was excited and proud to have such an interesting history. The mystery of Granny Malley fuelled my interest in genealogy and when I was older I began to look more closely into my family tree, but could never find any confirmation of the story. It was only recently, and thanks to the mother of a good friend of mine, that I uncovered the truth. Great-Granny's maiden name had not been Wolki, and she was neither Polish nor Jewish. It was the rather less exotic Wookey, a traditional surname from Somerset (not to be confused with the Wookiees of *Star Wars* fame). The Wookeys must have tired of the local Cheddar and moved to Merseyside. Sadly, that put paid to the Jewish-Polish legend.

James Malley was by all accounts a lovely man, very cultured and affectionate. He was a licensed victualler, and owned the pub where my mother was born. A middle-aged widower with no children from his previous marriage, he adored the two young daughters who had burst into his life when he had probably long given up any thought of having a family. He also loved music and was a fine piano-player. My mother would often reminisce about watching her parents at the piano at home as a little girl in the 1920s, trying to join in while they sang popular songs of the time, which they'd heard at the Music Halls. 'Only A Bird In A Gilded Cage' was one she particularly remembered. She always talked of her early childhood as a happy time. If the Malleys were not well off, they were relatively secure. But after a business partnership went wrong in 1925 they began to feel the pinch financially and then, in 1950, the family's comfortable, stable life was abruptly ended when James Malley died.

My mother was only eleven, and the death of her father had a huge and lasting impact on her. It was not a period on which she liked to dwell, but what she did tell me about it was enough for me to realise how terribly hard it must have been. Now Granny Margaret was a widow for the second time and had to bring up my mother with little income beyond her widow's pension of ten shillings a week.

There was not a lot of money or work around in the Liverpool of the 1930s. Day-to-day life was tough and keeping their heads above water became all that mattered. At the end of the day, my granny would often go to the market to buy whatever food was being sold off cheaply to put that night's tea on the table and as for clothes and shoes, they would have to be mended again and again and worn long after they had been outgrown.

My mother was a bright child, but there was never any prospect of her being able to stay on in education beyond fourteen - it was essential that she started earning money as soon as possible. She once told me that she and Ivy had had their names down for Notre Dame, the prestigious girls' school in Liverpool, but after her father's financial circumstances had changed, that was completely out of the question. Instead my mum got a job as a machinist in a factory before becoming a telephonist, eventually being conscripted into the fire service.

She was twenty-four when she met my father and soon they were courting - to use that wonderful word that conveniently covers all possible romantic behaviour, whether innocent or illicit, without going into detail. The early stage of their relationship was not without its difficulties. The war still had several years to run and my father began to suffer from a series of increasingly debilitating throat infections that were not helped by his work as a fireman, where he was constantly soaked to the skin, or the fact that he continued to smoke. There were no antibiotics then to properly clear up the infection and each time my father was afflicted, it became more virulent.

Perhaps his ill health brought my mother and father closer together, perhaps they were always meant for each other. Whatever the case, within a year they decided to get married. The wedding took place in 1943, back in Scotland at Dunfermline Abbey, a Church of Scotland kirk on the site of the original magnificent twelfth-century abbey, burial place of many early Scottish kings and queens, including maybe the most famous of all, Robert the Bruce.

The happy couple did not have much of a chance to enjoy their big day or their honeymoon. In the lead-up to the wedding my father had once more succumbed to a severe throat infection and, although he was able to get through the ceremony and the reception, that evening he had a very high temperature and fever and had to be rushed to hospital. The diagnosis was not good. The infection had developed into rheumatic fever, a disease that damages the heart and which at the time was life-threatening. My father did recover, but it took him nine months. He was only twenty-eight when he became ill and it was the fact that he was still a relatively young man that more than anything gave him the strength to pull through. But he was left with a permanent heart defect and although by 1944 he was able to return to work, he was not fit enough to go back to being a fire-fighter. He then joined the army for the remainder of the war but, again owing to his ill health, he never saw active service. He did at least get to drive Sherman tanks, which was not bad for a man who never learned to drive a car.

When the war ended in 1945 my father was not considered well enough to resume the job he loved, being a bobby on the beat, and the Liverpool Police Service pensioned him off. He decided to return to Dunfermline and I think that my mother was keen to leave Merseyside. His father James had died that year and my parents moved back to live with my Granny Dickson. My mother viewed the move to Scotland with mixed feelings. On the one hand it meant having to leave her friends and family and the city she had lived in all her life for the unknown foreign land that was Fife. On the other, after a childhood and early adulthood that had not been without its hardships, a fresh start with my father held out the prospect of better fortune and happier times.

Whether moving in with Granny Jessie and Uncle Bob at Chalmers Street was exactly the new beginning my parents had hoped for I am not altogether sure, but by early 1947 my mother had another new beginning to look forward to: she discovered that she was expecting her first child.

She had a shortlist of three girl's names - Lorraine, Elaine and Barbara - and when I was born she plumped for Barbara. She had been determined not to go with either of my grannies' names and in fact none of the three favourites were to be found anywhere in the Dickson or Malley families. I asked her once why she chose Barbara. She just said that she liked it, and that when I arrived she thought it suited me better than Lorraine or Elaine. It was as simple as that. Interestingly though, when my brother came along four years later he was named James Alastair, James after both grandfathers and Alastair after my dad. But he was always called Wee Alastair, to differentiate him from Big Alastair (my dad) and, even more confusingly, Alastair Dickson, our cousin, who was always known as Alastair Dickson.

I must admit that I have always thought my parents chose my name well and that I do suit being called Barbara. The name is Greek in origin and means 'foreigner' or 'stranger'; it also has the same root as the word 'barbarian'. St Barbara, a third-century Christian saint and martyr, was one of the most popular early saints. When I went to Liverpool my name was shortened to Barb, which I didn't like very much. There were quite a few Barbaras around in the 1940s and 1950s and in Scotland most of us were addressed as Babs, whether we liked it or not. I didn't. When I moved to Edinburgh in my teens I temporarily, and with very bad grace, gave up trying to correct everybody who abbreviated my name and so for a while answered to Babs, but I reverted to Barbara at the first opportunity.

My performing name was always, from the very beginning, Barbara Dickson and it never even crossed my mind to consider changing it when I turned professional. There was, though, a worrying moment in the late 1960s when I had to join Equity to appear on TV. Because there was already an actress called Barbara Dixon on their books I was told I had to choose a different name, even though mine wasn't spelled the same way and I wasn't actually acting. So I just took my full name, Barbara Ruth Dickson, added a hyphen and became Barbara Ruth-Dickson, which was generally considered highly pretentious.

When, a few years later in 1974, the musical *John, Paul, George, Ringo... & Bert* transferred to London, I was issued with a blue equity card that authorised me to work on the West End stage. Thankfully, this time there was no problem with me being Barbara Dickson the actress, Barbara Dickson the singer or Barbara Dickson the anything-elser, and that is how it has remained ever since. And even now, if ever you want to get my back up, shortening my name is usually a good way to start.

CHAPTER TWO
THE BOATIE ROWS

W hen I was still a baby - and I'm sure much to the relief of all concerned - we left my granny's house for a place of our own, first a wee rented house in Dunfermline in a lane called Buffie's Brae. In 1950, we moved again, to a little house with a garden in Rosyth, a mile south of Dunfermline on the Firth of Forth. Originally a suburb of Dunfermline, Rosyth grew into a town in its own right after the arrival of the Royal Navy dockyard just before the First World War. It was a major naval base during both world wars, and a significant employer not only in Dunfermline but throughout Fife. My Uncle Willie worked there and my father got a job on the tugs that brought the ships into harbour. He was not a bad cook - he made fantastic chips (recently commented on with great relish by Artie Tresize of 'The Singing Kettle', Scotland's foremost musical show for children) - and among his duties was responsibility for all the meals on the boat. Once a year they would have Navy Day, when families were invited to the dockyard, and I remember going into the galley of the tug where my dad made lunch for the crew every day. I couldn't get over how tiny it was.

We lived in a large complex of brick houses so small that the locals christened the area Dollytown, because it resembled a collection of dolls' houses. They're gone now: they were knocked down in the 1970s and 1980s to make way for a new estate. Soon after we moved in, in 1951, my brother, Wee Alastair, was born.

I was sent to nursery school in Rosyth but I wasn't there long before my poor mother was asked to remove me. I was miserable and unsociable, apparently, and would not talk or interact with anybody. When the morning hymn was sung I would stick my fingers in my ears and keep them there until the noise stopped. Perhaps even then I knew good singing from bad. I would have been three, nearly four at the time, and don't remember much about it, so I can only surmise that the arrival of Wee Alastair was not a development I was especially happy with. The escape bid I launched shortly afterwards would probably bear out that theory.

I must have put some thought into my plan to leave home. I wasn't a particularly girly girl, but all the same I loved my dollies and teddies, and going off without them, especially my favourite teddy, Big Ted, would have been out of the question, so I had the doll's pram all ready for the journey and had carefully filled it with my most precious toys. What I had neglected to pack was any food or drink for my journey. Well, I was only three. I had decided to head in the general direction of the nearby town of Inverkeithing, just over a mile away, and after pushing the pram for what seemed like ages, I was becoming tired and thirsty. I met a kind-looking woman along the road and asked her if I could have a glass of water.

The kind-looking lady was, thankfully, kind-hearted, too. She took me to her house, gave me some water and asked me my name.

'My name is Barbara,' I replied.

'And where are you going, Barbara?'

'I don't know.'

Unable to get much more out of me, the kind lady took me to the police station where I waited for my mortified and distraught mother to come and pick up her three-year-old runaway (plus pramful of dolls). I never went back to nursery. But you'll be glad to know that Big Ted is still with me, enjoying a comfortable and well-deserved retirement in Lincolnshire.

When I was five I started at the local school, Camdean Primary. After the nursery episode and the disappearing act my parents must have been apprehensive about how I would get on. As it turned out, I loved my first day at school, meeting all the other children, and the classes. But when I realised that I was expected to go back the next day, and the day after that, I was not pleased at all. I had been there, done that, and didn't understand why I had to go again. Surely once was enough? By all accounts, for the first few weeks, even getting me to the school gates was a battle for my mother.

I really don't think I can have been an easy child at all, despite what my mother used to say. Although I never ran away from home again, I did have a tendency to hide. When I was six I came home from school one lunchtime as usual, but instead of going into the house I decided to hide in the shed, and again my poor mother found herself frantically searching for her missing daughter. It took her some time to track me down as once I'd had enough of hiding, I simply went back to school for the afternoon. I remember that by the end of the day I was absolutely starving, not having had any lunch.

I'm told that the sweet, calm infant who had been no trouble at all grew into a rather solemn and serious little girl (in fact, I am still rather solemn and serious today), and the few family photographs taken at the time seem to back this up. There is not a lot of smiling going on. Yet my childhood memories are happy ones, and my solemn demeanour was probably just an outward manifestation of my thoughtful temperament. I was very imaginative and creative, the kind of child who would become quite obsessed with whatever I was interested in at the time and want to know anything and everything about it. My brother Alastair was similar and we would pretend to be other people and invent fantasy conversations that made absolutely no sense to anybody listening but perfect sense to us.

Eventually I settled in at school, and soon joined the Brownies, too, where I was an Elf. I still have my badge. I enjoyed Brownies, apart from the odd embarrassing incident.

Once, I remember, they organised a fancy-dress party and for some reason my mother decided to dress me up in a Japanese kimono. I have no idea where my mother got this kimono, and have my doubts about whether, so soon after the end of the war, choosing a Japanese outfit would have been seen as the best of ideas. Although I was too young to appreciate the subtleties of postwar sensitivities I must have had subconscious reservations of my own, because when we arrived at the church hall I simply refused to go in. I did not want everybody looking at me. No matter how lovely my mum said I was I could not be persuaded to enter the room.

The experience didn't leave me with a permanent antipathy towards the kimono. In 1978, when I was at the Tokyo Music Festival, I ended up buying one myself, having decided it would be the ideal thing to wear in my dressing room when I was changing costume and putting on my make-up before going onstage. And being the frugal Scot that I am, not only was I still wearing the same kimono thirty years later but I wouldn't have contemplated getting ready for a concert without it. It was only very recently that it finally became just too shabby to be seen in and though it should have been consigned to the great wardrobe in the sky, even then I couldn't bear to part with it. Call me superstitious, but it is still hanging in my cupboard, clean but frayed at the edges.

In general, I loved dressing up and would go to great efforts to make my costumes as fantastic as possible which, in the 1950s, sometimes took a great deal of imagination, not to mention quite a bit of Mum's make-up. I'd transform Alastair and me into cowboys or Indians or crusaders or Romans or whatever characters we had seen at the pictures that week.

When I was six I became obsessed with the character Calamity Jane, played by Doris Day in the 1953 film of the same name. I went with my mother to the Palace Cinema in Rosyth to see it and was immediately enthralled by the movie, the music and by Calamity herself. Like me, she was not a girly girl: she rode the stagecoach; wore buckskins and a Yankee army hat; she had a shotgun and she knew how to use it. Jane was as tough as any man, if not tougher, and I thought she was just wonderful. I could think of nothing better than becoming someone like her when I grew up. I was much less interested in the part of the film where she falls in love with Howard Keel and takes to wearing a dress, but even then she redeems herself by revealing that she keeps her trusty shotgun under her skirts. Doris Day was a fine singer and actress and as Calam she became my heroine.

There are so many terrific songs by Sammy Fain and Paul Francis Webster in that film, and I learned them all off by heart. Wherever I was, at home, on the bus, at school, I'd be singing and whip-cracking away. From a very early age I seem to have had the ability to remember songs easily, but even so, I have always wondered how I was able to memorise all those lyrics and tunes at only six years old, because I'm sure we never had the record of the soundtrack in the house. The only other explanation is that I must have made my mother take me back to the cinema to see *Calamity Jane* on several occasions.

It's not all that surprising that I was so keen on music so young as the Dickson household was always full of it. While my father went to work in Rosyth my mother stayed at home and every day she would be either listening to music on the radio or playing records on the gramophone. My grandfather James Malley had been a great fan of classical music and had passed on his passion to my mum - she was especially fond of Beethoven, Chopin, Mendelssohn and Schubert. To me, hearing classical music around the house was normal.

My mother also loved Deanna Durbin, Bing Crosby, Nat King Cole and Louis Armstrong, among many other popular singers of the time. And when she moved to Fife she discovered Scottish music that she liked: she thought the songs of Robert Burns were wonderful, having had a Scottish school teacher in Liverpool who initiated her charges into the joys of his poetry, and adored the now often overlooked Scottish tenor Kenneth McKellar, one of Scotland's biggest singing stars from the 1950s to the 1970s. She had a fine voice herself, so she would sing along to her music all the time, and I would sing along with her. And when she was not in the room I would sing along on my own. It is thanks to her that I have such catholic taste in music.

Not that all the musical genes came from the Malleys. My father also had a good singing voice, but he used it rarely. My Aunty Ella was an excellent pianist and my Aunty Mabel, who was also my godmother, played the piano at parties. In general, most of the Dicksons had good voices, which they exercised when they went to the kirk. There was, too, a musical brother of Grandfather Dickson's who settled in Crieff, Denis Lawson's hometown, where he was in charge of the town band. He was also the manager of the cinema on the High Street in nearby Auchterarder. It cost 4d to sit at the front, 6d in the gallery and worldly-wise usherettes would guide courting couples to the back row so that they wouldn't distract the rest of the audience.

When I was five my parents decided I should have piano lessons. For my mother in particular, who loved music so much and had never had the chance to learn to play an instrument, it was really important that my brother and I should be given the opportunities she had missed out on. She thought I might have some ability, and my father was happy to go along with her plans as long as it didn't cost too much. They bought a piano for me and I took lessons for the next seven years.

I was also enrolled in Miss Holroyd's Dancing Academy in Rosyth, where we learned tap and ballet, and in 1955, at the age of five, I gave my first-ever public performance (not counting singing to the postman from my pram at eighteen months) with Miss Holroyd's class at the Carnegie Hall in Dunfermline. It's fair to say that I was never the greatest dancer, but the name B. Dickson is preserved for posterity in the programme my mother carefully saved and I still have the tap shoes I wore. Nearly a quarter of a century later, in 1977, when I played my very first headlining gig at the Carnegie Hall in Dunfermline, I remember going backstage before the show and catching that evocative smell of carbolic and gym shoes. It immediately transported me back to the time I was a tiny wee girl dancing on that stage.

On a bitterly cold day in January 1955 the Dicksons moved back to Dunfermline. The house in Dollytown was by this stage just too small for us and my father was keen to return to his hometown, so when the Brucefield estate was built there, with three-bedroomed houses and bigger gardens, my parents put their names on the list of hopeful tenants. When we arrived at our new home at 66 Ochil Terrace in Brucefield, it was so new that the plaster was still wet and the garden hadn't been dug yet. Inside it was, not surprisingly, absolutely perishing, and we hadn't thought to bring any coal with us. There was no central heating at that time. But it didn't take us long to settle in and my father, who was not averse to a spot of gardening, soon had the plot ready and planted with roses and vegetables - the traditional garden staples in Scotland at the time.

The brand-new house was very exciting as it had an upstairs for the bedrooms and bathroom. Sometimes I would lock myself in the bathroom and just look out of the window, fantasising about being a film star or just daydreaming about nothing in particular.

I spent quite a bit of time in the bathroom because my mother had this theory that everybody should 'go' to the lavatory on a daily basis, whether they actually needed to or not. So every day, when she decided that it was time for a 'visit', I would head upstairs. Often I'd just sit on the edge of the bath and pretend I was Doris Day for half an hour, punctuated perhaps by a rendition or two of 'The Black Hills of Dakota', and then come downstairs again. My mother would ask, 'Have you done anything?', to which I'd reply, 'Oh, yes,' and the whole routine would be repeated the following day.

To me Dunfermline seemed like a huge metropolis. We never had a car, so we would either walk or take the bus and since we lived on the outskirts it felt as if everywhere was miles away, although nowhere was, really. Not that Dunfermline is small: it has a population in excess of 40,000 and a long and illustrious history, too. In fact it was the ancient capital of Scotland and in the eleventh century held the court of King Malcolm III, who succeeded Macbeth, and his wife Queen Margaret, who would be canonised as Scotland's first female saint thanks to her piety and support for the Church. When I was growing up Dunfermline was a city, but at some point in the 1970s, as a result of local government reorganisation, it became a town. I am not sure whether officially it is now considered a city or town, but as Dunfermline people are fairly modest by nature they wouldn't make too much of a fuss about such distinctions. All I can say is that visitors are always welcome at the beautiful Dunfermline City Chambers.

As well as the City Chambers and the historic abbey that gave its name to the church where my parents got married and where Alastair and I were baptised, the town is home to the long-since ruined Dunfermline Palace, a royal residence until the sixteenth century. In 1600 it was also the birthplace of King Charles I, he who became embroiled in the English Civil War and lost his head in the process. Other famous people who hail from Dunfermline include the nineteenth-century industrialist and philanthropist Andrew Carnegie, who left Scotland when he was thirteen, became the wealthiest man in America and then proceeded to give most of his millions away. The legendary Carnegie Hall in New York and the almost-as-legendary Carnegie Hall in Dunfermline are both named after him.

The town also has a rich and vibrant musical heritage. The singer-songwriter Ian Anderson of Jethro Tull, who is known for playing the flute on one leg, was born in Dunfermline just one month before me. Scottish rock band Nazareth were formed in Dunfermline in the late sixties and the seventies saw the arrival of punk band the Skids, one of whose number, Stuart Adamson, would go on to even greater success with another Dunfermline band, Big Country, in the 1980s.

Unlike Edinburgh, Stirling and Perth, however, one thing Dunfermline did not have in the 1950s was a repertory theatre (the Alhambra, which was a picture house, would not be restored as a theatre until the new century). I have occasionally wondered whether, if there had been such a place, this seven-year-old Doris Day obsessive might have decided that acting rather than music was the life for her. Luckily for me, the way my career panned out I was eventually able to do both. But we were not short of culture: we had the Dunfermline Opera House, which opened in 1905 and remained a famous landmark until it was demolished in 1982. The interiors were removed and, rather incongruously, taken to a theatre in Florida: a little piece of Fife on the Gulf of Mexico.

Obviously the move back to Dunfermline meant a new school: Pitcorthie Primary, ten minutes' walk from our house. I loved my time at Pitcorthie and made lots of new friends there. I think at first because I was the new girl, as well as being naturally shy and lacking in confidence, I assumed the role of the class clown. One day, when we stacked our chairs on our desks at the end of lessons, I decided it would be a good idea to put my head through the back of mine. Everybody found this highly amusing, but it wasn't so funny for me when I discovered that I couldn't get my head out again. The school janitor had to be summoned to extract me and I was terribly embarrassed.

One of my class teachers at Pitcorthie was Miss Wallace who, at the time, seemed very scary and ancient, although thinking about it now she was probably only in her forties. Miss Wallace was a good teacher but of all the subjects she taught us, the one that has stayed with me the longest is needlework. I really enjoy sewing and have collected needlework samplers for many years. One of my favourite ways of relaxing when I have an evening at home is doing a little bit of needlepoint of an evening, while half-watching - and no doubt becoming increasingly annoyed by – some television programme or other. It's a great way to unwind. I owe such needlework skills as I have to Miss Wallace. She was very strict with us: if our stitches were too big, which initially happened a lot, she would make us unpick them all and start again, and not surprisingly it didn't take us long to learn to keep them small and neat. Though I wouldn't want to blow my own trumpet too hard, many years later, when I had to sew labels into my sons' school clothes, my sewing was far neater than that of other mothers, thanks to Miss Wallace's expert tuition at Pitcorthie. They don't teach girls, or boys, for that matter, sewing in school any more. Far too useful.

Brucefield, on the southern side of Dunfermline, was very close to the countryside. Our street was on a hill, with a wonderful view of the Forth, although the position had its disadvantages, notably the biting wind that whipped across the terrace on a good many days. There were lots of children on the estate of about my age and we all played together. With hardly any cars around then we idled away hours on street games like Hopscotch and What's The Time, Mr Wolf. In those more innocent days kids had a lot more freedom. Parents would let them go off on their bikes and do whatever they liked, more or less, as long as they were home safe and sound in time for tea. At eight I was roaming the countryside with other Brucefield girls and boys, or we'd go to Pittencrief Park, next to the abbey, known locally as the Glen. The Glen had once been a private estate, with no access for local people. When Andrew Carnegie was a young lad, so the story goes, he used to peer through the gates of the Glen and imagine how marvellous it would be to be allowed to go inside. In 1902, after Carnegie had made his millions in America, he bought the whole estate and opened it up to the public so that no child would ever be locked out again.

In Calais Wood, just outside Dunfermline, we'd light a fire and bake potatoes we'd brought along - our very own barbecue - or build a gang hut. Once a group of us out exploring discovered a secret gang hut buried in the woods. It was a fantastic place. We investigated it carefully, making sure we didn't disturb anything so that the 'owners' of the secret den wouldn't know that we had been there. We would hide in the wheat, lying flat and invisible on our stomachs, before chasing each other round the fields, or go to the Blue Waters to look for frogs.

My brother did much the same with his own gang of wee friends. They were not renowned for their good timekeeping. One day, after they went off to the woods and built a campfire to bake potatoes, Alastair lost track of time. It was getting dark and still he hadn't returned. An Ochil Terrace search party was formed and everybody went out looking for him. As the hours passed, panic began to set in. Eventually, long after night had fallen, Alastair appeared, sauntering up the road; stinking of smoke from the campfire but otherwise without a care in the world. Even my mother skelping him on the bottom in front of all the neighbours didn't seem to bother him too much. But the episode clearly left an indelible memory: to this day Alastair insists that I was the first person to spot him, and claims I went up to him and, with unconcealed glee, said, 'Just wait till Mum gets you.'

It was a fantastic time, full of adventures and excitement and good fun. Having said that, it was Scotland, so there was also plenty of rain and wind and sleet and cold, cold days, but you tend to forget that when recalling your childhood.

Alastair could be an irritating wee monkey sometimes and we fought constantly, but because he was three and a half years younger than me, he had his own pals and did his own thing most of the time. And needless to say, if any bigger boy decided to pick on him, I immediately went into protective-big-sister mode and steamed in to sort out the bully. Besides, if anyone was going to beat up my brother, it would be me.

Wee Alastair has many, many talents and at an early age he showed great proficiency as a fisherman. We often went down to the Wedderburn, a small stream that ran through Brucefield and straight past our school, to catch sticklebacks and put them in jars. Alastair was very keen and very good at this and one day, when he was about ten, he caught an especially large stickleback (admittedly still not very big compared to most fish). He was extremely pleased with his feat and determined to keep the thing alive as long as possible. He set his sights on the forthcoming Dunfermline Pet Show, at which he thought his stickleback would have a strong chance of winning a prize. Along he went to the show in the Drill Hall with his 'pet'. We didn't hold out much hope but the entire Dickson family was very proud of him indeed when he came home with the prize for Best Stickleback in Captivity. If anyone suspected that this category had been invented on the spur of the moment by the judge, the local vet, who cared?

We didn't often trouble the judges at the pet show, as that was our first venture into petdom, and almost our last. The Dickson household never had a proper family pet, like a cat or a dog. Dad didn't like cats and didn't believe in keeping dogs in towns. Apart from the stickleback, and Thumper, our rabbit, the only animals I can ever remember having in the house were mice. I haven't a clue why my mother and father thought this was going to be a good idea, but one day they gave me a little white mouse as my pet and Alastair a black one. My parents had been told that both mice were female, but it soon became clear that either this was not the case or some sort of miracle had taken place when our two mice suddenly turned into a whole litter. That was the end of us having two mice as pets.

In Dunfermline Alastair and I would be sent off to St Ninian's kirk every Sunday. My parents did not go to church and we hadn't attended Sunday School in Rosyth, but the St Ninian's minister, who was a sort of benign forerunner of the Childcatcher in *Chitty Chitty Bang Bang*, saw it as his mission to round up all the local children and make sure they went to Sunday School, regardless of whether their parents were churchgoers, and the newly arrived Dicksons were no exception. I think this sort of three-line whip was fairly common practice back then. If the adults were lost causes, there was always hope with the children if you got them young enough.

When the minister found out that I played the piano, I ended up being the Sunday School pianist, and despite the aversion I'd shown to hymns at nursery, I quite enjoyed church and turned out faithfully for Sunday School, and later Bible class, for years. My mother and father never really commented on what they felt about it. Most parents in the 1950s thought it was good for their kids and they were probably only too pleased to get a couple of hours' peace on a Sunday morning.

I had been learning classical piano and had managed to get to Grade 4 by the age of eleven, although I was not enjoying the lessons or the piano as much as I should have been. Around that time I was put forward by my piano teacher, Miss Stewart, for a competition in the Assembly Rooms in Edinburgh. Miss Stewart was an excellent teacher, but to be honest I was not a very good student. I never practised enough. Already very nervous about the competition, when it was my turn to perform I walked on to the stage and sat down only for the adjudicator to announce me in a loud voice as 'Barbara Dogson'. My wrists immediately seized up and I did not play well at all.

With all my dancing classes and piano lessons and my love of Doris Day, I always knew that I could sing, and that I could sing well, but I never had the confidence to believe that singing was something I would ever have the opportunity to really shine at. I was part of the Pitcorthie School Choir and, shortly after my Assembly Rooms appearance, I delivered my first solo when I was given a verse of the traditional Joanna Baillie song 'The Boatie Rows' to perform at the school concert. Oddly, I don't remember much of it, with the eyes of all the parents upon me, singing on my own, but I do remember the words of the song:

> *When Sandy, Jock and Janetie are up and gotten lear*
> *They'll help to gar the Boatie Rows and lichten*
> *a' the cheer.*

When I think back to my childhood now I remember it as being a happy, carefree time. We were just typical working-class folk, the same as all our neighbours in Rosyth and Dunfermline. Nobody had much money to throw around and the family budget didn't stretch to pocket money for Alastair and me, but if we'd been good we always got sweets at the weekend and my parents made sure that we never went without, willingly spending anything they had to spare on trips and treats for the pair of us. Alastair never had piano lessons, though, as he wasn't interested - too busy with his sticklebacks. He was mad about all animals and during his childhood had an ambition to be a vet.

Never having owned a car, we were not big on family holidays. Many of our neighbours would go to Butlin's in Ayrshire, but wild horses couldn't have dragged my mother to set foot in a holiday camp. We did, however, go every year to Liverpool to visit Granny Malley, Aunty Ivy and my cousins Ivy and Sylvia. And every so often Aunty Ivy and the girls would make the return trip to Fife. Ivy and Sylvia are, to this day, my closest friends.

The pilgrimage to Liverpool always had a certain ritual to it. We would leave Dunfermline very early in the morning and take the train to Edinburgh, where we changed at the now defunct Caledonian Station for Carstairs Junction. My mother always ensured we were facing the rear on leaving Edinburgh as at Carstairs a different engine would be hitched to the other end of the carriages and we'd be facing forwards for the rest of the journey, which she always considered very important. We were invariably laden with luggage. Mum would bring stacks of food to keep us going as well as presents and clothes for our cousins. Our cases weren't any lighter on the way home, either, as in Liverpool my mother would go and buy old 78 records, which weighed a ton, to take back to Fife. I have no idea how we managed.

Perhaps, to our friends and neighbours in Rosyth and Dunfermline, my parents might have seemed a bit different: while my father was, like many men of his generation, a quiet, rather reserved Scotsman, the kind of man who didn't like to make a fuss, my mother, as well as being an Englishwoman, was lively, chatty and funny. But to Alastair and me, Mum and Dad were just our mum and dad, and we just got on with being kids.

CHAPTER THREE
LET IT BE ME

The rheumatic fever that had struck my father down around the time of his marriage left him, as I mentioned, with a heart defect, and in 1957, when he was only forty-two, he suffered a heart attack. It was a terrible shock to us all but thankfully he got over it and was able to lead a reasonably normal life afterwards. He went back to work at Rosyth, although only on light duties, but, significantly, continued to smoke and drink.

Like many Scotsmen then, and indeed now, my father liked a drink. Alcohol gave him a self-confidence that, when sober, he did not naturally possess. It is probably true that sometimes he drank too much, and that drink perhaps allowed him to put off or sidestep the things he did not want to face, but it would also be fair to say that he was always brighter and happier with a drink in him. Alcohol certainly never turned him sour. Dad was above all a nice man, and I don't remember him ever being anything but thoughtful and kind.

Although my father was shy, he was also funny, with a droll delivery, not unlike the late, great Scottish comedian Chic Murray. He used to make me cry with laughter, sometimes at the silliest of jokes. A favourite of mine was the one about the man who walks into a barber's with the biggest head of hair you have ever seen. This was the time of Afro hairdos. He asks the barber for a trim. The barber starts cutting the man's hair, a job that is clearly going to take him some time. After a while the barber asks the man if by chance he was ever in the Boys' Brigade. 'Yes! ' says the man, surprised. 'Why do you ask?' To which the barber replies: 'Because I've just found your hat.'

Although Dad had a good singing voice and liked music, he did not have the same passion for music as my mother. His passion was sport and particularly football, and on Saturday afternoons he would head for East End Park to watch Dunfermline Athletic, for reasons lost in the mists of time affectionately known as the Pars. The 1960s were a golden era for Dunfermline Athletic. The legendary Scottish football manager Jock Stein, who would go on to even greater success with Celtic and Scotland, began his managerial career with the Pars in 1960 and a year later they won the Scottish Cup for the first time in their history. We all went to the victory parade through Dunfermline. It didn't take long, as it's not a big place. Sometimes my father would take Alastair and me to a match, but, in spite of living through such a thrilling period for the club, neither of us became great football fans, and generally, like most dads then, he'd leave us pretty much to our own devices to enjoy the things we liked to do.

Neither of my parents ever tried to control or direct our interests. I cannot remember my mother at any point being one of those pushy mums determined to put their daughter on the stage. There was a talent competition in the Glen every summer but she hated them. She certainly assured both Alastair and me that we capable of achieving whatever we set our minds on doing, and she did spot that I had an interest in and aptitude for music and nurtured that embryonic talent with those piano lessons. But I'm sure her love of music, and the musical atmosphere she created at home, influenced me in choosing the path I eventually followed. My mum was always, throughout my pop and theatre career, my biggest fan. She kept programmes, scrapbooks of newspaper cuttings and other mementos dating all the way back to my days with Miss Holroyd's Dancing Academy. By contrast, I have kept very little in the way of memorabilia - it has never been something that has particularly fascinated me - but I must admit that going back over my life in such detail now without the help of all Mum's scrapbooks would have been nigh-on impossible. Regarding my mum's fan worship, I remember seeing a magazine article about a singer and in the photograph of them in their living room their gold albums were displayed above the fireplace. I would never have done that. Mine are in the loo or in my office. My mother was furious at this as she wanted me to have them prominently displayed and I thought that vulgar. She also used to turn to members of the audience at shows and say 'I'm her mother, you know!'

Like all close relationships, ours had its difficulties over the years. As I was an only daughter, and given that my mother and I were descended from a long line of strong-willed, opinionated women, it would have been surprising if sparks hadn't flown occasionally. But that is not to say that I ever doubted her love for Alastair and me or her pride in what we have done with our lives. She was a truly wonderful grandmother to her grandchildren, too.

Throughout primary school I was, I think it is fair to say, an above-average pupil. I did well in class, I worked hard and I liked to learn. If I had any sort of plan for the future at that age it would have been to go on to Dunfermline High School, where I would study exciting subjects such as Latin and French, and then perhaps to become a teacher. All I had to do to begin the next phase of my life was pass the Eleven-Plus exam, and nobody, not my teachers, not my parents, not I, thought that would be any problem.

I have no recollection of sitting the Eleven-Plus. I wasn't especially nervous or worried about it either before or afterwards. I didn't for one moment expect anything other than a safe pass. When the results eventually came through I was astonished. I had failed. And not only had I failed, but I had failed comprehensively, which left me in a state of complete shock and bewilderment.. I simply could not understand how this had happened. Although my parents, outwardly, at least, had never been particularly academically ambitious for me, they were pretty flabbergasted, too. They knew that I was bright and able and had more or less assumed I would go on to high school. They investigated whether there was any way I might be able to move across at a later date. There was a possibility of transferring at the end of my fourth year, once I had completed my O-Levels, but that seemed like a lifetime away. As far as the first four years of your senior education were concerned, if you failed your Eleven-Plus there were no second chances.

It was one of the pivotal moments of my life. Once the initial shock and disappointment had faded, my overriding emotion was one of resentment. I didn't blame the system that made the Eleven-Plus such a crucial watershed that a child's whole future could rest on the outcome of one exam on one particular day - the system was the system, and you just had to get on with it. And I didn't blame myself, either, for having failed, because I had done the best I could on that day. But the rug had been pulled from under my feet and everything felt different. That feeling hardened into a determination to make something of myself. It was a case of 'stuff that, I'll show them.'

Now, as the mother of three sons, I have spent many sleepless nights worrying about whether they would achieve the required qualifications to further their education and to do the things they wanted to do, IF they knew what they wanted to do. I don't think this is because I am a pushy mother. I simply wanted them to have the best possible start and not to be blighted by limited horizons. I'm sure my fear is a legacy of my experience and of the impact failing the Eleven-Plus had on my own life. I have always admired academics and academic success, probably more so because I never went to university myself. Deep down, I've always wanted to be respected above all for my intelligence and for what I have to say and it is imprinted somewhere inside me that learning is a great asset and a precious gift. My parents, like many working-class people of their generation, saw education as the road out of poverty and into a better life, and the importance of schooling that was absorbed by Alastair and me as children has remained with me all my days. And the schooling in Scotland, although mythically held up as a shining example, was indeed very good at that time.

The early 1960s was a time of near full employment in Britain and we were all able to get jobs when we left school, with those who were less successful academically moving into trades or office work. That wasn't the kind of job I had envisaged for myself but now, instead of going to the high school, I was enrolled at Woodmill Junior High School in Dunfermline, where I was put into the secretarial stream. Although it wasn't what I'd have chosen, Woodmill was in fact a very good school with many excellent teachers and I did enjoy my time there. My English teacher, Mr Forrest, who would read classic English and American literature to us, and also our Art and Science teachers were wonderful, though my favourite academic subject was definitely history. But the teacher who was to have the biggest influence on me was Sandy Saddler, who taught me music.

Sandy was only twenty-four when I went to Woodmill, but he retained his youthful charisma, enthusiasm and dedication throughout his career. He still has it in spades today! I remember him once asking me to sing alto while the rest of the class sang the melody line. Although mine was the only voice singing that part, Sandy could still hear me clearly. When we'd finished the song he said, 'Well, Barbara, you may not be the best singer in the class, but you are certainly the loudest!'

Sandy believed that music was good for the soul and that it could and should stimulate and invigorate. He organised the Woodmill school orchestra and made sure that, with a little encouragement, everybody could be involved. There mere a lot of musical boys and girls in that school. He would track down as many instruments as he could - recorders, violas, violins, piano - and transform them into a musical ensemble. He hated the idea of any instrument lying around not being played. I was the pianist in the ensemble he created.

It was Sandy who introduced me to a new world of folk and traditional music about which, until then, I had known very little. Although our home was always full of music, the only old songs with which I was familiar were those by Burns or the ones we learned at primary school, which could be a little dry. Sandy would let us listen to modern American folk artists and later, when I won a music prize in my third year, he gave me a copy of *101 Scots Songs*, edited by Norman Buchan, one of the best and most important modern collections of traditional songs from Scotland ever published. I quickly became completely wrapped up in exploring this rich and diverse heritage, and it was a revelation. These songs were far more grown-up than the ones we sang at school. I would pore over the words that told stories from the past, discovering the meanings of Scots words I'd never heard before. The stories were sad or tragic or funny or magical and sometimes all of these in one song. I also bought my 6rst guitar, subbed by my parents. And on this guitar I would patiently learn the tunes that could lift your spirits or break your heart or send shivers up and down your spine.

My new love of folk and traditional music did not in any way diminish my enjoyment of the kind of music I'd grown up with or, indeed, the pop music for which I'd developed a passion in the late 1950s. My parents' broad musical tastes didn't extend to rock 'n' roll or pop, so Elvis and the other early rock 'n' rollers hadn't really impinged on my consciousness and it wasn't until 1957 that I first heard the Everly Brothers singing 'Bye Bye Love' and 'Wake Up Little Susie' oui the radio. I was immediately blown away by them.

I have always believed that the best popular music combines the words and the emotions they express with the melody and the feelings that evokes. Don and Phil's music had all these characteristics plus superb harmonies. They liad so many great songs that still sound fantastic today: 'All You have To Do Is Dream', 'Cathy's Clown', 'Walk Right Back' and, two of my particular favourites, 'Let It Be Me' and 'So Sad'. It was through the Everlys that I began to appreciate country ballads. Radio I did not exist in the late 1950s, of course, and I never had the money to buy my own records. When I was a little older and had my own transistor radio I would tune in of an evening, like millions of other British teenagers, to the crackly sound of Radio Luxembourg to hear the hit records of the day, but before that getting to listen to new music was difficult.

Fortunately for me, I had the Yardley family as neighbours. The Yardleys lived in the same street as us and had two boys, Jim and Johnny, who were around my age. I was great friends with them and loved going round to their house. What was more, Jim and Johnny not only had all the latest singles, they had guitars as well. So whenever a new record by the Shadows or the Everlys came out, the Yardley boys would go and buy it and we would all meet up at their place to listen to the record over and over again and learn how to play it on the guitar.

So keen were Johnny and I on the Everly Brothers that we became members of the Everly Brothers Fan Club and wore our official fan club badges with pride. I would later discover that the singer-songwriter Rab Noakes, a great friend of mine for many years, was also a member of the Everly Brothers Fan Club and was sporting his badge in the nearby Fife town of Cupar while I was going around Dunfermline in mine. As well as being keen on the Everly Brothers, Johnny and I were quite keen on each other, and he became my first boyfriend. Johnny was the first boy I ever kissed. And very nice it was, too.

Although my enthusiasm for music was wide-ranging, as I grew more and more focused on the guitar, I grew less and less keen on playing classical piano, and when I was twelve I gave it up altogether. Even though I had been having piano lessons since the age of five, I cannot say, hand on heart, that I ever really enjoyed them, and I found the music I practised less interesting to play as time went on. Now I regret not becoming more adept on that instrument and my reading skills are not great as a result. The guitar, by comparison, just had this amazing feel and wonderful sound. It is perfect for the accompaniment of songs because you can play it and sing and transport the instrument! It took me ages to get back to the piano again and when I did I regained my love of the keyboard. I recall playing a harmonium in Yorkshire, revisiting my skills, in about 1970 with the great folk musician Nic Jones. We sang 'The Plains of Waterloo', so I hadn't forgotten everything and I loved the sound of thatorgan. I think I was just bored by my lessons and that's why I gave them up.

While the Everly Brothers remained big favourites of mine for years, by the early sixties - along with the rest of the country, and soon the rest of the world - I found myself swept along in the tide of Beatlemania, By the end of 1962, the Beatles had had only one minor hit single, 'Love Me Do', but within a few months they were the biggest-selling act in the country, bigger even than Elvis. So meteoric was their rise to fame that many of the venues they had booked in 1963, which had been arranged months in advance, were now far too small to cope with h public demand. There are numerous legendary stories about the Beatles going up to the Scottish Highlands and playing concerts in town halls in Elgin and Dingwall, and among their ports of call on their Scotland tour was the town of Kirkcaldy in Fife.

Kirkcaldy is fifteen miles east of Dunfermline and, until the arrival after the Second World War of the new town of Glenrothes, had vied with Dunfermline for the status of Fife's main town. Today Kirkcaldy is best known as the hometown and constituency of Prime Minister Gordon Brown, who I have always thought of as a good Fifer and a decent man, but back then it was a place that, although not far away, I didn't know at all.

The concert was to take place on 6 October at the Carlton Cinema. I was told that the tickets would be on sale at the Raith Ballroom, also in Kirkcaldy. Nothing was going to stop me seeing the Fab Four and I knew I had to get there immediately to grab tickets before they sold out. The only thing for it was to cycle all the way to Kirkcaldy. So off I went on my great adventure, following the road signs to Kirkcaldy, where eventually I found the Raith Ballroom. I parked my bike outside and raced up to the box office. I was in such a hurry that I didn't stop to wonder where all the other Beatles fans were and why there was no queue.

When I arrived at the box office, completely out of breath, they were pleasant and polite, but told me that I had been misinformed. There were not and never had been any tickets for the Beatles on sale at the Raith Ballroom and the only way you could get them was to apply for them by post. I was absolutely heartbroken. Worse still, I then had to cycle the fifteen miles back to Dunfermline, perhaps the most miserable journey of my life, although at least this time I knew the way.

Once I got back to Dunfermline, I vowed that I would not be defeated and decided to apply for tickets by post, even though it was a vain hope. I was sure that by now it was far too late and they would all have gone. Waiting to hear if I had been successful was torturous, far worse than waiting for any exam results. Finally a letter arrived... and, incredibly, I had got my tickets! I was hysterical with delight. I was going to see the Beatles!

I went to the concert with three friends and thankfully there was no cycling in the dark involved: the father of one of my friends had a car and he drove us to Kirkcaldy and picked us up afterwards. We couldn't wait for the Beatles to come onstage and when at last they appeared the whole place went crazy. The Fab Four looked very cute with their signature haircuts and grey collarless suits. I have never been good at screaming, but everybody else around me was yelling their hearts out, so I did my best to join in with the shouting and whooping. In the early 1960s bands did not play long sets and the Beatles couldn't have been out there for much more than half an hour. And for not one of those thirty minutes did I hear a single note they played. I couldn't even have told you which songs they were singing. All the same it was absolutely fantastic and one of the best nights of my life.

It was at Woodmill that I began to appreciate how naturally singing came to me and realised that I had the ability to excel at it. I found it very easy. I joined the school choir and also entered a Burns Singing Competition, where I had to sing two songs, 'Ca The Yowes' and 'The Learig'. Memories of the Assembly Rooms recital returned to haunt me and I was very nervous beforehand. I had expected to have to sing in front of a large audience but, as it turned out, I only had to face two judges and the performance went well. I was delighted. I'd always known I could do it. Now, with the support of Sandy Saddler, I was given some solos in the school concerts, and duets with Sheila Meldrum, my best friend, who also sang.

I would be absolutely terrified and sick before those concerts. I had no idea whether I would be able get through my spot without losing my voice or forgetting the words, or even whether I would manage to walk on to that stage. But by this time I knew singing was something I was meant to do. I have never been the kind of performer who, when he or she gets out onstage and into the spotlight, flicks some metaphorical switch and becomes this other being. For me the performing Barbara Dickson is just the same as the other Barbara Dickson. In the early days, when I came on, I often used to feel like a tiny speck carrying a huge burden of responsibility. And all these years later I still get nervous before I go onstage, sometimes cripplingly so if at an event I have no control over. The nerves never completely dissolve when I am singing, either, but once I have begun the desire and the need to sing is so strong that it overcomes them. It is only when a concert is over and has gone well that I can truly relax and allow myself to enjoy the warm feeling of a successful night that makes it all worthwhile. Troy Donockley, my musical collaborator, and I dream of performing our 'winning song' at the Oscars ceremony in L.A. I sometimes think I'd be too nervous to do it and would have to ask Eddi Reader to sing it for me instead!

It has always seemed to me the strangest dichotomy that while touring and performing are what I enjoy the most, they are also what cause me the most anxiety. This contradiction is not uncommon among performers, or unique to them, of course, but in my case I suspect it has a lot to do with the contrasting traits passed down by my parents. From my father I have inherited a Scottish reserve that hates fuss and is easily embarrassed, and from my Liverpudlian mother an outgoing, strong-minded element to my nature which, while lacking in self-confidence, enjoys public approval and loves 'quietly' showing off. I can clearly see all those characteristics in myself as a person, and combining the two sides of that split personality as a performer has never been easy. It is said of actors that they often tend to have no self-confidence but huge egos, an observation which makes me smile as I think it sums me up very well, too.

At school I kept to myself any ambitions and dreams I might have harboured about becoming a professional singer. I still had my O-Levels to sit and, having been assigned to the secretarial stream at Woodmill, it was expected that I would get an office job when I left. As part of the curriculum I was taught how to type and take shorthand. I became a very proficient typist and even today, when nearly everybody uses a computer, if ever someone in my family needs someone thing typed swiftly and accurately, I'm the person who gets the task. I'm a demon e-mailer, too. The same could not be said of my shorthand, however. I was absolutely appalling at that, usually only managing to get down 'Dear Sir' at the beginning and 'Yours faithfully' at the end and missing absolutely everything in between. My teacher, Mr Tulloch, completely despaired of me ever finding employment.

Although I enjoyed my years at Woodmill I did not excel academically. Deep down, I think I was still depressed that because of failing the Eleven-Plus I would never get the chance to go college or university, and sometimes I just didn't see the point of trying hard or always paying attention. Inside I was still angry that I was not allowed to get my teeth into the subjects that interested me and was not deemed academically bright. So I just clowned around and did very little. There seemed little point in trying to impress. The one and only time I received corporal punishment - the belt - was in my first year. It was in a geography lesson, a subject I liked and in which I happened to be top of the class at the time. I had spent ages intently studying a map of the Middle East, to which the geography teacher took great exception as the subject of that day's lesson was the southern uplands of Scotland. Top of the class or not, I was punished. The swine.

At sixteen I sat four O-Levels in total: English, modern studies (a combination of history, geography and politics, concentrating mainly on the twentieth century), art and arithmetic. I passed the first three, but rather ignominiously failed at arithmetic. Initially I had toyed with the idea of going on to Dunfermline High to sit more O-Levels, but by the time my exams came round at Woodmill I had lost all interest academically. I was sad to be finishing school, but now I needed to find work and earn a living. I had already had a Saturday job for a while, at a local baker's in Brucefield. I loved working there: the pay was pretty good, the people were very nice and, best of all, at the end of my shift I could take any unsold cakes home for nothing. But I never had any intention of going full-time there when I left school. Apart from anything else, if I had done I would soon have been the size of a house.

I had my three O-Levels, no secretarial skills, aside from typing, and absolutely no desire to become a secretary. Instead I decided to try the civil service and applied to be Temporary Clerical Assistant with the Ministry of Defence Navy Department at the base at Rosyth where my father worked for so many years. After signing the Official Secrets Act I started my job in the naval stores department, where I spent my time shipping the personal effects of civilian personnel all over the world. My first pay cheque was £3 7s 6d. Funny how you remember details like that. I worked in this little Nissen hut with a great bunch of people, and I really enjoyed the job. It was always interesting seeing the names of the far-flung places where the items I was handling would be going. All that studying of the map of the Middle East in geography wasn't wasted after all and there were at that time a huge amount of bases overseas stuffed full of British civilian personnel. Those were the days I suppose when Britannia did indeed rule the waves.

CHAPTER FOUR
I ONCE LOVED A LAD

In 1961 a folk club opened in Dunfermline in the cellar of 58 Chalmers Street, the same street where James and Jessie Dickson had lived and where my mother and father had been living when I was born. The club was called the Howff (a Scots word meaning 'meeting place') and from the very beginning it was very popular, attracting top singers all musicians from all over Scotland and beyond. The Howff was run by John Watt, who eventually realised that the Chalmers Street cellar was just too small for the number of members, and in January 1964, he moved it to the Brucefield Hotel, not far from where I lived.

Although I was still at school, I had been to the Howff a few times and loved it, so when the club moved to the Brucefield I was really keen to see the new venue and a group of us from Woodmill arranged a night out there. It was an evening when anybody could get up onstage and perform, but I had absolutely no intention of volunteering. Aside from the fact that I was far too scared to sing in front of all those experienced musicians and the folk enthusiasts who had paid to get in, I was only too aware of the small matter that, at sixteen, we were all under-age and shouldn't have been at the Brucefield in the first place. The music that night was great and we were all really enjoying ourselves when John Watt stood up and asked whether anyone would like to go up and sing. By this time it's possible that some of my friends had had a few libations and it had slipped their minds that we might easily be thrown out at any moment, because they started pointing at me and calling out: 'She does! She can sing!'

I had nothing prepared. I didn't even have my guitar with me. But with so many expectant eyes on me it was almost as difficult to refuse as it was to stand up. My trepidation mounting, I was persuaded to make my way to the front of the crowd. Somehow I got to the rostrum without falling over, sat down on the stool and crossed my legs in an attempt to stop them trembling which only made it worse! My knees were knocking.

Someone passed me a guitar. I had no idea what to do next. At that stage I had yet to learn the words to any Scottish folk songs and had never sung on my own before, I decided to sing something I knew well, 'The Cruel War', a traditional American song taken from an LP by Peter, Paul and Mary. I don't remember ever being as terrified at any time in my life as when I began to sing that night. All I recall even now is the trembling in my legs and the round of applause when I finished.

Yet, terrified or not, I was hooked. Nothing was going to stop me returning, but next time I would bring my own guitar. I soon became a regular and got to know everyone at the club. There is no point in claiming any false modesty about my ability: I knew I could do this, and John Watt must have thought so, too, as he began to invite me to sing. Since I wasn't au fait with very much traditional material he would suggest Scottish songs that would suit me, the first one, I remember, being 'I Once Loved A Lad'.

The Howff was a wonderful introduction to live performing. Although I was always nervous, there was absolutely no pressure as regards how I sounded, what I sang or even whether I wanted to sing every week at all. Nobody was getting paid - folk music was a hobby for us all and we went to the club for the sheer pleasure of it and to hear what other performers were doing.

If Sandy Saddler was my first mentor, it was John Watt who developed my passion for the wonderful world of folk and traditional music. For the remainder of my teenage years I was obsessed with learning as many new songs as possible as quickly as possible. From *Calamity Jane* and the Everly Brothers I progressed not just to Scottish folk music, but English and Irish too. I soaked everything up like a sponge. As soon as I heard a song I liked, I had to memorise all the words and play it on the guitar. Later on in my career it would astonish other musicians when, if they happened to strum a few notes or sing a couple of bars of a song, sometimes a really obscure old song, I was able to play and sing it back to them, or at least a reasonably accurate rendition of it, without even thinking about it. I can still do that now. Fragments of ancient ballads stream back through the mists of time.

I began to collect the words and music of my favourite songs, sheets of music and scraps of paper with lyrics scribbled on them, and squirreled them away in a shirt box of my father's. Once it became the designated receptacle for my burgeoning hoard, I wouldn't have dreamed of keeping my songs anywhere else. I still have that shirt box of songs today.

I was soon being asked along by the Dunfermline Folk Club when they went to perform at other clubs in Fife like the Elbow Room in Kirkcaldy and the St Andrews Folk Club. One of the groups I met playing the Fife folk circuit was a trio called the Farriers, originally the Tarriers, made up of Jack Beck, Jim Millar and Moray Sladen from Dunfermline. Our styles seemed to fit and they invited me to join them. I jumped at the chance. It meant more gigs and playing at weekends. Suddenly, I found myself in my first group, with Moray playing the banjo and the rest of us with guitars.

It was such an exciting time to be involved in folk. The music was radical, political and alive, We would listen to the songs of the great American folk singer and political activist Pete Seeger and the equally great British singer-songwriter Ewan MacColl, who wrote such classics as 'The First Time Ever I saw Your Face' and 'Dirty Old Town', and whose daughter Kirsty MacColl later became as well known as he was. That year, 1964, was the year we also became aware of a young American folk singer and songwriter who had recorded the album *The Freewheelin' Bob Dylan*. One of his songs, 'Blowin' In The Wind', had been covered by Peter, Paul and Mary, who were extremely popular at the time. I have been a huge fan of Dylan's since the first moment I heard him sing. The term genius is vastly over-used, but it is warranted, in my opinion, in Dylan's case. His music and lyricism mark him out as a huge milestone in popular culture as far as I am concerned.

Eventually the Farriers shrank to just Jack Beck and me, so we relaunched ourselves as a duo called Jack and Barbara, playing together until 1967. Jack had been involved with the Howff since the very beginning and, at the almost geriatric age of twenty-two, he was six years older than me and far more sensible and worldly-wise. Crucially, he also had a car, so he would drive us to gigs in and around Fife and deliver me safely home to Dunfermline afterwards. He was like a big brother to me, keeping his eye on me to make sure I didn't drink too much or get myself into any mischief. I had a great time singing with him and really enjoyed the years we played the circuit. We sang lots of Scottish songs together and I learned a great deal from him.

Meanwhile, at work at the naval base at Rosyth, my job as Temporary Clerical Assistant was soon made permanent and I was moved to reception in the personnel department, housed in a new building. I met lots of new people there and eventually my friend Elizabeth McVitie and I decided to take a two-week trip to Ireland. We had a fantastic, wild time. The chic was mighty and from the musical point of view, too, Ireland was an exciting place for me. Dublin in particular was jumping. We would go to O'Donaghue's in Merrion Row, where Luke Kelly, Ronnie Drew and the Dubliners were virtually a house band, playing every night in the back room of the pub.

Moving on to Wexford, we found the *craic* somewhat less mighty and returned to Dublin sooner than we'd planned. As a result we had no accommodation booked, and when the crowd we fell in with at the pub heard we had nowhere to stay they said, 'Not to worry, we'll find you somewhere.' Sure enough, at the end of a great night we were taken to this big house in Upper Baggott Street and given beds in someone's room. There were a lot of rooms in the place and there seemed to be a lot of people there, too. Elizabeth and I, young, properly brought up and still naive about many things in life, could not work out why the women we met in the house were going out in the middle of the night, all dolled up, long after the pubs had closed. It was very strange.

It was not until several days later, when we mentioned the Upper Baggott Street house to some other people we met, that we were finally told, amid much hilarity, that the house we were staying in was one of Dublin's most notorious brothels.

Though I've never returned to that brothel, or been to any other brothel, for that matter, I loved that first trip to Ireland so much that I went back on my own every summer for the next few years. I would go to Dublin and then head west, to wherever there were *fleadhs* and good pub sessions going on, mainly in Clare, a haven for musicians. I would hitchhike or blag a lift and stay wherever I could find a bed or, failing that, a tent. If drinking was compulsory, washing was optional and all I needed was my backpack, sometimes my guitar and a precious Irish bus driver's hat I'd been given with drunken solemnity by Mary Jordan, a great Dublin girl I knew. Ireland still has a special place in my heart and I'm happy to say that the audiences there always seem pleased to see me, too. Nowadays I spend as much time in Co. Mayo as possible as some close friends have a house at the foot of the Holy Mountain of Croagh Patrick. Overlooking Clew Bay, it's the most beautiful, peaceful spot. The family all take guitars and mandolins, bodhrans etc as we have mighty *craic* both in the house and Stauntons, the local pub.

Back home in Dunfermline, I was beginning to get itchy feet. Jack and I were playing more and more folk clubs and being invited to more and more parties, so there was generally a lot more drinking, smoking, staying up late and having a great time. I was seventeen, I loved the life and I wanted even more of it. In particular what I really wanted to do was to leave home and move to the big city: Edinburgh, Scotland's capital and home to a thriving folk scene. When Jack Beck and I had gigs in Edinburgh I would often stay at a flat in Rose Street belonging to Jack's friend Aileen, who later became his wife. Rose Street runs parallel to Edinburgh's main thoroughfare, Princes Street, and was then, as now, known for its numerous pubs. But unlike today, back in the 1960s it was full of dark alleyways and dingy doorways. On the positive side it had a thrilling bohemian feel, and those doorways were ideal for 'courting'. Which brings me to another important reason why I wanted to move to Edinburgh. I had fallen in love.

Jack and I had been invited to a party one evening at the home of Robin Harper in Largoward, near Leven in Fife. Robin was a folk enthusiast and familiar face on the scene then and a regular at the folk club at St Andrews. He was quite a wild, crazy guy (he was known as 'Robin Harpic - clean round the bend', a reference to a television advert for the lavatory cleaner) but was much admired and liked and his parties were not to be missed. Later Robin would enter Scottish politics and become the leader of the Scottish Green Party. Though he is now one of the most respected members in the Scottish Parliament, I'm sure he is still the same wild and crazy guy at heart.

Everybody that was anybody in the Fife folk world was at Robin's party that night. I remember chatting in the garden with Archie Fisher, the great Scottish folk singer who, along with his sister Ray and later Cilla, was part of a well-known musical family, and who was to be a huge influence on my career. It started to rain and, to avoid having our beer diluted, we went back into the house where the party was in full swing. In our absence there had also been a new arrival: there, in the griddle of the room, stood Ian McCalman.

Ian was eighteen, a year older than me, an up-and-coming folk singer and an integral part of a trio, the McCalmans, that would become one of Scotland's most famous folk groups. That night he was wearing a brown cord jacket and a polo-necked sweater - the height of cool. I took one look at him, across all the smoke and chatter, and fell for him completely there and then and I hadn't even spoken a word to him.

Ian came from Edinburgh and lived off London Road-near the city centre. He was studying at the Architecture School of Edinburgh's School of Art. The only member of the McCalmans who was actually a McCalman, he was in Fife with the other two members of the trio, Derek Moffat and Hamish Bayne, fellow students at the Architecture School, where the three of them had met. Having discovered that they had music in common, they had decided immediately to form a group and had had their first gig just two weeks later.

I had never felt anything like the heart-stopping attraction that I experienced that night. I'd had a couple of boyfriends at school, but these were innocent times - and I was very innocent. This was different. This was grown-up. It was instantaneous and unstoppable. Ian gazed at me through the wreaths of smoke, I gazed back at him and by the end of the party we had had a wee canoodle and arranged to meet up in Edinburgh.

Ian and I began to see each other regularly and when I went to Edinburgh at weekends I would stay with his family. They were lovely to me, but as you might imagine, I was now even more determined to move there and find my own place so that we could see more of each other. I had been studying for my clerical officer's exam and once I'd passed it, I put in for a transfer from Rosyth to a new post at New Registrar House in Edinburgh.

My parents had never tried' to stop me from singing or from going to folk clubs or even parties. They might not have been happy about the increasing late nights and the amount of time I was away, but I was still coming home at night (usually), and at the weekends they knew I was in safe hands with Ian's family. But when I announced that I had got a transfer and would be moving to a flat in Edinburgh they were extremely worried and tried to talk me out of it. My mother in particular was aghast and very hurt. If I'd been going to college, or getting married, it would have been easier for her to accept, but the idea of her seventeen-year-old daughter leaving home on her own was hard to take. She just did not understand why I wanted to go and made her opinion known frequently and with some force. But nothing my parents said was going to change my mind, I wanted to be in Edinburgh and that was that.

I found a flat in Northumberland Street in the salubrious New Town, less than ten minutes' walk from my new office at the east end of Princes Street. Although the department was quite large, the section where I worked was fairly small. We were responsible for recording causes of death, which in 1960s Scotland were, sadly, much the same as today – mostly lung cancer and heart attacks. I spent my days going through death certificates to identify the primary cause of death and feeding this information into a sort of early type of computer. Eventually the data was processed into the yearly statistics on Scottish health.

It might sound a strange job for a young girl, but actually I found the work quite fascinating, although sometimes the material I was dealing with could make me very sad, especially if the person who had died was young. While I was at New Registrar house I was also able to do a little research on my family tree. I settled in fairly well, and my new colleagues were very nice, but I don't remember much in the way of socialising with them outside work as I devoted all my free time to the music scene. With my new job, my new flat and my new boyfriend, I felt terribly grown-up.

Edinburgh was the epicentre of Scottish folk and now that I was living there and didn't have to worry about getting home to Fife I could immerse myself in its many and varied clubs, pubs and parties. There was a society called the Royal Antediluvian Society of Buffaloes in Albany Street, just along from my flat, which held a weekly folk club on a Monday night. Not surprisingly, it was more commonly known as 'the Buffs', which was slightly less of a mouthful. On Tuesday night there was a folk club at the Crown, organised by Archie Fisher, and folk music every night of the week, except Sunday, at the legendary Sandy Bell's pub near the university, which still hosts live music to this day.

Not that the Lord's Day was a day of rest for us musicians, or our livers. Although back then the pubs had to close on the Sabbath, the licensing laws exempted hotels on the grounds that weary travellers far from home might be in need of liquid refreshment after a long journey. So we would repair to the Learmonth on Queensferry Road or the West End Hotel on Palmerston Place, where the islanders would congregate, and you could have a session, both musical and alcoholic, even if you had no intention of ever booking in for the night, thus avoiding the wrath of the law.

At that time also the place to be seen was the Waverley Bar on St Mary's Street, just off the Royal Mile. The Waverley, like Sandy Bell's, is still there and has changed little, if at all, since the 1960s. Behind the bar there is a picture of the Queen and the Duke of Edinburgh, although I couldn't say whether they've ever had a drink in there. Another pub that became popular a few years later at weekends was the Halfway House on Fleshmarket Close, near Waverley train station - one of those historic steep stairways, narrow and dimly lit, for which Edinburgh is famous, and not a place for the faint-hearted: forty years on, my fellow Fifer Ian Rankin, the thriller writer, would name one of his popular Inspector Rebus novels after it. The Halfway House was, appropriately, halfway down the close. It was a small, traditional pub, not ideal for singing if there was a big crowd, but if that was the case we would just enjoy the *craic* and stay till last orders anyway.

After the pubs and clubs closed everybody would head for whatever parties were going on, making sure, of course, that they had purchased their 'carry-oots' first, and the singing and drinking would continue. The 'carry-oot' would be supplied in a brown paper bag which, according to Ian, could be converted, once your drink had been safely stashed away, into a makeshift lampshade to create 'ambient vibes'. Ah, happy days.

Later in the 1960s, 47 Forrest Road, round the corner from Sandy Bell's, became the in meeting place, largely because the licensing laws required Sandy Bell's to close at 2. 30pm and not open again until teatime. So in the meantime we would head round to Forrest Road to play music through the afternoon, fortified by a wee dram or two, and then it would be back to Sandy Bell's. The process would repeat itself when the pub closed again at 10pm, and the evening would stretch into the early hours of the morning. I was too much of a lightweight to stand the pace so at this stage I would usually go home. I did have to go to work in the morning, after all.

If I felt the need for some tranquillity I would go to the Catholic church and spend some time there in quiet reflection. Having faithfully attended Sunday School and then Bible class at St Ninian's kirk in Brucefield, while I was still at Woodmill I had started going to the Episcopalian church with a friend. The Episcopalians were the Scottish equivalent of the Anglicans, and I much preferred their more ritualistic style of worship to that of the Presbyterians. But the church that had always fascinated me the most as a child was the Catholic St Margaret's Memorial, near Carnegie Hall in Dunfermline. The Catholic Church seemed mysterious and alluring, no doubt largely because it was out of bounds to me. My father, though not a churchgoer of any stripe, came from a very

Protestant background and I knew he would not approve of his daughter being seen in a Catholic church. When I moved to Edinburgh, however, beyond the range of my family's watchful eye, there was nothing to deter me from crossing the threshold of the local Catholic church. I would also go to the Catholic shop, now long gone, and buy little sanctuary candles which I would light in my flat.

I might have had my own flat, job and boyfriend, but I was living away from home for the first time, still only seventeen and still incredibly naïve. When I think of the mistakes I made and the numerous times I came a cropper in my first couple of years in Edinburgh...But it was all part of growing up and finding my way in life, and without the experience of those early years I could never have gone on to do what I did. One of the worst nights I remember was actually before I moved away from home permanently. I was at a party in Stockbridge given by a friend of Jack Beck's called George Craigie, and for some-reason I took it into my head to start knocking back dark rum and orange juice as if it were going out of fashion. Rum and orange are a lethal combination. The stuff looks hideous and it tastes like paint-stripper - not that I have ever tasted paint-stripper, but it tastes how I imagine paint-stripper would taste. I am mortified even now when I remember how many hours I spent that night clamped to the lavatory and I'd like to take advantage of this belated opportunity to apologise profusely to George, Jack and anybody else who needed to go to the 'wee room' that night and couldn't get in.

At Easter 1965 Ian and decided it was time we took a holiday together. We didn't have much money so we plumped for an adventure through the breathtaking Scottish Highlands and on to the idyllic destination of the Isle of Skye. We didn't have a car so the idea was to hitch there and back. What could be more romantic for two teenagers looking for a wee bit of privacy?

When we told my parents about our plans, my father, much to Ian's discomfort, became very inquisitive and persistent. 'What exactly are you planning to do?' he asked Ian. And how was Ian intending to take his daughter away without a car? Maybe we should have listened to my dad, because it ended up being a holiday neither of us would ever forget, though not necessarily for the reasons we had anticipated. The journey up worked out well enough. On the way north we had managed to hitch as far as the middle of nowhere in the Trossachs, where the traffic wasn't exactly heavy. Suddenly, over the horizon came this gorgeous new car, just off the production line. We knew it was just off the production line because it was perched on the back of a transporter lorry, along with several other brand-new cars. To our surprise the lorry stopped for us and, rather than asking us to get into the cab with him, the driver let us sit in one of the pristine cars on the trailer. We headed into the Highlands with a bird's eye view of the beautiful scenery, only travelling backwards.

Arriving at last at Broadford in Skye, we booked into a B&B as Mr and Mrs McCalman. The proprietor made no comment about the marital status claimed by his teenage guests, but we were aware of a distinct quizzical raising of an eyebrow as we signed in. We were both nervous about pretending to be married - deep down we were both respectable young people - but here we were in beautiful Skye, unsupervised and with plenty of hormones tearing around. We had a lovely time.

But of course we still had to find our way home. Once again we hitched all the way. There was no car transporter this time; instead we ended up travelling from Crianlarich to Stirling on the back of a flatbed truck, clinging on for dear life in temperatures that had probably dropped below freezing. I have never been as cold in all my life as I was on the back of that lorry, and when we arrived home we resembled frozen bog people who had been dug up after thousands of years. I don't think I fully thawed out for at least a week.

Ian and I had a great time on our Highland odyssey, but it was not long before our relationship began to encounter problems. We were both very young and an attractive guy like Ian had plenty of attractive women interested in him. With the sexual revolution getting underway, he was quite happy with the idea of 'meeting' other girls. I, on the other hand, was more than happy with the one man I had. So when he started talking about 'needing his space' I just couldn't believe what I was hearing but because of that, we soon after broke up.

I was absolutely distraught. I was completely smitten and I could not believe that something so wonderful had ended. I remember going to a party in Portobello, Edinburgh's seaside resort, shortly afterwards and seeing Ian there. Not only was he at the party with someone else, but the someone else was draped all over him, the brazen hussy! This was not my idea of him 'needing his space'. I was still hurt and it was just too much having to watch him cavorting with some other girl right in front of me. Although Ian was not officially my boyfriend any more, I wasn't going to let this minor technicality stop me making my feelings known. I got a pint of beer, walked up to Ian and his 'friend' and, with great deliberation, held it upside down over his head. Everyone at the party was looking on in silence, mesmerised as, just for a split second, it seemed as if a large, brown jelly in the shape of a pint glass had formed on Ian's head before the beer cascaded down his face and neck. My point made, I turned smartly on my heel and, without a word to anybody, stormed out of the party and walked briskly all three miles back to Northumberland Street. Safe inside, I slid down the inside of the door into the foetal position and burst into tears.

When I think back to that time and my relationship with Ian I realise that, although we were only together for a short time, it was at least seven years, perhaps more, before I could honestly say I was over him. I went out with other guys, Ian went out with other women; we tried becoming friends; I tried avoiding him, as being friends was too difficult for me; I tried again to be friends when avoiding him proved even more difficult. Whichever phase we were in, I was stuck on Ian long after we had ceased to be an item.

Many years later, in the early 1980s, when we were both older, if not necessarily wiser, we found ourselves considering giving it another go. But perhaps I was afraid of all that history. Whatever the reasons, our relationship wasn't to be. Soon afterwards I was to meet the man I would marry and later on, Ian met Ellen, who would become his third wife. But we have remained the best of friends and I am very glad and grateful that throughout everything, I have kept in touch with this funny, clever and talented man. Over forty-five years after the McCalmans were first formed, Ian still leads his group all over the world. They do, however, plan to retire in 2010. It has been over forty-five years, too, since I first clapped eyes on him in his brown corduroy jacket at that party at Robin Harper's house in Largoward. So, in the words of a certain well-known song, I think I can claim that 'I know him so well'.

CHAPTER FIVE
GOOD VIBRATIONS

I f I hadn't decided to leave Dunfermline, Jack Beck and I might well have carried on singing together for much longer, but Jack was a Fife boy through and through and preferred to remain there. Although we still performed together for a while after I moved to Edinburgh, we began to drift apart and eventually went our separate ways. Jack later became a college lecturer and head of construction subjects at Lauder Technical College, now Carnegie College, but he has remained involved in the folk scene and a highly respected singer of Scottish songs. On his retirement Jack, the dyed-in-the-wool Fifer, surprised me by moving to the United States, but we have managed to keep in touch and I still have very fond memories of the years we sang together. As performing apprenticeships go, I couldn't have had a better one than partnering Jack Beck.

As I spread my wings in Edinburgh I rubbed shoulders with so many talented performers that it's impossible to mention them all, but I must pay tribute to a few of those who inspired me, or who went on to become household names. Two giants of the folk scene at the time were Roy Williamson and Ronnie Browne, better known as the Corries. The band had started out as a folk trio in the early sixties when Roy and Ronnie sang with Bill Smith and were occasionally joined by Paddie Bell, a lovely singer from Northern Ireland who played a five-string banjo longer than herself. Roy and Ronnie quickly became massively popular through their concerts and TV appearances, notably as the main feature of *Hootenanny* (a Scottish television show long before Jools Holland borrowed the name), which was filmed at the Place in the West Bow in Edinburgh's Old Town.

I was a huge admirer of Roy and Ronnie. They were friendly and down-to-earth as well as being smart and talented. They were also instrumental in revitalising the Scottish music scene with their passionate arrangements and reinterpretations of traditional songs in addition to writing and recording great 'originals. The Corries took Scottish music around the world, where they played to enthusiastic audiences of ex-pat Scots and plenty of others who had no Scottish connections at all, but secretly wished they had.

When the Edinburgh Festival came around in August the Corries would host and headline a show at the old Caley Cinema, which recently reopened as a music venue called the Picture Show, and would invite other folk artists to do a spot. Their 1968 festival line-up was especially stellar, including among others, the influential Irish band the Chieftains, led by Paddy Moloney, and Roger Whittaker, who would have a hit record the following year singing and whistling 'Durham Town'. And yet who should Roy and Ronnie choose to open such a prestigious event but wee Barbara Dickson from Dunfermline.

Roy and Ronnie were great supporters of new singers and performers, and the chance they gave me with the 1968 festival show was a really big break for me. Roy and his wife Vi also hosted some bloody good parties, and since their flat was on the same street as mine, I never had far to stumble home. Roy sadly died in 1990, but his name will forever be remembered for his most famous song, 'Flower Of Scotland', Scotland's unofficial national anthem.

Other fantastic musicians around the scene were Robin Williamson and Clive Palmer, a folk duo who became the incredible String Band when Mike Heron joined them. They had a series of bestselling albums and were known for their unique psychedelic folk sound. Then there was the extraordinary Shetland fiddle player Aly Bain. I first heard him play in Edinburgh when he was just seventeen and he took everyone's breath away with his virtuosity and his talent. Aly went on to found the acclaimed Scottish-Irish band Boys of the Lough before establishing an enduring partnership with another virtuoso Scottish musician, Phil Cunningham. He's never lost the mischievous Shetland twinkle in his eye. I remember one evening, when drink may have been taken, Aly taking me aside and telling me in his island dialect: 'Du kens, Barbara Dickson. If anybody kens, du kens.' I nodded sagely at this insight although to this day I still have no idea what he was on about.

The fantastic folk singer and guitar player Dick Gaughan, who was born in Rutherglen, had moved to Leith as a child and became one of the most famous performers on the Edinburgh folk circuit. An early member of the Boys of the Lough, Dick appeared on their first album but is best known for his solo work. With albums such as *Handful Of Earth* he established a reputation as one of the most powerful and important voices in Scotland. His song 'Both Sides Of The Tweed' remains one of my all-time favourites.

I knew Dick well in the late 1960s and we even talked about forming a band with Tom Smith, brother of Bill, original member of the Corries. Tom was a great singer and guitarist and a gorgeous-looking guy who was tragically killed in a car crash in his early twenties. The three of us met in my flat with the intention of working on material, but we ended up spending more time hanging out and drinking than being musically productive and the idea soon fizzled out. It was a shame, as we would have been a fantastically good line-up. I wonder what we would have sounded like, all together. They were both great guitarists too.

Isla St Clair, born in Grangemouth, was also in Edinburgh then. She had gone to school in Buckie and Aberdeen and made her name as an unaccompanied singer of the traditional songs of the north-east of Scotland. Isla, younger than me by a few years, was glamorous and bubbly and she, of course, went on to find national fame in the 1970s as the co-presenter with Larry Grayson of the TV game show *The Generation Game*. With my appearances on *The Two Ronnies* and Isla on *The*

Generation Game, there was a period when the pair of us were being watched by tens of millions of viewers every week on primetime Saturday-night TV - not bad for two lassies from the Scottish folk circuit. Who would have predicted that ten years earlier?

I loved living in Edinburgh. Even in winter, when it would be bitterly cold, there was always Christmas to look forward to. One year I had a brainwave: with all the brilliant singers and musicians there were in the city, why didn't we get together and go carol-singing to raise some money for Cancer Research? I persuaded a big bunch of friends and acquaintances, including the McCalmans, to congregate at a prearranged time outside the old General Post Office at the east end of Princes Street and, for the next two hours, the cream of the Edinburgh folk fraternity sang their hearts out. Our efforts were rewarded with the grand total of three shillings.

Granted, this was a long time ago, but even then it was an embarrassingly paltry haul: three shillings would only have bought you three half-pints of beer (not that we would have spent any of our charity money on beer, of course). Disgruntled and disheartened by our failure to entice the good people of Edinburgh to part with a more generous portion of their loose change, we agreed to repair to the Abbotsford in Rose Street to discuss our options. First, though, we needed a couple of pints, and once we'd had a couple of pints, we decided to sing one of our Christmas carols in the bar. It was like a scene from *It's A Wonderful Life*. As soon as we began we were inundated with donations and by the time we had finished our collection tin was impressively heavy. Emboldened by our success, we then trawled all the pubs on Rose Street, of which, as I mentioned, there are many, having a half-pint and singing a carol in each of them. Checking our takings in Scott's bar, where we wound up, we found we had collected over £20.

That was the start of a Christmas tradition in Edinburgh that continued for a good many years and raised hundreds of pounds for charity. I have always wondered whether the reason for the initial generosity of the pub regulars in Rose Street was their appreciation of our wonderful singing or whether they realised that the quicker they paid us, the quicker we would leave. According to Ian McCalman, the Christmas carol-singing experience convinced him that singing to drunk people indoors was always preferable to singing to sober people outside.

As well as all the musicians living in Edinburgh, every week, it seemed, there would be someone visiting from Glasgow or the Highlands and Islands, or from even further afield - England, Ireland, Europe or America - who had brought their guitar, fiddle or banjo with them and wanted to play. There were some great sessions: whether in a pub, a club, or somebody's flat, there was always music going on. The wonderful Martin Carthy would come up from London, the Dubliners or the Chieftains would be over from Ireland on tour, Tom Paxton arrived from America. Rab Noakes even managed to get down from Fife. Word of their whereabouts that night would spread and we'd all turn up not only to hear these fantastic musicians play but to play alongside them and socialise with them, too. It was magical. We even had our own resident academic genius in the shape of Hamish Henderson, from the School of Scottish Studies at Edinburgh University. He who wrote the wonderful 'Freedom Come All Ye', recognised as one of the most iconic Scottish songs of the twentieth century. Hamish was a regular at Sandy Bell's and was most convivial company. When Nelson Mandela was imprisoned in the 1960s Hamish wrote the wonderful 'Free Mandela' which called for his release. We all sang that song.

Edinburgh may have been at the heart of the Scottish folk scene, but the sixties were an incredibly fertile period for music up and down the country. In the north-east of Scotland Arthur Argo was running an important folk club and festival in Aberdeen and when Jack Beck and I were just starting out, Arthur booked us for a week at the Music Hall during the Aberdeen Music Festival. Arthur came from an illustrious musical family: his grandfather, Gavin Greig, had compiled the definitive song collection of the area, *The Folksongs of the North-East.* As recently as 2008 I dipped into this wonderful book for the haunting 'Lady Franklin's Lament', which I recorded on my *Time and Tide* CD. Arthur also attracted big names to the Aberdeen Folk Festival. One year the iconic Pete Seeger himself played at the Music Hall. I remember watching him there and finding it hard to believe that I had stood on the very same stage as the man who wrote 'Turn, Turn, Turn' and 'Where Have All The Flowers Gone?'. Even now, whenever I return to the Music Hall in Union Street, with its fantastic acoustics and echoing memories, it immediately brings that night to mind. I'm also hoping one day to play 'Turn, Turn, Turn', a huge favourite song of mine, which I heard played first by The Byrds.

In Glasgow there were many great singers. Hamish Imlach, who was later to have a major impact on my career, and Danny Kyle, both sadly no longer with us, would come through to Edinburgh to play. Also hailing from the west were two young guys who called themselves The Humblebums. When I first saw The Humblebums the line- up consisted of Tam Harvey and a Glaswegian welder by the name of Billy Connolly who specialised in bluegrass songs such as 'Foggy Mountain Breakdown' and 'Cripple Creek'. Tam played the guitar and Billy played the banjo and told jokes in between the songs. They were a great double-act on the circuit and attracted big crowds.

One night when The Humblebums were playing at the City Halls in Glasgow, Billy asked another young musician, Gerry Rafferty from Paisley, to play with the band. When Tam left the group The Humblebums became a duo again, now consisting of Billy and Gerry. Billy still sang, wrote songs and played the banjo, all interspersed with jokes, while Gerry sang and wrote unique, original songs such as 'Her Father Didn't Like Me Anyway' and 'Patrick the Painter'.

The first time I ever heard Gerry sing was in 1967, one lunchtime when I happened to be in the famed Scotia Bar in Glasgow. After that Gerry often popped up at sessions and on nights out in Edinburgh and, although he was quite shy, I got to know him well and really liked him. Our voices complemented each other and when we sang together I could intuitively tune my sound into his. He became great friends with Rab Noakes and spent a lot of time in Fife, writing and performing. And Billy was a wonderful man too. He was very generous, and still is: one of the many nice things about him is that big success and worldwide fame don't seem to have changed his basic outlook at all. He is the same funny, charming person I met back in the 1960s with that underlying Scottish modesty which is very attractive. At the core of his talent are his acute powers of observation, which are as sharp now as they have ever been.

Billy is an inspiration. Throughout his career he has never looked back or repeated himself. He has progressed from one phase of his life to the next without ever losing his excitement and enthusiasm for living to the full. He is still a great folk fan and remains part of the great union of banjo players - once a banjo player, always a banjo player. In 1994, when I brought out *Parcel Of Rogues*, my first folk album in over twenty years. Billy very kindly said that it was one of his favourites - although, rather worryingly, he has never mentioned any of the albums I made after that. It was probably inevitable that Billy and Gerry would eventually part company as it was always clear that, with Gerry's rare singing and song writing talent and Billy's gift for comedy, The Humblebums comprised two great solo acts with greater potential than they could realise in combination. While Billy focused on comedy, Gerry went on to form Stealers Wheel with a Paisley buddy, Joe Egan, and had a number one hit record with 'Stuck In The Middle With You'.

When Gerry was recording his solo albums *City To City* and *Night Owl* he asked me to sing backing vocals and, years later., repaid the favour on my album of Bob Dylan songs, *Don't Think Twice, It's All Right*. I find his vocals on my version of 'Times They Are A-Changin'" very moving. Gerry is one of' the most talented people I have ever worked with, a sensitive and intense man, but a great artist and a really immense talent in popular music.

While I've never believed that one era of music is better than any other, for someone like me, still finding her way, to have artists such as the Beatles, Bob Dylan, Paul Simon, John Sebastian and the Beach Boys around to emulate was such a privilege, and the temptation to perform some of their songs was far too strong to resist. I also loved The Who and Jimi Hendrix, and the rock trio Cream - Eric Clapton, Ginger Baker and Jack Bruce from Glasgow - but it was the singer-songwriters, Dylan, Joni Mitchell, and later on, Crosby, Stills, Nash & Young and James Taylor, whose songs I began to incorporate into my set alongside those of my contemporaries, Rab Noakes, Gerry Rafferty, Gallagher & Lyle and Alan Hull of Lindisfarne.

To some of the folk fundamentalists - the people Billy Connolly once memorably described as 'bearded men wearing Aran jumpers singing about dead sailors', this was heresy. I have nothing against beards, Aran jumpers or sailors, living or dead, and I have been rooted in folk and traditional music since I was a teenager, but as far as I was concerned, singing songs by artists like Dylan and James Taylor was perfectly natural. These songs had their foundations in a proper musical background and, even more importantly, they were fantastic to sing.

Not having been exposed to traditional music as a child, when I eventually came to it as a teenager, I had no preconceptions about the way certain songs should sound or how they should be delivered and never felt under any pressure to copy any particular singer or style. When I learned a new song I would simply interpret it as I felt it should be interpreted. I applied the same principle to music I had already heard on the radio or on a record: I was able to ignore the version of, say, a Beatles or Bob Dylan song I might have heard hundreds of times, strip it back to its musical bones on the guitar or piano and then reinterpret it. When I was twenty, I started playing the piano again to help me do this.

There were some great songs with which I found I could do nothing. No matter how hard I tried, there was no fresh interpretation I could give them. So if something wasn't right for me, however much I loved it, I would just leave it and move on. When covering a song I have always resisted setting out to make it sound as close as possible to the original. What on earth is the point in that? All you will end up with is a pale imitation. I was recently pleasantly contradicted though by hearing a version of 'Witchita Lineman', the great Jimmy Webb song, sung by James Taylor. I really believed that song to be uncoverable as the original version, which James credits with affection, was legendary and sung so well by Glen Campbell. He did, however, pull it off.

As a performer, although I was very nervous before a gig, once I was onstage I was confident enough in my abilities and my material to overcome the jitters. While I wasn't one for jokes like Billy Connolly or Bill Barclay, the Dalkeith equivalent, I was happy to introduce my songs and to talk to and banter with an audience. But offstage I was still very shy and unsure of myself and uncertain about the way I looked, how others saw me and what it was I was looking for in life. There has never been anything wrong with my appearance, but that has never stopped me being unsatisfied with it. I had this great friend in Dunfermline called Lilian Cheyne, who was blonde, bubbly and fabulously curvy (she is still a very attractive woman). I, on the other hand, was serious and gauche, with an unruly mop of curly hair that has always been the bane of my life, and I was constantly, aged about twelve, comparing myself unfavourably with Lilian who seemed so feminine to me. As time went on, my inclination was to cover myself up. I usually wore a full-length cardigan that went from my neck all the way down to my ankles, and if it had been feasible to wear a balaclava when I was singing onstage I would have done so. For all that I wanted people to hear my voice, I never felt comfortable with them looking at me. I thought I was such a beanpole that I sent off to a girls' magazine for a set of exercises to make my legs fatter.

I had never been fond of my curly hair but when Twiggy set the tone for us all in the 1960s it became imperative that I somehow managed to straighten it. I used to spend hours and hours bent over the ironing board trying to iron it, but no matter how much progress I thought I'd made, I could never get at the curls on the top of my head. And it was a disaster whenever it started to rain. Hours of preparation could be ruined in a couple of minutes of even the lightest drizzle. Even now, a hat is an essential accessory whenever I venture outdoors, just in case the heavens open and I end up looking like Leo Sayer. No offence, Leo.

I was never happy with the colour of my hair, either. When I was at school I decide to bleach it with a powerful product called Bandbox Spray Tint from Woolworths and then discovered, to my horror, that the tint wouldn't wash out and instead of my natural brown or the hoped-for blonde, I was stuck with a not very pleasant orange colour. When I came home from holiday it had so completely transformed my appearance that when I got out of the taxi, my mother didn't even recognise me at first.

Before I left school I was dyeing my hair jet black with stuff I bought in Boots. After the release of the epic film *Cleopatra*, starring Elizabeth Taylor and Richard Burton, in 1963 we all wanted to look like Liz's beautiful Cleopatra, with her raven hair and copious amounts of dark eyeliner. The eyeliner was easy - you could get easy-peel eyeliner which simply peeled off - but not only did the requirement for black locks make the whole business of getting my hair right take longer and longer, when it went wrong I could sometimes have been mistaken for a black poodle. Not a good look.

And of course, back then, as well as having to be straight and the right colour, hair also had to be big. I remember talking to the singer Helen Shapiro, who had been a child star in the sixties and

Above: Dad as an apprentice grocer in Dunfermline, aged about 18, so around 1933.

Top left: My parents standing on the steps of the beautiful Dunfermline Abbey after their wedding in 1943. My dad was very ill and looks painfully thin in this picture.

Left: Me in a 'posh' photograph, aged about two and a half. Taken by Norval's in Dunfermline, my mother used to say that the photographers displayed the print in their window because I looked so charming.

NORVAL PHOTOGRAPHERS

Above: A groovy cowboy brother, a.k.a. Alastair Dickson, in 1953, in the back garden of our Dollytown house. See Big Ted in the background, looking brand new.

Left: Outside my Granny and Aunty Ivy's house in Carrington Street, Liverpool 8, about 1955. It looks like the *Blood Brothers* set! *Back left to right:* Aunty Ivy, cousin Ivy, Granny holding Robin, Ivy's baby and my mum. I am in the front with Alastair who is obviously trying to escape.

Below: I think this is my favourite old family picture. My dad obviously got down to make Alastair look at the camera, so Alastair crouched down as well.

Above: Alastair and me at Glenview, my Aunty Mabel and Uncle Jock's house in Dunfermline, about 1955. It was directly across the road from Pittencrieff Park, the 'Glen' so we could just walk across and into the park on our own from there.

Right: My mother Ruth, Alastair, our rabbit Thumper and me in the back garden at Ochil Terrace, about 1958.

Below: I can't believe The Beatles played two shows a night in 1963! And in Kirkcaldy! Look at the other forthcoming attractions: Del Shannon, American superstar, appeared, plus other big Mersey band names of the time. I like the mention of dancing 'till 4 a.m.' at the bottom of the page. They had stamina then.

Right: Jack Beck and me, snapped by Bill May, the son of the local pharmacist in Brucefield, Dunfermline. Bill was very much into taking pictures, hence the 'arty' feel of these.

ALAN KING presents TOP ENTERTAINMENT at the
Carlton Theatre, Kirkcaldy

SUNDAY, 10th NOVEMBER, 1963 6.30 and 9 p.m.	SUNDAY, 24th NOVEMBER, 1963 6.30 and 9 p.m.
The Big Beat Show	**TOP POP 1963**
with DEL SHANNON GERRY AND THE PACEMAKERS THE FOUR MOSTS and Full Supporting Programme Tickets—17/6, 15/-, 12/6, 10/-, 7/6.	with THE SEARCHERS· MARK WYNTER EDEN KANE and Full Supporting Programme Tickets—12/6, 10/-, 7/6, 5/-.

All seats can be reserved in advance for either show.
Booking Office at the Raith Ballroom, Kirkcaldy.
Open Daily 10 a.m.—5 p.m. and 7 p.m.—10 p.m.

The BEATLES in Scotland
SUNDAY, 6th OCTOBER, 1963—6.30 and 9 p.m.

PROGRAMME

1. **ANDY ROSS AND HIS ORCHESTRA**
   featuring **Sue Taylor and Bryce Wilson**

2. **HOUSTON WELLS AND THE MARKSMEN**

— INTERVAL —

3. **THE CLIFTON HALL STARS**
   featuring **The Fortunes**

4. **THE BEATLES**

AFTER THE SHOW ---*DANCING THROUGH THE NIGHT*--- AFTER THE SHO
At the Raith Ballroom Kirkcaldy—Midnight till 4 a.m.—5/-
TRANSPORT LEAVES THE CARLTON THEATRE AFTER THE SECOND PERFORMANC

ALL PHOTOGRAPHS BY BILL MAY

Top left: The Tarriers/Farriers folk group in full spate, singing at a pub near Dunfermline in about 1964.

Top right: I think this must have been an early publicity shot from 1965. I've got my set list for singing taped to the top of the guitar!

Left: Me photographed near Falkland, Fife, about 1970 in my mum's vintage 1950s Astrakhan coat. I wasn't really riding the bike in a miniskirt – I was just clowning around.

Below: A production still from *Once Upon A Song*, taken at the Gateway Theatre in Edinburgh. *Left to right*: Iain MacKintosh, me, John MacKinnon and Archie Fisher.

Top left: Me playing at the Hexham Folk Festival in 1973 looking very serious. The frizz indicates an outdoor gig in the North!

Top right: On tour in 1977, my first headlining dates. Not sure about all those stripes, but I am wearing a Willie Nelson T-shirt, so not all bad news. My American Mountain Dulcimer – with which I used to play Bill Withers' 'Lean on Me' – is resting on the flightcase in the foreground.

Left: By the outfit, I know this is 1976 and dates from when we used the pianos belonging to the venues. This is a fabulous Bosendorfer 9' grand, so it must be Birmingham Town Hall or the Manchester Free Trade Hall, where concert pianists would play regularly.

Right: Made it! Accompanying The Flying Burritos on my first tour as a solo pop artist in 1976.

Below: Bat wings and skin-tight trousers, 1978. I don't know how I managed to sit down on the stool with those trousers, but at least I didn't get stuck on top of a stage monitor as I did in Edinburgh on that tour. By this time I have an electronic piano, seen in the background.

Above: Me being a DJ in about 1980 for Tees Radio, an independent station run by Dave Cousins of the Strawbs. He asked me to come up and stand in for two weeks which was loads of fun.

Right:
Appearing on
TV's *Rock School*
with Ian Gillan
in 1981.

had two number-one hits at the age of fourteen, about how she got her hair so magnificently bouffant and she told me that the secret was loads of shellac hairspray from Woolies. It set hard and was really for varnishing sideboards! Not Elvis sideboards, but pieces of furniture.

As if my body and my hair weren't bad enough, to my mind, having to wear glasses as well was something I could have done without. I had first been prescribed them when I began suffering nightmares at eight. The doctor suggested I might be suffering from eye-strain-induced headaches and that spectacles might help. I am convinced now that, as was the case with many children, there was nothing really wrong with my eyes and that being made to wear glasses so young actually made them lazier and my eyesight worse. Whatever the reason, by the time I left school I really couldn't see very well at all without glasses, although I was stubbornly determined only to wear them when I absolutely had to. Men didn't make passes at girls who wore glasses and all that. I felt I had enough defects already. So I would wander round in a constant blur, ignoring friends and acquaintances and blanking attractive men. Many a time I'd have to apologise to a disgruntled friend for some perceived slight or general standoffishness. Getting on the bus could be an ordeal if I was on my own, as it was only at the very last second that I'd be able to make out the number, and if it turned out to be the one I was waiting for I'd have to make a dash for it.

If I disdained my glasses in the street, I certainly wasn't going to wear them onstage, so it wasn't until the 1970s, when I purchased a tinted pair and convinced myself that they resembled sunglasses and were therefore just about cool enough, that I performed with twenty-twenty vision. Even those tinted glasses I would whip off if I was going to be photographed. I really used to loathe having my picture taken. To be honest, I still dislike it. I fully understand the belief in some parts of the world that the camera steals your soul, and if it was going to steal mine, it wasn't going to get me wearing glasses into the bargain or without a fight. Almost all of the photographs taken of me in the 1960s show me peering uncertainly into the camera, not a pair of spectacles in sight, although perhaps, at that time in my life, I always looked uncertain. It is safe to say that nobody would ever describe me as happy-go-lucky. I was a serious child and, for good or for ill, I've always been a serious adult.

For all the socialising and parties and drinking on the Edinburgh folk scene, my priority was always the music. It was a predominantly male world and, rather than emphasising my difference as a woman, I tried to fit in by becoming one of the boys. I dressed accordingly: my standard attire was jeans, black polo-neck and black boots, accessorised with the obligatory packet of Woodbines and a Zippo lighter (everybody smoked then). I was never a student in Edinburgh, but I made a great effort to look like one and it was probably the student lifestyle I really aspired to. The jeans, of course, were always men's Levi's 501s. You bought them too big, put them on at home, sat in a bathful of water and stayed there until they had shrunk enough to fit perfectly. The boots were black, ankle-high Chelsea boots, as worn by the Beatles and the Stones, although you dreamed that one day, somehow, somewhere, you'd be able to get your hands on - or, to be more accurate, your feet into - that most prized item of footwear, the cowboy boot. The only part of the uniform I was missing was the huge duffle coat, something I always wanted but never had. With one of those, the look would have been complete.

The men and the women on the folk scene all dressed more or less the same, and as both sexes wore their hair long and parted down the middle so that it hung over their faces like curtains, with only their noses sticking out, it was often said that there were only two ways to tell a male and a female folkie apart: the women would have a poetry book clutched to their bosom (though in my case it was as likely to be philosophy as poetry) and the men all had beards. Technically, it could work the other way around, I suppose, but thankfully this was quite rare.

Although as a rule I was reluctant to reveal any more of my body than was absolutely necessary, the time came, around 1967, when I bought minidresses and skirts. I remember going to a party in a harlequin-patterned short tent dress. The night passed off without any major incidents, but it was not the most relaxing of outings as I constantly had to remember to take special care, when bending down or sitting, to ensure that it was only my legs I was showing off. Not easy in the days before tights, when stockings and suspenders were the only option. You had to sort of curtsey if you dropped your ciggies and lighter.

Shy and unconfident as I was, I don't want to give the impression that I was some sort of shrinking violet interested only in the music who went home every night to a single bed and a cup of cocoa. There was far too much around in the way of drink, parties and men for that to be true. If you take the well-known phrase 'sex and drugs and rock 'n' roll' and replace 'rock 'n' roll' with folk and 'drugs' with 'drink' then you'll have a reasonably accurate picture of my Edinburgh.

While I always had to balance the social scene with working full-time, I had my moments. After the split with Ian McCalman, I met a charming and attractive drama student from Selkirk. Ian Dempsey was studying at the Royal Scottish Academy of Music and Drama in Glasgow and we stepped out for a time. He went on to become a highly respected actor under the stage name of Peter Blake, working regularly in the theatre and appearing in countless popular TV shows. It was through Ian that I was first introduced to the theatrical world and its denizens - actors, directors, producers and stage managers - although it would be many years before I would ever be professionally involved in it myself. The relationship with Ian Dempsey was fun but short-lived: the wounds left by the break-up with the other Ian were still fresh and, deep down, I wasn't ready for any serious commitment.

By the time I turned twenty in 1967, I had lived in Edinburgh for the best part of three years. On many levels everything was going well. I had made a new home in a city I loved, I was relatively secure financially, I had lots of new friends and I was following my dream. My singing partnership with Jack Beck came to an end that year and I began to perform, albeit still on a part-time basis, as a solo artist. My musical career was progressing steadily with more gigs, more bookings and more opportunities; I was becoming more experienced and more self-assured. But I was still very unsure about what I wanted out of life and whether I was ever going to find someone to share it with.

CHAPTER SIX
THE CLIMB

By 1968 I was earning around £3 or £4 a gig which, together with my civil service salary, kept me fairly comfortable financially. But with bookings still financially sporadic, the money I made from singing was nowhere near enough on its own to allow me to give up the day job. I might have carried on the way I was for years if my hand had not been forced but, as we all learn sooner or later, when your life changes dramatically it usually happens when you least expect it.

That year a Danish folklorist called Thørkild Knudsen came to Edinburgh with the purpose of collecting Scottish folk music. Thørkild and his family rented a flat in Forrest Road, and from there he travelled all over the country, as far as Lewis, where he recorded the haunting Gaelic psalm singers, in his quest. We were happy to help Thørkild with his mission and in the process met a number of people from the Danish folk scene who came over to visit him. It was through these new contacts that I was asked if I would be interested in three weeks' work in the summer of 1968 at the Tivoli Gardens Folk Club, the Vise Vers Hus, in Copenhagen. While Thørkild was in Edinburgh I recorded with him the fantastic song 'The Early Morning Rain' written by Gordon Lightfoot, accompanied by Martin Carthy and Dave Swarbrick, all done on Thørkild's fantastic tape machine, a state of the art Nagra.

I was really excited at the prospect of going to Denmark. Other than informally on my trips to Ireland, I had never performed abroad. And not only was I being given the chance to sing in one of Europe's most famous capital cities but I would be paid, for the privilege. Although I was not entitled to more than two weeks' leave from my job, in the circumstances I did not foresee this being a major problem. After all, I had been with the civil service since I was sixteen and had been a conscientious and dependable employee. I couldn't imagine that they wouldn't look kindly on my request to bring forward a week from the following year's holiday allowance to take advantage of this once-in-a-lifetime opportunity. And if they did refuse, I could always fall back on taking it as unpaid leave.

I went to see my personnel manager - none of your human resources then - and explained the situation. He listened to what I had to say but, apparently without giving it a moment's consideration, immediately told me that it was out of the question for any member of staff to bring forward holidays. Disappointed, if not completely surprised, I resorted to Plan B. 'If that isn't possible, then could I take unpaid leave instead?' My second proposal, which I was sure no reasonable person could conceivably turn down, was hardly out of my mouth before the personnel manager responded that, while he was sympathetic, rules were rules. 'It is not possible to authorise such an application,' he said firmly.

I was totally shocked to have my request so summarily dismissed; more than that, I was also extremely angry. Before I'd had time to think about what I was saying, I found myself telling the personnel manager that in that case, I was resigning.

Giving up my job of four years and my main source of income had not been my intention, but I was just so outraged at this rigid attitude that I felt I had no alternative. In my heart and in my head I had already decided that I was going to Denmark no matter what. There are certain chances in your life that you instinctively know you must take or you will regret it forever, and this was one of them.

Although my decision was made on the spur of the moment, looking back, I realised that almost subconsciously I had been building up to it for a while, and if it had not been the Copenhagen offer, there would have been some other catalyst. It simply wasn't feasible to combine a successful singing career with a nine-to-five job, and if I was going to achieve that I would have to put all my energies into it. With the die cast, I now had to break the news to my parents. Understandably, they were both extremely concerned. What was I going to do when my three weeks in Denmark were over? It was a fair enough question, because, to be honest, I hadn't a clue. For my father in particular, the idea of anyone voluntarily giving up a secure job was difficult to comprehend. And, as he repeatedly pointed out, I was also sacrificing my civil-service pension. That was hardly a major consideration for me then, as it wouldn't be for most twenty-year-olds, but of course it might well have given me pause for thought later on in life.

My poor parents must have been very worried. They did not have the money to support me if all went badly and I came home with my tail between my legs. But I think that, what with first Alastair and now me confounding their expectations, they were more bemused than anything else.

Alastair had experienced none of the tribulations I had suffered with the Eleven-Plus. He breezed through it without a care in the world, going on to the promised land of Dunfermline High School. Always artistic and creative, once he had finished school, he went on to study sculpture at Edinburgh School of Art. At the time I resigned from my job to try to make it as a singer, then, Alastair was studying to become a sculptor. With both children earning no regular income, and neither planning careers that could ever be described as steady and secure, my father must have been scratching his head and thinking to himself, 'Hell's teeth, how did I produce these two?'

Despite the almost four-year age gap and going to different schools, Alastair and I always were close. When I'd moved to Edinburgh at seventeen, thirteen-year-old Alastair would come and visit me in my flat. While I was determined that my wee brother would not cramp my style, I felt at the same time that it was my sisterly duty to initiate him into the ways of the world or, more specifically, into the ways of the Edinburgh folk scene. So Alastair would be dragged - and I must say he always seemed quite happy to be dragged - to whatever event, concert or party I happened to be going to while he was there. Some of the parties could be a little on the wild side, and I always kept a vague eye on him to make sure that he didn't get himself into too much mischief, but I am proud to report that he never let down the Dickson family name and would often have far more fun than I did. I remember the night he heard he'd passed his 0-Levels as being a particularly raucous one, although I'd be surprised if he had the same memories of it. Or any memories of it, come to that.

When Alastair went to Edinburgh School of Art he was, therefore, already a veteran of the big city and thoroughly enjoyed himself studying there (he also thoroughly enjoyed himself when he was not studying). On his twenty-first birthday, he and his art-student flatmates - they all lived on London Road, not far from Ian McCalman's parents - decided to hold a fancy-dress party in honour of the occasion. For reasons that I have now forgotten, wildlife was the chosen theme. Alastair, rather uniquely, went as a warthog. He had made a gigantic head out of papier mâché, which looked fantastic but proved difficult to manoeuvre through doorways and a bit of an obstacle to circulating. More importantly, it wasn't too conducive to the consumption of alcohol, either, as he had to take the head off every time he wanted to have a drink. My most abiding memory of that evening was not the party itself, but the journey there, as it is the only time in my life, so far, that I have been on a bus dressed as a bee. And furthermore it is the only time in my life that I have been accompanied on a bus ride by a finch and a ladybird. At least when I saw the ladybird get on I knew I was on the right bus.

Alastair grew into a thoughtful and talented man, and certainly takes the prize for the best brother I've ever had. After graduating from Edinburgh in 1975 he became an excellent sculptor: his work was featured in a short film called The *Stone Of Folly* that went on to win the Jury Prize for Short Films at Cannes in 2002. I am immensely proud of him. We are not dissimilar in character, although Alastair is quieter than me, and he is someone I have always been able to talk to, laugh with and confide in. He now lives with his family, Kathleen his wife and children Liam and Neve, in Canada and I don't see as much of him as I'd like – holidays and visits are always too short - but even though he is now approaching sixty and a continent away he will always be my wee brother and I will always be his big sister, telling him what to do.

My three weeks in Copenhagen in 1968 were everything I'd hoped they would be. I had a fabulous time playing at the Vise Vers Hus - the 'song and verse house' - at the Tivoli, meeting other singers and performers, some of whom, like Eddie Sköller, went on to be national favourites there. I loved Copenhagen and the Danes seemed to like me, too, as I was invited back the following year. By the next summer, 1969, Denmark was truly swinging. Everyone was wearing paisley shirts, velvet pants, exceedingly long hair and shades at all times, day and night, outdoors and in. I had not only dispensed with my bra, but had decided I could do without shoes as well. On this trip I had planned to learn the songs from the latest James

Taylor album, *Sweet Baby James*, and to this end had surreptitiously 'borrowed' Rab Noakes's copy, squashing its corners in my guitar case. As it was, I ended up spending less time with James than I did with a lovely Danish man called Lief. The song 'Wonderful, Wonderful Copenhagen' was never more appropriate.

Meanwhile I had to deal with the pressing question of how I was going to keep my head above water. On my return from my first visit to Copenhagen in 1968 I gave up my Northumberland Street flat and initially returned home to Dunfermline. With no work and no money, I was forced to sign on as unemployed for a depressing six weeks before moving back to Edinburgh and renting a fairly tatty flat in Grove Street, near Haymarket railway station. I shared with my friend Diane Halley and Chuck Fleming the fiddler, and we attempted to make it as cosy as we could. It certainly was no fun having no money and needing to rely on unemployment benefit to get by, but I honestly cannot recall now how miserable I was or how seriously I considered giving up the dream of singing full-time and looking for another day job. All I do remember is my strong conviction that music was my vocation. Those three weeks in Denmark had encouraged me to believe that if I could just break through, I could make a living out of it.

It was mainly through the friendship and support of two of the biggest names on the Scottish folk scene, Archie Fisher and Hamish Imlach, that I began to get regular work. Archie, who had been born in Glasgow before moving to Edinburgh and had made his name first with the Fisher Family, then as a solo artist, was a regular performer on radio and TV. It was through him that I was asked to make my first TV appearance up in Aberdeen on the Grampian Television show *My Kind Of Folk*, in which many of Scotland's top performers appeared. Disaster almost struck two days before my television debut when I woke up in the morning to discover that I had completely lost my voice. Nothing was coming out at all. I was in a complete state and, with no sign of any imminent recovery, I had no choice but to do something I normally avoid at all costs: go and see the doctor. Luckily, the pills he prescribed did the trick and forty-eight hours later a television career was born. I sang the traditional song 'The Rigs O' Rye' which, forty years on, I would finally record on my *Time And Tide* album.

My radio debut followed not long afterwards, on a BBC show called *On Tour* that was produced by the highly respected BBC producer Ben Lyons from an outside broadcast at the village hall in Kinlochbervie in the former county of Sutherland, way up in the north-west Highlands. It would be difficult to imagine a more remote place to get to while still remaining on the mainland, plus I had no car – my travel expenses from the BBC were around ten times my appearance fee. I had to commandeer a friend called Alan Wynne to drive me up and back again in a hired car. However, I remember thinking that it was a good move to do that show and it gave Ben Lyons a chance to see me play. He produced a lot of radio programmes.

Headlining the show was Calum Kennedy, known as the Frank Sinatra of the Highlands and very popular with the ladies. Calum was late arriving, I recall, and it was panic stations as there would have been a riot if he hadn't appeared. I came further down the bill, sandwiched between the children from the local school and their headmaster, who played the fiddle. I'll never forget that headmaster: he is the only musician I've ever seen perform in his slippers. Well, it was radio. Everyone heaved a sigh of relief when Calum turned up, crumpled from the excesses of the night before in Oban.

Archie Fisher was, and remains, an authority on the history of Scottish music and a fantastic interpreter of traditional music. Today he is best known in Scotland for presenting the long-running and highly popular BBC Radio Scotland show *Travelling Folk*, which has been featuring the best of folk music since 1983. When, in 1972, he was commissioned by Scottish Television to make a series of programmes on the music of Scotland, Archie asked John MacKinnon, who sang and played violin and mandolin, and me to appear with him. *Once Upon A Song* was a fantastic series to be involved in. Each programme concentrated on a specific subject - the Jacobite risings, Scotland at war, Scotland at work, Glasgow and Edinburgh - and featured songs that were relevant to each topic with introductions from Archie setting them in their historical context. We also appeared together in another television series, again for Grampian in Aberdeen, called *Silver City Folk*. Both were very successful and achieved high ratings. This was very good profile for me in Scotland.

In October 1969 Rab Noakes - my great friend, fellow Fifer and fellow member of the Everly Brothers Fan Club - and I, together with a number of other Fife musicians, were asked by Fergus Woods from Queen's University to play a concert in Belfast. Afterwards, with Fergus and a few others, I headed to Donegal for a couple of days and ended up in Ballyliffen on the wild Atlantic coast. We had a great weekend there and on the Sunday morning, after a heavy night, I was given the mission of finding sausages for our fried breakfast. Even though it was Sunday, in rural Ireland the shops and pubs would open after Mass. In fact, most of the shops were pubs as well. My instructions were clear: I was to buy a 'clatter' of sausages which, I was told, was an ancient Irish measure. Of course, a clatter was no more an ancient Irish measure than I was - it was just a colloquial collective noun, so all it meant was a large quantity of sausages. This led to a certain amount of confusion in the local shop-pub before it finally dawned on me that I had been set up. It might have been the Lord's Day, but boy, was there a clatter when I finally got back to our hungover cottage.

We had so much fun, not only during the show, but on that whole trip to Ireland, that on the ferry back to Stranraer, after yet more refreshments, the idea that we should all go on a proper tour took root. And so the Great Fife Roadshow was born. My mentor from the Dunfermline Folk Club days, John Watt, was brought in as our star tour organiser and in the summer of 1970 we played a series of concerts for whoever was able to put us up and pay us all - by this time we had become quite a horde.

It was at the Great Fife Roadshow that I first got to perform one of John Watt's best-known songs,' 'The Kelty Clippie' (a 'clippie' being a bus conductress and Kelty being a village in Fife). The show required me to appear in full bus conductress outfit, complete with ticket machine, and, during the song, to shout out in my best Fife accent: 'C'mon, get aff.' I suppose that must qualify as my first acting job.

After the summer of the roadshow Archie, Rab and I began to play occasional gigs together and over the next couple of. years we performed in Scotland and the north of England, doing solo sets on the same bill and then combining to sing together as either a duo or a trio. It was a real privilege to work with them and those nights in the early 1970s remain, for me, a highlight of my performing career.

For all the bookings with Archie and Rab, the Great Fife Roadshow and the TV programmes, from 1968 through to the early 1970s I didn't have enough work to make a full-time living out of singing. At the time the most popular artists in Scotland were also entertainers who could crack a joke and make the audiences laugh. I was comfortable enough talking to a crowd and introducing my songs with light-hearted stories, but telling jokes just wasn't me. In 1969, as I considered how I could build and direct my career, Hamish Imlach gave me some valuable advice. He told me that he thought I was always going to struggle to get enough gigs in Scotland and should consider trying my luck on the folk circuit in the north of England. In that milieu, he reckoned, a performer who was female, Scottish and a guitarist as well as a singer would stand out among the other musicians on the circuit.

Hamish was a big man on the Scottish folk scene and a big man physically, too. In addition to his talents as a singer and musician, he was a natural raconteur and his style of mixing music with humour paved the way for many other performers. Hamish was also generous and had a big heart. Not only did he willingly give me his advice, but he helped me to follow it. He offered to take me with him on a weekend of dates he had booked in the north of England in some of the biggest folk venues at that time.

So off we went, and on the Friday I appeared at the Londonderry Hotel in Sunderland. On Saturday it was the Highcliffe Folk Club in Sheffield and finally, on the Sunday, I played the Mitre in Liverpool. Each night I was given what was known as a 'floor spot'. I had carefully chosen what I thought were the best three songs in my repertoire and I put everything I had into all of them. The venues were packed and I was given a very positive reception.

Hamish had been spot-on about the potential for a singer like me in England. There they didn't mind that I didn't tell jokes or sing humorous songs. All three venues immediately arranged for me to come back and I got further bookings from other folk-club organisers who had been in the audiences that weekend. For the first time I could envisage the possibility of earning a regular income and felt entitled to describe myself as Barbara Dickson, professional artiste. At last I had a sense that I'd arrived.

For the next few years, up until 1973, my life revolved mainly around the folk circuits of northern and central England. I would do a small tour of one of the regions – the north-west, the north-east, Yorkshire or the Midlands - usually playing either seven nights out of eight or ten out of fourteen. Occasionally - thankfully, not too often – audiences were disappointing and I'd be performing only for a devoted few, but generally the venues would be packed. Given my roving lifestyle, there seemed little point in continuing to pay rent on my rarely occupied Edinburgh flat, so I gave it up and moved what few possessions I had back to my parents' house. I finally felt vindicated in my decision to give up my civil service job: I was now playing around four tours a year in England and earning £8 to £12 a gig, which could amount to £50 a week - a lot of money then. If I had still been a clerical officer I would only have been making around £7 a week. Of course, there were many weeks in the year when I was not touring and not earning anything, so I had to make sure that I managed my money to tide me over when I wasn't working. All the same, it was exhilarating to be earning a proper living doing something I loved. I also used the money to buy a new guitar, songbooks and LPs as well as cigarettes and alcohol, although I also paid board and lodging to my parents.

All I took with me was my trusty guitar and one small suitcase of clothes. I would take the train from town to town and be picked up at the station by the organiser. When I got to the venue - usually a local pub - I would change in the ladies' lavatory. In the loo I'd find myself peering into a minuscule mirror in dim light, trying to apply my lippy somewhere in the approximate area of my mouth. I'd usually stay overnight at the house of the organiser or a committee member with a bed or a sofa, depending on their circumstances. They never charged for accommodation. Somehow it made everything more friendly and informal and I made good friends by staying with people in that way. I'll never forget though the horsehair mattress I slept on in Accrington once. I don't think I got a wink of sleep that night, it was so lumpy.

However, I met one of my closest friends, Dave Emery, in those days. Dave worked with Bill Leader, who produced the Jacobite album *The Fate o' Charlie* but comes from Whitley Bay in the north-east. He used to organise tours and dates for me in that area and kindly ferry me about in his van. I even used to stay with his family and was made most welcome by his mum and dad. I had a great following in that region partly due to his hard work and I used to be able to fill the Guildhall on the Quay in Newcastle long before I was a household name elsewhere. Also I had a great patron in Ray Fisher, Archie's sister, who also lived in the area. I was by no means the only female singer on the circuit, but there were not many of us and even fewer who sang solo and played the guitar. But that honestly never bothered me, and I never felt under any pressure to be glamorous or sexy. I tried to look my best onstage, of course, but it was always the music that really mattered and I felt I could compete with the boys.

Being on the road on my own, with only my guitar for company, might sound like a lonely life, but it really wasn't anything of the kind. I was always meeting new people and making new friendships, and touring around the country gave me the chance to visit and stay with old friends, too. Above all, I just loved being a professional singer. I still do. I immersed myself in music, learning new songs, striving to improve and relishing the opportunity to perform every night. It was exactly the life I had dreamed of for so long, and now that I had achieved it, I was determined to make the very most of it.

Recently someone kindly sent me a recording of a gig I did in Leeds around 1973 and, with more than a little apprehension, I sat down to listen to myself across the distance of thirty-five years. My set consisted mostly of traditional songs, interspersed with contemporary numbers by Archie Fisher, James Taylor, Gerry Rafferty and Gallagher & Lyle. It wasn't quite as terrifying as I'd anticipated: my voice was fine and, best of all, my guitar-playing actually sounded really good, even if it was sometimes difficult to make out over the background noise of clinking glasses.

Although most of my work was now in England, I had not forsaken Scotland and would go back to play there whenever possible. And it was in my home country that I got the opportunity to work on my first album. Once again it was Archie Fisher I had to thank for that. Of all the influences on my early singing career, Archie has probably had the greatest impact. In 1969 he had been responsible for my first television appearance and now he asked me to join John MacKinnon and himself on his next album. He is an extraordinary talented guitarist, songwriter and arranger and I've always felt he sprinkled a little of his special gold dust on me throughout our association.

Along with producer Bill Leader, who would release the album on his own record label, Trailer, we began recording *The Fate O' Charlie*, a collection of Jacobite songs, in a back room of Archie's home at Torbain Farm Cottages, just outside Kirkcaldy in Fife. The Jacobites were, of course, the seventeenth- and eighteenth-century supporters of the exiled Stuart dynasty who made several unsuccessful attempts to restore the family of James II of England (or James VII of Scotland) to the throne lost in 1688, culminating in the ill-fated rebellion of 1745 by the Young Pretender, Charles Edward Stuart, and the final defeat in 1746 at the Battle of Culloden. Most of the songs were about Charles Stuart, the Bonnie Prince, and the 1745 Rebellion. We also recorded one of Scotland's most famous songs, 'The Flowers Of The Forest', a lament for another disastrous chapter in the country's history, the 1513 Battle of Flodden Field.

I had done a little bit of recording before, but this was my first experience of working on a whole album. I immediately fell in love with the recording process and felt at home 'in the studio' or, in the case of *The Fate O' Charlie*, in the back room of Archie's cottage. It liberated me from the nervousness I always felt onstage and from the pressures of trying to please an audience and having only one shot at getting it right. With recording you could concentrate solely on the music and the songs; you could experiment and rearrange and work at a piece until you were satisfied with it. Another pleasure was playing Arthur Argo's Martin New Yorker acoustic guitar which he'd loaned to me on a semi-permanent basis. The instrument recorded beautifully: I especially love the last note of 'The Flowers Of The Forest', which simply refused to die away while being recorded. The *Fate O' Charlie* was a wonderful introduction to the disciplines of making an album. It garnered good reviews and remains highly regarded. It also led indirectly to Archie and me being signed by one of the major record labels, Decca.

In 1970 Archie and I recorded two more albums - the collaborative *Thro' The Recent Years* and my first solo album, *Do Right Woman*, named for the Dan Penn classic – at Craighall Studios in Edinburgh. Rab Noakes also featured on these albums. The three of us worked together and we interwove vocals on each other's songs with other musicians chipping in as well. What could be better than making music with Archie and Rab? But the recording was less than ideal as Decca gave us only three days in total to put together each album. Yes, you read that right, three days. It allowed us no breathing space to make changes, to improvise or even to go for another take very often. Not surprisingly, *Do Right Woman* is rather uneven. There is some good material but some of the songs could definitely have done with more work.

If *Thro' The Recent Years* and *Do Right Woman* had been recorded at breakneck pace, the publicity and promotion they were given was leisurely to the point of being non-existent. I was not at all happy with the lack of support we received from Decca, but our contract with them obliged us to make one more album for them. So in 1971, again with Archie's help, I recorded my second solo effort, this time at the Decca studios in West Hampstead in London, and *From The Beggar's Mantle* was released in 1972. The full title is *From The Beggar's Mantle ... Fringed With Gold*, a reference to James VI's description of the kingdom of Fife. It had the same strengths and weaknesses as *Do Right Woman* as, yet again, we had just three days to record it: there were some great musicians playing on that album, among them the wonderful Nic Jones on fiddle and guitar, and some great songs, including one of Archie's finest, 'The Witch Of The Westmerland', which I still sing in concert today, but a few of the songs ended up just so-so at best. Both *Do Right Woman* and *From The Beggar's Mantle* were unavailable for many years, but a few years ago they were digitally remastered and it was fascinating to hear them again. I was pleased at how well some of the material stood up. I think I was a little over critical of them at the time.

The release of *From The Beggar's Mantle* marked the completion of my contract with Decca. Given the time constraints they imposed and my dissatisfaction with their lack of input it was no great surprise to me that they didn't offer me a new one. I loved recording with Archie, but I knew he'd had his own difficulties with the label over his solo album and if the conclusion of this contract was to spell the end of my budding recording career I was not overly disappointed. I don't suppose Decca were, either.

As far as my career was concerned, life was great. I loved playing live gigs and doing tours and it was in those first few years as a professional that I worked hard to lay foundations for the future, learned my craft and became proficient at what I did. So not having a record contract wasn't by any means the end of the world. I was earning enough on the circuit not to have to pay too much heed to my dad's warning about the perils of giving up my civil service pension.

For my first four years as a professional I didn't have a manager. With the help of Archie and Hamish Imlach I had made some initial contacts and thereafter all bookings and tours, and payments, were arranged directly with me. I really was a one-woman band in every sense. My mum answered the phone enquiries when I wasn't there, which led to many long-distance relationships for her, with amongst others, a monk from Uddingston near Glasgow. Handling the bookings was not, however, a part of my job I much enjoyed. I always found it difficult evaluating my own worth and invariably had to battle to secure a decent fee: often I found myself being beaten down. In the Midlands I had been finding some of my work through a folk agency called Fingimijig, run by Robert Davis and John Starkey.

Robert was also a folk singer, about the same age as me. He was one of those performers who was great at bantering with audiences and told jokes between songs. This part of his routine became so popular that, as happened with Billy Connolly, he was doing more and more jokes and fewer and fewer songs until he ended up, as Jasper Carrott, being hailed as Birmingham's most popular comedian (or, as Jasper himself puts it, 'world famous in Birmingham').

In 1972 it was through Jasper's partner John Starkey, who would later take over as his manager, that I met a man called Bernard Theobald, whose parents lived in the same street as John and who I met at a party locally. Bernard had been staying with his sister in Shropshire but came one night to hear me play at a folk club in Wolverhampton. He told me that he had £150 saved up, which he had been planning to use to go abroad to Greece for the summer. After seeing my performance, he was prepared to invest every penny of that £150 in my career if I would agree to allow him to manage me. Once the money had been spent, if I decided I was not happy with the arrangement, we would call it quits and go our separate ways. It was an offer I could hardly refuse.

So I now had a manager and, as it turned out, our partnership worked so well that it lasted for the next thirty years, through all the tours, record deals, hit singles, musicals and TV roles that were to follow.

Bernard's first move was to get me a minimum of £15 a show, and not a penny less; where possible, he would get that figure up to £25. Whenever he was told by the caller that this was too much, he would always say: 'I'm sorry that you can't afford Barbara. Come back when you have saved up.' I was convinced I would end up with no work at all, but to my surprise, I soon discovered that most people were willing to pay what Bernard asked. It opened my eyes to how important it is in this business to have somebody fighting your corner. It's difficult putting a price on yourself.

In 1973 I left home for the second time - well, you can' t live with your mum and dad forever - and moved to England, initially to Bernard's home county of Lincolnshire, where we shared a cottage in Navenby. Now that most of my work was in England, it made sense to be based south of the border.

If my career was shaping up nicely, on a personal level the outlook was rather less rosy. At twenty-six, I still hadn't completely recovered from Ian McCalman. For me that relationship was such a hard act to follow that I probably didn't give others a proper chance. Yet deep down I was restless and felt I'd reached the stage where I wanted someone to share my life with. Thinking about it now, I must have been a nightmare for any man to deal with.

Even if the folk scene of the 1960s and early 1970s was less sex, drugs and rock 'n' roll than sex, booze and folk music, hard partying still wasn't really my thing, especially once I began to mature. I had some great times and did plenty I might easily look back on now and regret - though actually, I don't. In my heart I know that if Ian had asked me to marry him when I was seventeen then my life would have turned out very differently. But he didn't, and it would be a long, long time before I finally met the man who would become my husband. When I did, as is often the way, he came along when I least expected it and was nothing like what I thought I was looking for, or indeed like anyone I'd been involved with before.

In truth I don't think I really knew what it was I wanted, or for that matter where to find it, which goes a long way to explaining the badly thought-out and usually short-lived relationships in which I found myself in the 1970s. The Barbara of 1975 was certainly older than the wide-eyed teenager who'd moved to Edinburgh in the 1960s, but as far as men were concerned, whether she was any wiser was, at the very least, debatable.

CHAPTER SEVEN
WITH A LITTLE HELP
FR⊕M MY FRIENDS.

have no idea how many people I have met in the course of my career. It must run into thousands. You never can tell, of course, on a first meeting which of those people you will never set eyes on again and which are going to change your life completely. So it was with a young student teacher from Liverpool whose path happened to cross mine in the summer of 1967. Willy Russell was up for the Edinburgh Festival and happened to be in Sandy Bell's one Saturday lunchtime. I am much more hazy about when our second meeting was (Willy will have a far better idea, I'm sure), but I think it was after a gig I did in Liverpool, probably in a folk club at Gregson's Well that has long since disappeared. Willy had left school and worked as a hairdresser before going to teacher-training college. He was a huge folk fan - hence his presence in Sandy Bell's - and ran a folk club for a time at his college in Liverpool. Whenever or wherever it was that we met again, I soon became great friends with Willy and his wife Annie, and would often stay with them when I was in the north-west.

I've always loved Liverpool. I felt a great affection for and allegiance to the city because of my mother's roots and family. I have another great friend there: Rosemary Clark, whom I'd first met at fourteen on a school cruise to Spain, Portugal and Gibraltar, was one of a group of girls I got chatting to from Seafield Convent Grammar in Great Crosby. I also bought my second guitar in La Coruna and proudly carried it all the way back to Fife. We kept in contact and I was even a bridesmaid at her wedding. Whenever I went down to Liverpool I would visit Rosemary and her family, who were great to me, and she'd come up and stay with me in Scotland. After Rosemary got married and had four children, we lost touch for a while, but we've remained firm friends since contact was re-established and she gave me plenty of good advice when I had my own children. Once her own had grown up she took a law degree at LMJU in Liverpool. She was always a clever girl.

Back in 1963, at the height of the Merseybeat era, I would go to gigs in Liverpool with Rosemary. Her older sister, Jen knew all the best places and we went to the Cavern and all the other famous venues of the time. We never actually got to see the Beatles - although of course

I was able to declare with pride that I'd already seen them in Kirkcaldy (even if I hadn't actually heard them). Ten years later I was performing in and around Liverpool myself, though I doubt the people who came to see me were quite as excited as Ro, Jen and I had been as audience members in 1963.

It was at teacher-training college that Willy had begun to write drama. On one of my visits to Liverpool in the early seventies, he told me that he had been commissioned by the Liverpool Everyman Theatre to create a musical play about the Beatles from a Liverpool perspective, I remember thinking what a fantastic idea that was and of course I was very keen to find out what he'd written. He gave me a draft of the manuscript to see what I thought of it. I went to bed with a cup of cocoa, or maybe something stronger, and began to read the story of the Beatles as seen through the eyes of an 'everyman', a fellow Liverpudlian called Bert, and became so engrossed that I had to keep going until I'd finished it. It was 4.30 in the morning before I turned over the last page and was finally ready to sleep. I could hardly wait until it was time to get up again and I could tell Willy how absolutely brilliant I thought his manuscript was. Not for one second, though, did it ever occur to me that I could or would have any involvement in the project.

So I was astonished when, in 1973, Willy approached me and asked if I would be interested in appearing in his Beatles show, now entitled *John, Paul, George, Ringo... & Bert*. The play was to open at the innovative Everyman Theatre in May 1974 and was scheduled to run for eight weeks. Willy wanted a different interpretation of the classic Beatles songs featured in the production. He knew that having a soundalike band perform them onstage in Liverpool, of all places, was not going to work, as the audiences would without question always be comparing the unfortunate musicians to the real thing. For some strange, lateral reason, Willy thought of me and decided that this Scottish female folk singer was just the person for the job.

Not surprisingly, the artistic director of the Everyman, Alan Dossor, was not immediately convinced by my qualifications or suitability, and initially he was very sceptical about the whole idea of giving me such a crucial role. He accepted the argument that having an imitative band was not the answer, but felt the way to go was to have the actors in the company sing the songs.

My own immediate reaction to the call from Willy was also cautious. This was a long way from my comfort zone of folk music and what did I know about musical theatre? Bernard, my manager, was rather more confident. He was already convinced that I had something that could transcend the folk circuit and was keen for me to branch out into other musical areas, so he saw this as an ideal opportunity. With Willy's support and Bernard's encouragement, I decided to give it a go. I had loved the script from the first moment I read it in Willy and Annie's house, I had loved the songs of the Beatles since I was a teenager and it was only going to be for eight weeks, after all.

If the proposal hadn't come from Willy, who knows whether I would have accepted it and, if I hadn't branched out, what direction my career might have taken? As it was, even though I was Willy's choice, I was far from being a shoo-in. I still had to demonstrate that I was suitable. A meeting was arranged in February 1974 at the Everyman, where I would need to persuade Alan Dossor that I was the right person for the role. I'd decided that I should play the songs on piano, even though I'd never really played the piano in public before: with only three musicians in the band, I felt a keyboard would be necessary to generate enough noise to make the music work in the theatre and have impact.

On the day of the meeting - and, thankfully, unbeknown to me, as I don't think my nerves would have been able to deal with any more stress - Alan and Willy realised that there wasn't actually a piano in the theatre for me to play and spent a frantic morning manoeuvring the one from the downstairs bar on to the stage, complete with bar stool: the piano was on wheels and too high to play sitting on a normal chair. There were also drawing pins on the hammers to make it sound like a honky-tonk piano. So it wasn't exactly ideal for one of the most important meetings of my life thus far.

Having arrived at the theatre and clambered on to the stool, the first song I sang and played for Alan was 'With A little Help From My Friends'. Written by Lennon and McCartney and recorded by the Beatles on their Sergeant Pepper album, this song had subsequently been a huge hit for the great British singer Joe Cocker. I loved Joe's interpretation - he sang it in a kind of waltz time - and had had the idea of building on that, with the addition of some folk elements.

I wasn't trying to be clever, or to be different for the sake of it. I was just doing what I've always done when learning a song, no matter how familiar or famous: more or less ignoring the versions that have gone before, starting from scratch, though perhaps with influences from previous versions, and interpreting the music and the lyrics in an arrangement I felt was right for me and for my voice. Next I did the same with 'Penny Lane'. To my great delight and even greater relief, Alan loved it. He immediately understood what Willy had in mind in proposing me, saw how my approach would work as part of *John, Paul, George, Ringo... & Bert* and decided that this Scottish folk singer Willy knew was OK. I was in. When I finished singing, I heard a smattering of applause and I looked round. In the auditorium was sitting virtually the whole company, who'd been out in costume in the town, drumming up support for 'The Country Wife', their current production. Bob Hooper in pantaloons and a bald head. That was a sight! More of him later.

The days and weeks leading up to the rehearsals in March were spent learning and re-learning all the wonderful songs that were to feature in the show. As I was going to be mainly playing the piano, I had to memorise all the piano chords in double-quick time. When the rehearsals began I moved in with Willy and Annie, who were expecting their first child. So everyone was on tenterhooks, not only about the show but also over the imminent birth. It was a very exciting time. From the early days of rehearsals we all realised that *John, Paul, George, Ringo... & Bert* was something very special indeed; none of us, however, could ever have envisaged how big it was going to become.

From the day I auditioned for Alan Dossor, I knew I definitely wanted to do the show and needed no further persuasion. I was delighted, too, that it would allow me to spend two months in Liverpool. The local press soon picked up on my Merseyside connections, and suddenly I was no longer an unknown Scottish folk singer covering Beatles songs but a genuine daughter of Liverpool singing the music of its favourite sons. From *John, Paul, George, Ringo... & Bert* onwards, the reception I've been given whenever I've performed in Liverpool has been simply amazing. Walking out on to the stage at the beautiful art-deco Philharmonic Hall on my first headlining tour after doing Willy's show, I was greeted with an ovation unlike anything I'd ever known before. And over thirty years later, in 2007, when I once again appeared at the Philharmonic, the audience was so exceptionally warm and appreciative that I was almost moved to tears. That night, as everybody got to their feet to welcome me back to Liverpool, I was so overwhelmed that all my concentration and professionalism well and truly went out of the window. I could feel my eyes stinging. And I hadn't even started to sing. I remember turning around to my band: they were all wreathed in uncharacteristically soppy smiles.

When *John, Paul, George, Ringo... &* Bert opened in May 1974, the response was ecstatic from the outset. All the doubts about whether a Liverpool audience would accept a play about the Beatles and their music staged by musicians who were not the Beatles were instantly dispelled. The show was completely sold out: it seemed as if everybody in Liverpool wanted to see it. There were bus loads from north Wales there too!

There were three of us in the band: myself on piano, guitar and vocals, Bobby Ash on guitar and bass and Terry Canning on drums and bass. We were seated on a bandstand on the stage for the entire show. Aside from taking a bow at the end, we played no part in any of the action. However, we did do a wee bit of acting of sorts before the show began, when Bobby, Terry and I, along with George Costigan, who played Bert, would go outside and busk the queue. I wore a gigantic duffle coat that actually belonged to Geoff Durham, who later became the magician the Great Soprendo and married Victoria Wood. Once the audience were all safely seated in the theatre, the buskers would reappear and trot down the aisle to take their places on the bandstand, during the first scene.

I sang fifteen songs in total: twelve by the Beatles, two of Willy's and the traditional carol 'In The Bleak Midwinter' that segues into George Harrison's 'Here Comes The Sun', a fine combination that was Willy's brainchild. I still sing it to this day. As well as 'With A Little Help From My Friends' and 'Penny Lane', there was 'The Long And Winding Road', 'Help', 'Lucy In The Sky With Diamonds', 'We Can Work It out' and 'A Day In The Life'. After years of performing on my own with my guitar in small clubs and pubs, it was great to be part of a company, and especially one as talented as the actors of the Everyman, playing to hundreds of people.

Among them were my proud parents. As soon as I heard that they were planning on coming down to see the production I was worried. There was a lot of swearing in the show, and my father did not approve of swearing. So when I met them afterwards I was nervous about what his reaction would be, and broached the subject rather tentatively. 'For goodness' sake, Barbara,' said my dad. 'I used to be in the army.'

It wasn't only the audiences who loved the show; the reviews were great as well. Among the influential people who came to Liverpool to see *John, Paul, George, Ringo... & Bert* were Robert Stigwood, founder of RSO, the man who had brought *Hair* to the West End, and Michael Codron, the top producer of non-musical plays in London. They were bowled over by it and wanted to transfer it to the West End as quickly as possible.

It was the most exhilarating time. That production was to change the lives of everyone involved with it. Not only did it put Willy on the road to becoming one of Britain's finest playwrights, it was also the launch pad for many of the cast of young actors. John Lennon was played by Bernard Hill, who would become a household name as Yosser Hughes in Alan Bleasdale's *Boys From The Black>tuff* and has since appeared in numerous blockbuster movies including *Titanic* and *Lord Of The Rings*. Our Paul McCartney was Trevor Eve whose long television career includes the lead roles in *Shoestring* and, more recently, *Waking The Dead*. As Ringo we had Antony Sher - now Sir Antony. After starring in the highly acclaimed television production of *The History Man* he, of course, went on to become a highly regarded Shakespearian actor, painter, novelist and theatre director. George Costigan (Bert) was Bob in the film *Rita, Sue And Bob Too*. Elizabeth Estensen - whose partner, distinguished Welsh actor Phillip Joseph played George Harrison - was also in the cast, in the role of Bert's girlfriend. She later became a Liver Bird and is now to be found happily (or sometimes unhappily, depending on the twists of the script) pulling pints five nights a week as Diane Blackstock, proprietor of the Woolpack in *Emmerdale*. In the role of Beatles manager Brian Epstein was Robin Hooper, who has enjoyed a long television career and is also a dramatist. He remains a good friend of mine. Looking back, it is extraordinary that so many of today's prominent actors, almost all of whom were unknown then, should have been in the same production at the same time.

Most of us ended up working together for over a year and became a very close-knit company with a real sense of camaraderie. Even though I wasn't an actor and had no previous theatrical experience, everyone was supportive and friendly to me. When Annie Russell gave birth to her son, Robert, and they came home from hospital, I moved in to the 'theatre house' in Huskisson Street where all the actors boarded. The actress Kate Fahy kindly lent me her room as she was staying with her boyfriend Jonathan Pryce, another Everyman luminary - he was appearing at the Nottingham Playhouse at the time. Antony Sher, who came from South Africa, was generally considered the poshest member of the company, apart from Trevor. In addition to being the only one of us, apart from Liz Estensen, who had a car, he was the only one who had Southern Comfort in the drinks cabinet in his room. Come to think of it, he was the only one who actually had a drinks cabinet. Very sophisticated.

When the show transferred to London all but two of the original cast went with it. It was just unbelievable: suddenly, here we were, a bunch of unknown actors from Liverpool and an itinerant folk singer with no theatrical experience, performing onstage at the Lyric Theatre in Shaftesbury Avenue. *John, Paul, George, Ringo... & Bert* eventually ran in the West End for twelve months, winning both the *Evening Standard* award and the London Critics' award for Best New Musical. Throughout that year I had bookings in my diary but as the months went by I kept having to cancel them. So much for my eight-week break from folk clubs.

On the opening night in London in August 1974, famous names such as Peter Sellers and Rod Stewart were in the audience. The whole evening was simply sensational and incredibly exciting for all of us. Our co-producer, Robert Stigwood, had organised an opening-night party for cast and crew at his manor house in Stanmore in Middlesex. As you might imagine, Antony Sher and Trevor Eve knew how to behave in such opulent surroundings and conducted themselves impeccably, but the rest of us got stuck into the free drink and before long most of us, except Antony and Trevor, were absolutely blazing. Robert had kindly extended our invitations to our families, and my parents came all the way down from Fife to be there. It was incongruous to say the least to see my dad at Robert Stigwood's country pile with a gin and tonic in his hand, quietly observing the free-alcohol-fuelled debauchery going on all around him. Although perhaps stranger than the setting was the sight of my father holding a gin and tonic, something he had never drunk in his life, I remember asking him, 'Dad, why are you drinking gin and tonic?' His answer was: 'I don't want to get drunk so I thought I would have something I don't like.' There is, you have to admit, a wonderful logic to that.

As the evening wore on and more and more alcohol was consumed, more and more people seemed to think it was a good idea to take their clothes off and jump into Robert's outdoor swimming pool. You know what actors are like - any excuse to get their kit off. Thankfully, though, all three representatives of the Dickson family remained fully clothed and on dry land although I was tempted. Bernard pointed out the folly of nude bathing, so I was chastened by that and kept my clothes on.

During our stay in London, since there wasn't a theatrical boarding house like Huskisson Street in Liverpool, the cast were scattered across the city. Initially I was in a flat in Parsons Green in west London with Bernard and George Costigan. We all worked really hard on the show, but we would party hard too, when we got the chance - most of us were young, free and single. If London could sometimes be a bit intimidating, I for one loved living there.

John, Paul, George, Ringo... & Bert was so successful that RSO decided they wanted to make an album of the music from the show. Although the whole cast were involved in the recording sessions and there was one song by George Costigan as Bert, twelve of the fifteen numbers on the album were sung by me, so I spent a good deal of time in Scorpio Sound Studio. In between performances at the Lyric I would go off to play the piano and sing the same songs at the studio, situated at the foot of the Euston Tower, next door to Capital Radio. It caused me a certain amount of embarrassment as my fellow stage band members, Bobby Ash and Terry Canning, had not been invited to appear on the album, the record company having opted to employ session musicians. This is not to say that the guys I did work with were anything less than top notch - Kevin Peak from Australia played guitar, Pete Zorn from America played bass, and on drums was a great hero of mine, Dave Mattacks, of the leading folk-rock group Fairport Convention - and I had to be on my very best form to keep up with such a formidable line-up. We had a whizz-kid engineer called Dennis Weinreich all the way from Orange County, who was fantastic in the studio and full of beans on the sessions. It was a far cry from the three days allotted to my previous albums.

I was thrilled when I heard that the producer, Ian Samwell, had managed to book my old friend Gerry Rafferty and his fellow member of Stealers Wheel, Joe Egan, to sing backing vocals. I was really excited to be working with Gerry again, but when the two of them pitched up at the studio they were accompanied by a distinct clanking noise, even though neither Gerry nor Joe appeared to have brought any instruments with them. Further investigation revealed that they were in possession of that most traditional of Scottish gifts: the carry-oot. I had to leave the studio not long after they arrived as I was due onstage at the Lyric. When I returned the next day I discovered that in the course of their session they had polished off the entire contents of the carry-oot. Not surprisingly, there was not much of Gerry and Joe that was usable on the finished album, and Pete Zorn and I had to redo most of the backing vocals.

RSO decided to release 'Here Comes The Sun' as a single - my first ever. Although it received quite a lot of airplay, it didn't make the charts, unfortunately, but that wasn't the end of the world. RSO had already signed me to make a proper solo album once the show closed in mid-1975, and it looked as if my recording career was back on track. It had been three years since *From The Beggar's Mantle* had sneaked out, attracting the attention of almost nobody, and in the meantime I hadn't exactly been besieged by offers to make another one. But now Robert Stigwood was going to give me all the support and promotion and funding a major record label could provide.

While I was appearing at the Lyric, hardly a week went by when I didn't meet some casting director, television producer or record executive. Even now I still come across well-known people who saw the show and who tell me they have never forgotten how great it was. It was at this time that I was first introduced to Andrew Lloyd Webber, Tim Rice and Terry Hughes, producer of *The Two Ronnies*, all of whom would later be significant to my career. None of this hoopla did anything to dispel my innate cautiousness. I was fully prepared for it all to come to an end at any moment and quite expected to be back in the pubs and clubs of the folk circuit before long - and that would have been no hardship, because I did miss the music.

Having been such a fan of The Who in my youth, I was thrilled to be invited to the launch party for the film version of their rock opera, *Tommy*, in 1975. It was a lavish affair at a top hotel in Park Lane. There was a huge ice sculpture, I recall, and loads of famous people in attendance, many of whom I'd admired for years. I would like to list them all here but unfortunately my memory of that night is a little hazy. I'd gone straight to the party from performing at the Lyric and had had absolutely nothing to eat. Being the lightweight I am, after only a couple of glasses of champagne I was suddenly drunk and the next thing I knew I had somehow lost my balance and found myself upside down over a table. One of the guests at the party was the late John Walters, who was for years the producer of John Peel's radio show and a presenter in his own right and whose wife, Helen, was my press officer at RSO. The only reason I recollect John Walters being there was that it was his table I landed on, sending glasses flying and splattering everyone with champagne. John Peel might well have been at the table too, but so might Lord Lucan for all I remember.

After that I took off my shoes, apparently, and promptly lost them. Before I could do any more damage Bernard got me out of the party and took me home. On the King's Road I got out of the car and cheerfully waved him goodbye. I was still so inebriated that I hadn't realised we weren't there yet: Bernard had simply stopped for a red traffic light. Not surprisingly, after that night John Peel never played any of my records on his show. Although to be fair he had never actually played any of my records on his show before that night, either.

Perhaps surprisingly, the four people I didn't meet then were the Beatles themselves. So I had no idea what they thought of *John, Paul, George, Ringo... & Bert* or of my interpretation of their songs. I cannot recall any of them ever commenting on the show, although we did receive, via Capital Radio, a taped good-luck message from John Lennon, by then living in New York, in which he mentioned 'the great girl singer'. As you can imagine, that thrilled me to bits. I was also told that George Harrison came to one of the London performances but didn't stay to the end. And that was about it. However, Willy went on to do some work with Paul McCartney so he couldn't have been offended by the show.

It would have been nice to know if they did approve of what I did with their work - it is always good to get compliments - but to be honest, other people's approbation, as far as music is concerned, has never been an important issue for me. The only approval that has ever mattered has been my own. If a song works and sounds good to me, then I am satisfied; if it doesn't, I am not, regardless of what anyone else says.

Though, sadly, John and George are no longer with us and I will never get the chance to meet them now, in 2005 I did finally come face to face with my teenage heart-throb Paul McCartney, when he very kindly presented me with the Companionship of the Liverpool Institute for Performing Arts. We had a brief chat but didn't discuss *John, Paul, George, Ringo... & Bert*. What I did tell him in front of the assembled audience at Graduation was that I still had in my possession a big picture of him from 1963 that used to hang in pride of place above my bed in Dunfermline. I think he was impressed, although he did look a little alarmed when I asked him whether he thought it might be time I took it down.

My mother, of course, compiled a scrapbook of all my reviews and press cuttings for the show, some complimentary and others less so, although she tended not to keep the unfavourable ones. Of all the reviews I've had in my career I think it is the one of *John, Paul, George, Ringo... & Bert* in *Punch* magazine, written by Barry Took, that sticks in my mind the most for its surreal combination of good and bad:

'The surprise of the evening is Barbara Dickson who plays the piano and sings. Miss Dickson sings in a voice of slate and marble, brass and fire. It is a voice of the Liverpool Kop. It is a voice in love with what it sings, a voice made for singing.

'It is only during the curtain-call that the audience gets a good look at this large, gawky girl wearing gold-framed spectacles. When they do they show their appreciation in a manner reminiscent, of the Liverpool football crowd when Kevin Keegan scores the winning goal.'

Large and gawky? Just how every woman wants to be described.

CHAPTER EIGHT
ANSWER ME

I t is generally only in retrospect that you can pinpoint the key moments of your life. The crossroads in mine have been failing my Eleven-Plus, which put paid to any hopes of academic success; standing up to sing solo at the Brucefield Hotel in Dunfermline when I was sixteen, which gave me the confidence to sing in public; and putting a three-week folk-singing booking in Denmark above my job with the civil service. All of these events set me on the path to becoming a full-time singer. And now, as a result of my decision to accept Willy Russell's offer to sing in *John, Paul, George, Ringo...& Bert*, and all the unexpected success that brought, suddenly a flood of wonderful, potentially career-changing opportunities was coming my way. But did I really want them?

Having had a taste of London life for a year I was in no rush to leave it when the show closed. I stayed on in the fiat I'd been sharing with George Costigan and Bernard until 1976, when I moved to the King's Road, via a brief sojourn at a friend's house in Tufnell Park. On all other fronts, however, I was very uncertain about what I should do next. The cautious, reserved, self-conscious and bloody-minded Barbara had huge reservations and concerns over what was happening and where it was all going. I was a folk singer from Fife, just me and my guitar, and essentially that was all I had ever wanted. But the other Barbara, the inquisitive, wilful, adventurous, bloody-minded Barbara (bloody-mindedness appears to be a characteristic of both sides of my personality) was intrigued by the possibilities being dangled in front of her eyes. My manager, Bernard, having always believed I could and should break out of the folk circuit, was very enthusiastic about the prospect of my career taking a new direction. In the end I was persuaded to surf the wave of new opportunities, even though I felt - correctly, as it turned out - that in the process my opinion of what I ought to be doing was going to be subsumed by what others thought I should do.

Robert Stigwood's worldwide record label, RSO, had on its roster, among others, the Bee Gees, who were on the brink of becoming the biggest artists in the world with *Saturday Night Fever*, plus all the individual members of Cream, one of my favourite bands. So far, RSO had followed up my first single, 'Here Comes The Sun', with a stand-alone version of Irving Berlin's 'Blue Skies', neither of which had troubled the compilers of the Top 40. But I still had my first solo album proper to look forward to, and it was a mouthwatering prospect: Pete Zorn was once more to accompany me on bass, Richard Burgess on drums and Martin Jenner on guitar. The album was recorded at Eden, Scorpio and Morgan studios in London and I was delighted to find that my producer was going to be Junior Campbell.

Junior came from the East End of Glasgow and had been a founder member, guitarist, keyboard player, singer and songwriter with the popular sixties band Marmalade. While Marmalade might be best known now for their number one cover of the Beatles song 'Ob-La-Di Ob-La-Da', a real underestimation of what they could do in my opinion, they also had a whole string of hits written or co-written by Junior, including the classic 'Reflections Of My Life'. And when Junior went solo in the 1970s, he had further success with 'Hallelujah Freedom' and 'Sweet Illusion'. He was a great white soul singer.

The recording in 1975 of what would become *Answer Me*, and working with Junior, was a great experience for me. It was my first pop album and I was surprised at how straightforward the transition was. Having said that, it wasn't as if I'd never sung non-folk music before - I had reinterpreted plenty of contemporary songs in my folk club sets and had just spent nearly eighteen months singing Beatles songs, so it wasn't a complete shock to the system. Besides, I'd never allowed myself to get bogged down in pigeonholing music into rigid genres. As long as I liked a song and believed it was right for what I was doing, that was all that counted. By now I had become quite well known in folk circles all around the country - the weekly music paper *Melody Maker* ran a regular folk-scene column, reporting on who was playing where, and what we were up to, in which I'd been given quite a bit of favourable coverage - and no doubt there was some disappointment among folk purists at what might have been seen as a defection. But for me the only surprise was how creative I found the experience.

For *Answer Me* I even decided to write some of my own songs, something of a new departure as I was not confident about whatever song writing abilities I may have possessed and was therefore pretty reticent about them. It wasn't until thirty years later, with 'Palm Sunday' from the *Time And Tide* album, that I really felt I'd written a song that was as good as any of those I sang by other people. But back in 1975 singers were expected to write their own songs and, as Bernard constantly reminded me, you would always make more money where you had a writing credit as well as a singing credit on a record, so I did the best I could. I wrote six in total for *Answer Me*, and they are probably better than I have allowed myself to believe.

As part of my transformation into a pop star the record label had decided to make radical changes to my image. In the early West End performances of *John, Paul George, Ringo... & Bert*, as Barry Took had not been slow to notice, I'd still been wearing my large, square, gold-framed tinted glasses, though during the run I'd invested in a pair of contact lenses. This was not because I thought dispensing with my glasses would necessarily make me look more glamorous or attractive or showbiz or sexy, but for the more practical reason that when I was playing the piano they kept slipping down my nose and crashing on to the piano keys.

While I was still appearing at the Lyric, RSO had organised a photo session for the album cover, for which I selected a whole wardrobe of gorgeous vintage dresses from Antiquarius on the King's

Road. When I arrived at the photographic studio first thing in the morning for the shoot I met Regis, the legendary French hairdresser and make-up artist. He did not say a word to me. He just looked me up and down as I stood there trying not to look like a startled rabbit. Then he announced: 'Barbara, you have beautiful eyes, but I cannot see your eyes because of your hair.'

He picked up a pair of scissors and began, somewhat to my alarm, to cut my long, unruly locks. Then he turned his attention to my face, judiciously applying make-up from various mysterious tubes and pots. When I looked in the mirror I couldn't believe what I saw. The woman of the glasses and cardigans had morphed into a glamorous, sophisticated, sensual goddess - or as close to a glamorous, sophisticated, sensual goddess as I was ever going to get.

I'd spent my whole life covering myself up as much as possible and hiding behind the hair that gave me so much grief. Now I had a short, elliptical, almost pre-Raphaelite hairdo that I just adored. For the first time ever I was looking into a mirror and actually pleased by what was reflected back at me. The art-nouveau, turn-of-the-century style that was fashionable in the mid-1970s was perfect for me. It was theatrical, but not over the top. When I went to the theatre later that day I called into Phillip Joseph's dressing room and he didn't even recognise me. I was so grateful to Regis for drawing out the Barbara that had been locked inside me all the while and for making me feel confident about my appearance. I still had no real idea about hair or applying make-up or choosing clothes, but having been gently persuaded by the look Regis had given me, from then on I was willing to accept guidance from people who knew something about fashion and style. I really respond to the stories about the Princess of Wales being nurtured in the same way at the start of her celebrity. For a woman, self-confidence is a very fragile commodity and it was only now, at the age of twenty-seven, that I finally began to feel comfortable in my own skin.

Twenty years later, when Trinny and Susannah began their TV show, I would almost weep with joy when I saw ladies who had been stuck in a dowdy and unflattering rut and who were completely devoid of self-confidence being transformed, with a little advice and a fair amount of prodding and pushing, into the gorgeous women they had been all along. All shapes and sizes too. It doesn't matter. It's what's within those women which moves me so much. The confidence just breaks out of them. Trinny and Susannah did a great service to the sisterhood, in my opinion.

The *Answer Me* album was quite well received and sales were OK - if it didn't set the world on fire, it was by no means a disaster, either. The single 'Answer Me' was something else entirely. The song was an old standard that, uniquely, had been number one in the UK charts in two different versions, by David Whitfield and Frankie Laine respectively, one following on the heels of the other, in January 1954. The version I knew, however, was the one by Nat King Cole, which had made the Top 10 a couple of months later. It was the first song that Junior and I had recorded together and Junior's rearrangement was a completely new take on it. He had a hunch that the song would work with a Latin treatment, and it did - though we had a lot of trouble in the studio with the steel guitar and ended up having to use three different musicians. The bell-like harmonics in the introductory hook came courtesy of Gordon Huntley, of Matthews Southern Comfort fame.

We were all pleased with the result and it was decided that it would be the first single from the forthcoming album. 'Answer Me' was released at the tail end of 1975, initially to a generally indifferent response. The singles charts, dominated for over two months by Queen's 'Bohemian Rhapsody', were otherwise full of Christmas hits and nobody seemed bothered by our little song. But by January 1976, when everybody in Britain had bought their copy of 'Bohemian Rhapsody' and the radio DJs stopped playing all the festive records, we finally began to pick up some airplay and, slowly but surely, to creep up the charts.

'Answer Me' would eventually reach the dizzy heights of number nine. Not bad for my first pop single. Suddenly I heard myself being played on Radio 1 all the time. Not only that, but I was asked to appear on *Top Of The Pops*. In the 1970s, BBC Television's weekly chart show was at the height of its popularity. Millions would settle down on a Thursday night to watch it, although as many again, including my dad, hated it. He called it 'moral decline'. Whatever you thought of it, *Top Of The Pops* was gloriously democratic: no criteria whatsoever of quality or taste were involved in selecting the content of the programme - it was all decided on the basis of which singles had been selling that week.

For my *Top Of The Pops* debut the record company sent a white stretch limo to my flat off the King's Road to take me to the studio. This was long before white stretch limos became the must-have accessory for every hen party and I thought it was a very grand gesture. What I didn't realise at the time was that I was actually paying for the privilege. Also I wasn't allowed to take my recording band with me and had to play with the BBC orchestra. I didn't enjoy that experience at all. You live and learn.

I have great fondness for 'Answer Me'. It was my first hit record, after all, and the one that established my name, in the eyes of the general public, as a singer and solo artist. Strangely, though, after about 1985 there was a period of nearly twenty years when I didn't perform it in concert. This was not because I had fallen out of love with the song; it was simply inextricably linked in my mind to playing the piano, something I gradually did less and less of in the 1980s until I stopped altogether. And when the piano went, 'Answer Me' went with it. Just a few years ago, by which time I had returned to playing the piano as well as the guitar in concert, a man came up to me in Glasgow and asked, 'Why don' t you sing "Answer Me" anymore?' and I realised there was no longer any good reason not to include it.

So I went back to the original arrangement Junior Campbell and I had done all those years before and brought 'Answer Me' back into my set. I love performing the song and audiences seem to love hearing it again, too. Even better, 'Answer Me' is the old song of mine that my second son, Gabriel, likes the best. Or, as he succinctly puts it, 'Cheesy, but great,' which, from Gabriel, is high praise indeed.

With 'Answer Me' in the Top 10, the next stage of the RSO master plan was for me to hit the road. First of all I did a 'showcase' gig at the celebrated jazz club Ronnie Scott's in London to mark my debut as a 'pop star'. No more solo gigs with just me, my guitar and my specs: now I had my new hairdo, my expensive vintage clothes, my contact lenses and a band behind me as I sang the songs from my new album. This band comprised Pete Zorn, Martin Jenner, Jeff Allen on drums and Pete Filleul on electric piano. I also had a very cool new Dan Armstrong electric guitar with sliding pick-up, though at this juncture most of the time I was playing the piano and acoustic guitar. In addition, I was being encouraged to get out from behind whatever instrument I was playing and move to the front of the stage to 'strut my stuff'. I never felt comfortable with this; indeed, the very idea of strutting my stuff would bring me out in a cold sweat. I might have temporarily set aside folk music, but I was still Scottish and I had never in my life strutted my stuff, or anybody else's, for that matter, and certainly, not in public.

So if my advisers had worked wonders with my image, they were far less successful in their attempts to change my onstage behaviour. Because I had made my name singing and playing the piano in *John, Paul, George, Ringo... & Bert*, there were moves to package me as a female Elton John. That scared me rigid. I was not a show-woman, I was a folk singer, and while I was happy to play the piano rather than the guitar, I didn't feel right 'working the crowd'. It's just not my style and it's completely at odds with my philosophy that it's the music that is important, not outfits and routines. In that sense I'm not an entertainer, I'm a musician. I always console myself that nobody ever put pressure on someone like Bob Dylan to dance onstage and I didn't understand why they were asking me to do it. But in a bid to make me more of a 'pop star', I was sent off to a woman called Jo Jelly who was charged with trying to 'loosen' me up a little.

Jo was a great dancer and teacher who had worked with the cast of *John, Paul, George...* and ran movement and dance classes at the City Lit off Drury Lane. I had great fun working with her, but it soon became crystal clear that if God had blessed me with the gift of music, he had certainly not complemented it with the gift of movement, in spite of Miss Holroyd's early training. One of the techniques Jo used to relax me was to get me to lie spread-eagled on my back and imagine that I was full of sand and that it was all draining out of my coccyx. This exercise was very effective: I found it so relaxing that before I knew it I had fallen asleep. But for all her efforts, Jo wasn't able to turn me into a dancer, and a non-dancer I have remained ever since. However, I did manage 'Your Feet's Too Big' with flippers in *Seven Ages of Woman* but that was just for laughs. Many years later, when I was performing in the musical *Spend Spend Spend*, a young choreographer by the name of Craig Revel Horwood attempted to devise a gentle dance routine for me but my deep-rooted Scottish suspicion of dancing and all things extrovert was just too ingrained for me to manage it. And if somebody as witty and sparky as Craig couldn't get me to dance, then nobody can. So don't expect to see me on *Strictly Come Dancing* any time soon.

For my first tour of the UK and Europe as a solo pop artist I was the support act for the Flying Burrito Brothers. The Flying Burritos, who were not actually brothers - indeed there were quite a few changes to their line-up over the years - were a hugely influential country-rock band and I was a big, big fan of theirs. By 1976 Chris Hillman had departed and Gram Parsons, sadly, had died, but the great pedal steel guitarist Sneaky Pete Kleinow, a hero of mine who had played on my version of 'The End of The World' on the *Answer Me* album, had rejoined them in their latest incarnation.

We had a marvellous time travelling through the UK, France, Holland, Germany and Scandinavia. I loved touring but I soon realised that if you were not careful you could quickly burn out. No wonder so many musicians took drugs to keep going. My band and some Burritos would hang out after gigs for a couple of hours, drinking and smoking, before having to get up at the crack of dawn to move on to the next destination. I was reluctant to miss out on this quality time with such brilliant musicians, but it didn't take too many of these nights to tire me out. I also began to have problems with my voice. This was the first tour I had ever undertaken with a band and the first using stage monitors. I couldn't hear myself properly above the sound of the band and, being inexperienced, I'd find myself shouting into the microphone to compensate, which is the perfect way to lose your voice. As a result I spent a good deal of time on the road fretting about my ability to perform, but it was all part of finding my feet and learning the ropes in this new arena, which included the legendary Paradiso in Amsterdam and the Olympia in Paris.

At the end of 1976 I supported David Essex for a week at the London Palladium before setting off in 1977 on my first headlining tour of the UK. It proved highly successful and was to become the template for the national tours I have made every year (apart from when I was appearing in the theatre) from 1977 to the present day. In financial terms, touring has always been one of the most important elements of making a living in the music business. It maintains your profile, helps sell records and also allows you to try out new material in front of an audience. But to me it means much more than that because singing live is what I love doing above all else.

If 'Answer Me' had introduced my name to the national consciousness, another unexpected opportunity was about to make me a household name, whether I liked it or not. The producer of *The Two Ronnies*, Terry Hughes, who had seen me in *John, Paul, George...*, asked me if I would be interested in singing on the show, in the musical interlude between comedy sketches that was a staple of the format. Of course I was interested. Plus I didn't have to compromise at all with material. I could sing what I liked. *The Two Ronnies* was one of the most popular and best-loved programmes of the 1970s, with 15 million viewers watching Messrs Barker and Corbett every week, and I loved it. This was a highly prestigious spot and the invitation wasn't just for one show but for an entire series, eight programmes in total. So I was delighted to accept, and every week in the autumn of 1976, viewers would hear Ronnie Corbett introduce me with the words, 'Ladies and gentlemen, Miss Barbara Dickson.' And millions of them would be asking themselves, 'Who's she?'

I will always be grateful to Terry for giving me such a fantastic chance and it constantly amuses me how associated I remain in the public's mind with that show. *The Two Ronnies* ran from 1971 to 1987 and, whenever the subject comes up, everyone seems to remember me as the resident singer for about ten of those years. Nobody ever believes me when I point out that, except for my eight appearances in the 1976 series, I only ever sang on the programme a handful of times. A friend of mine once came up with an explanation of this phenomenon: 'Barbara, people always assumed it was you singing, even when it wasn't. They didn't notice who it was because that was the part of the show when most of them would go out and put the kettle on.'

Another backhanded compliment I have been paid many times over the years is people enthusing about my singing on *That's Life!*, the long-running consumer-affairs show hosted by Esther Rantzen. While it's always nice to receive unsolicited praise, unfortunately I never once appeared on *That's Life!* If I can safely take it that they are not confusing me with Esther herself, the only other possibility is that they are mixing me up with Victoria Wood, who sang humorous songs on the show for a couple of years. At least, I hope so. It's a lot less worrying than being mistaken for Richard Stilgoe.

Something else that surprises people is how little time working on *The Two Ronnies* actually involved. For the 1976 series I went to the BBC rehearsal studios in Acton one lunchtime, where I was introduced to Ronnie and Ronnie, and another day I went to Television Centre and recorded all eight songs chosen for the series. Once one song was in the can, I changed into another costume and moved on to the next one. And when I had finished them all, I went home. The recordings were then seamlessly edited into the shows. I was invited to watch the actual recording process of the last show in the series, which was great fun, and I have met Ronnie Corbett several times since, but that was the full extent of my role on *The Two Ronnies*. Yet even today I am asked what it was like working with Ronnie and Ronnie. Ah, the magic of television.

When I was invited by RSO's film department to play for the nominees and dignitaries of the highly respected Deauville Film Festival in Normandy in 1976, I decided that one of the frocks I had worn for *The Two Ronnies* would be ideal for the occasion. It was a long, diaphanous affair with little beads on the top, a sort of frill around a lowish neck and a long train.

Now, it is one thing wearing a frock to record one song for a television programme and quite another to play a whole show, complete with guitar and piano, in it. But this was a chic, sophisticated French film festival, and Bernard and I would be attending a black-tie dinner with the glitterati before the show, so I felt it was incumbent on me to try to look a bit glamorous. Jeans and stilettos simply wouldn't do.

I should probably have realised that the evening was not going to be a success in sartorial terms when Bernard tried on his dress trousers only to discover that the cleaners had shrunk them. When he tried to pull up the zip, it broke. With no back-up trousers, he had no alternative but to go out in his dinner jacket with his trousers at half-mast and a plethora of safety pins in a sensitive area that would make sitting down a somewhat hazardous experience. As it turned out, it wasn't Bernard who got into trouble, but it was Bernard who understandably distracted by his own plight - trod on my train, causing it to rip along its entire length. What a disaster. With the dinner about to get underway I headed for the ladies' to see if there was anything I could do to salvage the evening. There I found a helpful cloakroom attendant and, although neither of us could speak the other's language, we both knew what had to be done and, communicating through female empathy, we pinned up the train and said a prayer for the pins to hold. Somehow or other Bernard and I managed to get through the dinner without further mishap, but if I had already been feeling *un peu gauche* before the wardrobe malfunction, by the time I got onstage later that evening in my dress held together by safety pins, I was a quivering wreck. The floaty nature of the frock made it simply impossible to play the guitar and restricted my movements, and bits of it kept getting stuck on various pieces of equipment. I have never worn a gown onstage since. I was reminded of this when I saw Shirley Bassey perform in one of her frocks at Glastonbury.

While appearing in *John, Paul, George, Ringo... & Bert*, around the time I'd met Terry Hughes, I'd also been introduced to Tim Rice and Andrew Lloyd Webber, who had come to see the show one night. After their huge success with *Jesus Christ Superstar*, Andrew and Tim were working on a new concept album about the life of Eva Perón, the wife of the Argentine president Juan Perón, known to the people of her country as Evita, and, after hearing me at the Lyric, asked me whether I'd be interested in working on it. Originally, they wanted me to consider the lead role on the album, singing as Eva Perón herself.

In the spring of 1976 I had done some work with Tim and Andrew, but it had soon become clear to us all that my voice did not have the 'belting' quality they wanted for the production numbers and that I felt awkward with some of the material. So instead the role went to Julie Covington, an experienced theatre singer, who would have a massive number-one hit the following year with *Evita*'s most famous song, 'Don't Cry For Me Argentina'. Julie did a fantastic job, and I had no regrets about missing out on the part because I just wasn't right for it. But Tim and Andrew were still keen for me to appear on the album. They offered me another song by a different female character, the unnamed mistress jilted by Juan Perón when he met Eva. The song was 'Another Suitcase In Another Hall'.

After 'Don't Cry For Me Argentina' topped the charts at the beginning of 1977, the record label decided to release another single from *Evita* and chose 'Another Suitcase In Another Hall'. It came out in that spring and made the Top 20 in the UK - my second hit record. Whenever people are asked about their favourite songs of mine, 'Another Suitcase' is one of the two or three that are invariably mentioned, but although I loved it from the very beginning, I have never been fond of the version that was released as the single. In the story of *Evita* the jilted mistress is supposed to be a girl of fourteen and Andrew wanted me to sing in a very high voice, to convey her youth. I worked very hard to create the sense of naïveté and innocence he was looking for but the result, I've always felt, doesn't sound like me and therefore feels false. So I find that recording difficult to listen to.

When I began to sing it in concert I decided that I would reclaim it and make it sound like the real me. 'Another Suitcase' might have been written for a teenage girl, but the experience of being abandoned by a man is one women of all ages can relate to. I think you have to be honest with songs and with yourself. My long-time musical director, Ian Lynn, came up with the arrangement we still use today and once I had found my own voice for the song, it became one of the highlights of my concerts. I love singing it and it is always appreciatively received by audiences, even if it is not quite the version they first heard all those years ago. The rearranging of old hits is something I've become quite good at over the years.

With the success of the two singles it was inevitable that *Evita* the album was going to be huge: as big, if not bigger, than *Jesus Christ Superstar*. After the album was released in 1977 the musical opened to great acclaim in 1978 and became an international phenomenon. All these years later people still assume I appeared in the musical, perhaps because I am so closely associated with 'Another Suitcase', or perhaps through my subsequent collaboration with Elaine Paige who, of course, was the original onstage Eva. But in fact my involvement began in 1976 with the recording of 'Another Suitcase' and ended in the spring of 1977, when the single was in the charts. Andrew and Tim had only ever talked to me about the album and the possibility that I might appear in a West End musical was never even considered. It was Siobhan McCarthy who played the mistress and sang in the original run of *Evita* (she went on to feature in both *Chess* and *Mamma Mia!*). Barbara Dickson ACTING in musical theatre? What a bizarre idea!

CHAPTER NINE
CARAVAN

By 1977 I had settled into life in London. I had bought a three-bedroomed house in Clapham and had made a whole circle of new friends. My parents would come down from Scotland to visit and my mother, always my biggest fan, was proud and delighted with my new house, my new life and my achievements. Being out-going and sociable, she was in her element going out with me and meeting my London friends, though her confidence relied on having me close by her. My father was very proud of me too, but in his quieter, more unstated way. I'm sure he was as bemused as ever by my lifestyle. I loved having my parents to stay, although being an independent woman in her thirtieth year, I was invited to quite a few parties and gatherings where the last thing I wanted was having my mother tag along. My brother, who was mostly living in Germany at the time, would also come over and we had a great time catching up, seeing friends and going out. And now, for the first time, I had a house big enough for us all to be there at the same time.

Until I moved to London I'd never learned to drive – in my years on the folk circuit I'd depended on buses, trains and the kindness of those with cars. By 1976, I'd decided it was time I had lessons. I crammed an intensive course into two weeks and when I went to take my test I was a bag of nerves. Ever since I'd failed the Eleven-Plus I'd been very fatalistic about any kind of exam. I didn't see the point in working slavishly for them when it seemed that anything might happen on the day. Not very logical, I admit, but it was how I felt. I thought I'd driven really well in my test, apart from one glitch, but I knew better than to count my chickens. To my great relief the examiner announced that I had passed and let me loose on the roads of Britain. In fact it was 1978 before I bought my first car, a Mini Clubman Estate - practical and low-key, just like me. When I finally left London fifteen years later I refused to be parted from it, insisting that it went with me to Lincolnshire, where we used it to take us to and from the railway station fifteen miles away. Eventually it fell into disuse and rusted gently away in the garage. When I finally had to get a truck to cart it off to the scrapyard, I cried.

The 1970s seemed to fly by. I was working really hard, touring, recording, doing interviews and appearing on TV. In the little time I had off, there were always parties, dinners, friends to see and family visits. I was living in one of the world's great capital cities and my own world was full of people. My personal life, if not quite as chaotic as it had been before, remained complicated. During my time in London I had two consecutive long-term relationships, both with talented but not well-known musicians. I ended the first to begin the second, however the main problem lay in my selection process. Both were serious and when the second one collapsed I felt particularly hurt and let down. I realised that, in the latter, I was being exploited by a man I had trusted and I had to acknowledge that it was never going to last. The problem was not an uncommon one: our partnership was unequal and I felt that the guy was always uncomfortable with my success. I think he resented it and, therefore, me. So that was an unhappy period. But as painful as break-ups can be, you do live and learn, and you move on, you hope, to something better. At least I had my career to concentrate on. It is probably true to say that I was a late developer and although I had turned thirty in September 1977, in many ways I was far younger than my years. And as for finding a mature, stable and adult relationship, I still had a long way to go. I had given up a really nice person for someone less so and that was my problem at that time. I seemed to be going backwards, not forwards.

My transformation from unknown Scottish folk singer to a 'pop star' with two hit records and a regular performer on one of the biggest television shows of the time made 1976 and 1977 pretty surreal years. Not only did millions of people now know my name, but they knew what I looked like as well. I would often find myself doing promotions, such as appearing at shopping centres or on some live broadcast for radio, where I wouldn't even be playing live but miming to 'Answer Me' and looking out at hundreds of excited, occasionally hysterical people thrilled that this 'pop star' had come to their town. I was genuinely bewildered about why everyone was so excited. It was only me after all. What was all the fuss about? It was as if I had found myself in a parallel universe.

Somehow I had suddenly become famous. I hadn't sought or desired fame, but through the opportunities that had come my way I had attained celebrity whether I wanted it or not. I was only too aware, of course, that, in the line of work I had chosen, if I was successful, then becoming well known went with the territory, but when everything started happening for me in 1976 I instinctively knew in my heart that fame for fame's sake was not worth having.

I have been in the public eye for over three decades now and have spent all that time fighting the whole notion of celebrity. It's a false assumption based on the premise that famous people are different from everyone else. From the very beginning I was uncomfortable about being recognised when I wasn't working. Sunglasses, hats and scarves soon became accessories I never left home without. Even today, when I am doing my shopping or walking along the street in my hometown, I never make eye contact with anyone. This is not a legacy of my teenage years in Edinburgh when being too vain to wear my glasses, I couldn't actually see anybody, but a conscious effort on my part to be as invisible as possible. My husband Oliver finds it highly amusing when a neighbour or a friend waves at me as I go by and receives not a flicker of recognition in return, so oblivious am I of passersby when I'm out and about that I never look at anyone. At work I like meeting people, and at the end of every show I always go out and speak to any members of the audience who have had the patience to wait for me, and I'm delighted to sign whatever programmes or CDs they have. It is a part of the job I enjoy and

I've never had a problem with it. Going about my private business, however, I sometimes struggle to deal with strangers coming up and talking to me.

When 'Another Suitcase In Another Hall' went into the charts in Britain I was across the Atlantic making my second album for RSO. We recorded *Morning Comes Quickly* in Nashville, Tennessee, home of country music, even though it was not really a country album. Being in Nashville was very enjoyable and I even got to meet the country legend Willie Nelson, a thrill I'll never forget. My producer was Mentor Williams, who was also a songwriter best known for 'Drift Away', a US number one for Dobie Gray. I got on very well with Mentor and he brought together an excellent group of musicians to play on the album. Everybody was incredibly laid-back; in fact the whole atmosphere was very relaxed and stress-free, just what I needed for my first experience of putting together an album in the US. On keyboards we had David Briggs, who recorded and toured with Elvis Presley. We found out that Elvis was recording in Nashville at the same time as us and thought it would be great if we could engineer a meeting with him. Everyone got very excited at this prospect and tentative approaches were made. Not exactly my people talking to his people, but David knew the right members of Elvis's entourage to handle our request and a message came back that yes, Elvis would be happy to meet us. Mentor had met him once already, which helped.

Trying to find a suitable date was much trickier. Elvis lived in Memphis, of course, and was scheduled to fly in and out of Nashville on his private jet. He liked to record through the night, so he wouldn't ever be arriving at his studio till the evening. That wasn't a problem but he kept delaying his sessions due to illness. When we were finally given an appointment, on a Friday evening, our excitement reached fever pitch.

We were all set to leave when, at six o'clock, we got a message to say that The King remained unwell, had postponed his recording session yet again and was still at Graceland. Elvis had not left the building. I was disappointed but held on to the hope that our meeting could be rearranged.

To my great sadness, it was not to be, on that trip or any other. I had to return to London and only a few months after I'd been recording in Tennessee, on 16 August 1977, word came through that Elvis was dead at the premature age of forty-two.

Morning Comes Quickly was released in 1977 and did relatively well - it was the first of my records to make the album charts - but it didn't have an 'Answer Me' to break into the singles listings, an important component at that time. The album featured three songs I'd penned myself, but on reflection I'm not certain any of them were all that fantastic. It was my last one for RSO as in 1978 I was headhunted by CBS records, run by Maurice Oberstein who was very keen to have me on his label. I was classed as a 'major signing' at that point which was why they sent me to Los Angeles to make my first album for them, *Sweet Oasis*. It was my first proper visit to LA, aside from a brief trip at the end of 1977 for a blink-or-you'll-miss-me appearance in the finale of the film *Sergeant Pepper's Lonely Hearts Club Band* which starred, among others, the Bee Gees, Steve Martin, George Burns and Frankie Howerd (it would be safe to say it must have been the only time that particular bunch of people were ever all in the same place at once) and which was ultimately a box-office disaster. On the plus side, I got to meet Donovan and Jack Bruce, both of whom had been persuaded to appear in the last few frames of the movie with me, both of whom were heroes of mine and both of whom came originally from Glasgow. We formed a little Scottish cabal as the madness of filming unfolded around us. I also got to keep my director's chair, which was printed with my name.

I wrote all but one of the songs on *Sweet Oasis*, the exception being a version of 'City By City' by my old friend Gerry Rafferty, and the band included my long-time musical collaborators Ian Lynn and Pete Zorn. We recorded at the famous Wally Heider studio in Hollywood. It was great working there but I felt the album needed a bit of UK atmosphere, so we completed the project in Chelsea at Sound Techniques.

Sweet Oasis was not a great success and did not trouble the album charts so in 1979 CBS decided to team me with Alan Tarney, one of the hottest producers and songwriters in Britain at the time, who had recently enjoyed great partnerships with Leo Sayer and Cliff Richard - he had written Cliff's number-one hit 'We Don't Talk Anymore'. We began working on the record that would become *The Barbara Dickson Album* with half the songs written by me and half by Alan. The first single was to be a new song of Alan's, 'January, February', but before it was released another song of mine was to make the charts.

Caravans is a mostly forgotten epic film based on a James A. Michener novel, starring Anthony Quinn (one review accused the lead actor of being Zorba the Nomad). It was also the last movie to be made in Iran before the revolution. I never knew if there was a connection. The soundtrack was written and composed by Mike Batt, top songwriter and producer and the man behind the music of *The Wombles*. His greatest success came in 1979, with 'Bright Eyes', the theme song from the movie *Watership Down* and a number one for Art Garfunkel. That same year I was asked to sing Mike's theme song for *Caravans*, called 'Caravan Song', and it was released as a single at the end of 1979. Coincidentally, I sang a song for *Watership Down*, too. It was called 'Run Like The Wind' and it was for Hyzenthlay, the lead female rabbit. However, after it was decided that Hyzenthlay wouldn't sing after all, I ended up on the cutting-room floor.

'Caravan Song' became a minor Top 40 hit for me and, although it was nowhere near as big as 'Answer Me' or 'I Know Him So Well', it has since become the piece that elicits the warmest response from my audiences. Even now, nearly thirty years later, the hymn-like feel to the music and the inspirational lyrics resonate with them every time I perform it. As a live favourite, 'Caravan Song' usually appears in the second half of my shows. During my pregnancies in the late 1980s, an emergency 'pee break' had to be built into the second half, ostensibly as a costume change. So I would leave the stage as the band carried on playing a specially extended instrumental version of 'Caravan Song', much to the bemusement of the audience. If only they'd known what was happening backstage.

It really is a lovely song and I am glad I was given the opportunity to record it. To be honest, it probably should have been a much bigger hit than it was, but since CBS had decided that the first single from my new album was going to be 'January, February', which therefore had to be released in the first two months of 1980, all their efforts were focused on making that one count. 'Caravan

Song', meanwhile, quietly dropped off the radar.

CBS did a great job with 'January, February'. The single reached number eleven and was a terrific launch pad for *The Barbara Dickson Album* - my first Top 10 album in the UK, and also the first to go gold. With sales of over 100,000 copies, it was far and away the biggest album success I'd had so far. The odd thing about 'January, February' is that, although I like the way the record turned out and the tune is very catchy, I've never thought it was a great song. I much prefer 'My Heart Lies' or 'Can't Get By Without You', both also written by Alan Tarney but forgotten now. Alan did a fantastic job on both album and single; he's a lovely man and I really enjoyed working with him. But 'January February' just isn't one of my favourites, and I have to say I've never much liked singing it since. So, while I still happily perform 'Answer Me', 'Another Suitcase In Another Hall', 'Caravan Song' and 'I Know Him So Well' in concert, with various tweaks and reworkings over the years, recently I haven't played 'January, February' at all. I've found, too, that it relies completely on its original arrangement and doesn't seem to benefit from any fresh approach. Interestingly, in contrast to what happened with 'Answer Me', I have not been aware of any great public demand to bring it back. Maybe it is simply of its time and doesn't bear too much scrutiny. Nowadays, I feel I need more meaningful material, I guess. There's a huge difference between a great record and a great song, and both have their place. But for me, the song wins every time.

Rain or shine, wind or hail, every year I would set off on my annual tour. With hit singles and hit albums, the venues became bigger and the tours became longer as more people wanted to see me live. Ever since I stopped performing solo, I've always had a fantastic band behind me and I found I much preferred playing with them to going it alone. It has been a privilege to share my career with so many great musicians - some in the UK, some in America, others scattered elsewhere in the world - and I know I have been a very lucky girl in that regard. Sadly, a few of them, like Andy Brown and Martin Jenner, are dead now, but many of my working relationships have lasted for years. I believe part of the reason they have done so is that other musicians respect and appreciate my commitment and my burning desire for us collectively to make the best music we possibly can. That's what they want, too. It's why we all do what we do and why we continually come back for more.

When you have played as many gigs as I have, it is difficult to differentiate one tour from another in your memory. The outfits I wore are usually a reliable indicator of which year was which. Many were designed by Jackie Castellano. It was on my 1978 tour, for example, that, in our wisdom, we decided skin-tight trousers, bat-wing sleeves and a sequinned skullcap were the way to go. I don't think that look caught on. That was also the year, I recall, when I managed to get myself stuck onstage. One night in Edinburgh the trousers I had on were so tight that when I walked backwards at the end of a song in the fading light, my calves collided gently with a stage monitor, my knees folded - and they stayed that way. I sank gracefully over the back of the monitor and out of sight, legs stuck up in the air in a passable imitation of a sheep that has ended up on its back and can't right itself. There I was obliged to remain until, under cover of darkness, my roadie was able to manoeuvre me into an upright position just in time for the next song.

On that same tour, at a gig in Preston, I was still in my dressing room, completely starkers, when I heard the tour manager announce over the Tannoy, 'Ladies and gentlemen, Barbara

Dickson!' Hell's bells. There was nothing for it but to throw on my costume as quickly as I possibly could – I must have set a world speed record for getting into those trousers. As I ran on to the stage I was still buttoning my shirt and simultaneously fixing my sequinned skullcap. I passed the tour manager on my way and would happily have punched him, if only I'd had the time. I should have had a five-minute call, of course, but the tour manager hadn't quite got to grips with that part of his job description and neither had he checked to make sure I was at the side of the stage before announcing me. He also, I might add, told the hall manager every night I needed a bottle of whisky as part of my backstage rider. It was, needless to say, not for me.

Albeit more by accident than design, in general my bands have all been well behaved, not too rock 'n' roll, although a dishonourable mention must be made of my Spring 1982 band. I'm naming no names: you know who you are. And there was a particular drummer who used to read a book onstage behind the kit by torchlight while I was singing 'MacCrimmon's Lament'. Hardly up there among the worst excesses of rock 'n' roll history, I grant you, but it played havoc with my confidence.

The crew, however, could be another matter. I once had a crew member who was a complete cocaine fiend and constantly agitated, although I was so naïve I thought his red nose was a result of an unusually persistent cold. This fellow had decided that the set should include a lamppost and a staircase. The lamppost was so big it wouldn't fit into most of the theatres we were playing and when I walked down the staircase, all the audience could see was my feet. It might sound funny now, but at the time was an absolute nightmare. I had to cancel a homecoming concert in Dunfermline, which as you can imagine did not go down at all well, because we simply could not get the set into the theatre. There were mentions in the *Dunfermline Press and West Fife Advertiser*, I can tell you.

On another tour the crew were resident on a black double-decker bus, charmingly known as the Black Death, and to celebrate one of their birthdays they decided to throw a party on it. This featured copious amounts of beer and a local stripper. Thankfully, I was unable to make it owing to a prior engagement. And then there was the roadie who accompanied the band and me to the 1978 Tokyo Music Festival where, despite all my doubts about my songwriting abilities, I was awarded a bronze prize for 'Second Sight'. It was a very prestigious festival, with big names such as Al Green, Diana Ross and a young Kate Bush in attendance, and we were wined and dined and generally royally entertained for a week. One of the events to which my band, my crew and I were invited was a sake party. I was there only briefly as I had to be somewhere else that evening, but Bernard and I later received a message telling us we would have to return to the party as an 'incident' was taking place. When we arrived we were confronted with the sight of our roadie, stripped to the waist, standing in a giant barrel of sake, swirling the sake ladle around his head like a claymore and beating off all attempts by the waiters to remove him. Eventually we were able to persuade him to get out and a diplomatic incident was averted, although suffice it to say I have never received any further invitations to the Tokyo Music Festival.

The follow-up to *The Barbara Dickson Album* was also produced by Alan Tarney with, once again, half the songs written by Alan and half by me. We all had high hopes for *You Know It's Me*, which was released in 1981. Unfortunately, it soon became clear that either the public didn't know it was me, or they did know and decided not to buy it anyway. CBS responded to this disappointment by resorting to one of the great maxims of the record industry: if in doubt, bring out the greatest hits. *All For A Song* was duly released in January 1982 and included 'Answer Me', 'Another Suitcase', 'Caravan Song' and 'January, February', along with some new tracks recorded in Holland and produced by Mike Batt. It became my most successful album yet, reaching number three in the charts and selling an incredible 300,000 copies - my first platinum album. Even more remarkably, it came out in Scotland before hitting the shelves in the rest of Britain and sales there were so high that it reached number nine in the UK charts on the Scottish figures alone. In fact *All For A Song* was such a hit that the tour planned for 1982 had to be expanded and split into two, with more dates and even larger venues.

In the 1980s, when I was at the height of my success as a 'pop star' you were expected to do the rounds of the television music and entertainment shows to promote your records. Today about the only regular music programme on mainstream TV is *Later...with Jools Holland*, but back then there was a plethora of them. If you were fortunate enough to have a hit record you would go on *Top Of The Pops*, but there were all sorts of other variety-type shows for which you could be booked to sing your single, such as *Little and Large*, *Des O'Connor* or *Crackerjack*. I think over the years I must have done all of them, with the notable exception of the *Basil Brush Show* which, for some reason, I turned down - probably too many 'boom-booms' for my liking. These appearances were a part of the job that held little appeal for me and I don't remember ever being particularly keen on them. As happened with *The Two Ronnies*, sometimes you would go and record your song separately and it would later be edited into the show. Other times the extent of your encounters with the host would be when you found yourself being introduced by Syd Little or Ed 'Stewpot' Stewart. It was all very unreal and slightly weird, but it was what was required of you and you just got on with it. The record company required cooperation with promotion.

Perhaps because I had started in pop music so late and had a long apprenticeship on the folk scene behind me, I always prided myself on being professional and taking television work as seriously as I took everything else. I didn't know any other way of working, to be honest, and if it meant my image was never edgy or cool and I became known as one of the acceptable faces of pop and light entertainment, then so be it. I couldn't imagine myself acting like a diva, throwing tantrums or otherwise behaving badly: I would turn up, smile and say hello, sing my song, say goodbye and go home, where I would put my feet up, have a glass of wine and ruminate on the peculiar life I led.

But if I didn't much relish promoting my work on TV, I loved singing and performing and I loved recording. In the 'pop years' it was fantastic to have the time, money and support to make my albums as good as they could possibly be - a far cry from the frustrations of helping to produce those Decca folk albums in three days. I loved having my own house and my own little car in London, and all the financial and material benefits that came with pop success. For someone like me, who had always dreamed of making a career in music, it truly was a wonderful life. As Billy Connolly would say when experiencing the occasional setback, 'When all's said and done, it's still better than welding.' Not that I have ever welded, but I know exactly what he means.

By 1980, thanks to my good fortune, I was in a position to offer to buy my parents a new house, and they opted to leave Dunfermline for Southport on the Lancashire coast. My mother was the driving force behind the move. I think it would be fair to say that she had never quite seen herself living in Fife for the remainder of her days and her restlessness had been compounded by both Alastair and me first leaving home and then leaving the country altogether. In Alastair's case first for Germany and then Canada. So, after thirty-five years in Scotland, she decided that this chance of a new home would be the ideal time to make a fresh start. My father was at first very reluctant to leave his hometown that had been his life for so long, but being the man he was, he not only chose to go along with my mother's wishes but then settled into his new surroundings surprisingly well.

I suppose I had a sense of being in showbiz but not of it. I never felt I was some kind of imposter who didn't deserve to be there, but I wouldn't claim, either, to have felt completely at ease with it, or with the fame it brought. I've never in my life wanted a fur coat or to travel around in a Rolls-Royce. So I saw myself as an outsider, really, one step removed from many of the celebrities I worked with. What it did give me was a priceless opportunity to meet some very interesting people. I might not have come face to face with Elvis in the end, but I did meet Nana Mouskouri and Eric Clapton. If you've ever wondered what sort of person would be equally excited to encounter two such disparate artists, you need look no further than me. Among other musical heroes of mine to whom I was fortunate enough to be introduced (I've already mentioned Jack Bruce) was Levon Helm, the singer and drummer from The Band who had started out as Bob Dylan's backing band before going on to great acclaim in their own right with one of my favourite-ever albums, *Music From Big Pink*. His was the amazing voice on 'The Night They Drove Old Dixie Down'. And when I was playing at the Royal Albert Hall, I had the privilege of meeting the legendary Ray Charles, who said to me 'Baby, you're a great singer.' Life doesn't get much better than that.

There was still plenty of room for improvement, however, in my personal life, for which the early 1980s was a fairly disastrous period. My second long-term relationship ended in a messy spell of rancour and bitterness that left me feeling somewhat dented, and then came the second blow of a failed reconciliation with Ian McCalman. So I was at a very low ebb, and desperate to get some fun back into my life when, right on cue, I met Desmond Lynam.

This was in 1982, when Des was one of the main sports presenters on the BBC and regularly presented *Grandstand* on a Saturday afternoon. We hit it off immediately: Des is very funny, interesting and great fun to be around. He genuinely loves sport and took his career very seriously; indeed, we did seem to spend quite a lot of our short time together watching it on television when I'm sure there was something more interesting we could have been doing instead.

It is fair to say that I have never been the biggest fan of sport in general, although I do love rugby union. In spite of those childhood visits to East End Park with my dad to see

Dunfermline Athletic I'd never really got into football and by the time I met Des my knowledge of all things sporting was rather limited, to say the least. But I knew how important sport was to him, so I tried my best to take an interest. Des was always very patient as I asked him for the twentieth time to explain the offside rule, although in most cases whatever information he took the trouble to impart went in one ear and out the other. In the two months we went out together Des was sent by the BBC to do several outside broadcasts around Britain or overseas and I would feel it was my duty to make sure I got up early or stayed up late to watch him live on TV, even if I rarely had much inkling of why he was there, let alone what he was talking about.

It was never destined to be a long-lasting relationship - at the time Des didn't much go in for long-lasting relationships, and I was hardly one of the Brigitte Nielsen lookalikes that seemed to be his usual type. I enjoyed our time together, although it didn't end that well, which was a shame. It kind of fizzled out. Sadly, I didn't get the opportunity to pour a pint of beer over his head, but even if I had I'm not sure it would have resulted in anything more than a sardonic raising of an eyebrow.

Many years later I was invited into the hallowed Dictionary Corner on Channel 4's *Countdown*. Although it was still being presented by a Des, by this time it was Des O' Connor, who had replaced Des Lynam as host. I had great fun on the show with him and Carol Vorderman, but I think viewers might have enjoyed the added frisson if I'd appeared on it earlier, when the other Des was presenting - frisson, of course, being a seven-letter word consisting of five consonants and two vowels.

CHAPTER TEN
TELL ME IT'S NOT TRUE

In 1982 I was approaching my thirty-fifth birthday and it was not a landmark I was anticipating with great joy. The relationship with Des Lynam had fizzled out, leaving me once again well and truly single and with no prospect of a potential partner on the horizon. Yet, for the first time I could remember, I had no great desire to find a new man. I was tired of being hurt and fed up with being fed up. By now I was convinced that there had to be something in my own make-up that was causing my relationships with men to end in failure and I decided to do something about it. I started going to see an analyst, an experienced doctor with a practice in London's Wimpole Street.

After a nervous beginning I found I was surprisingly comfortable talking about myself. My Scottish reserve was soon abandoned as all the feelings and emotions of the previous few years, and all the changes there had been in my life, came tumbling out. As is always the case when dealing with this kind of introspection, it takes a good and perceptive analyst to get you to open up and I was very fortunate in that respect. The doctor was a wise old owl. He was patient and courteous, but at the same time he could be blunt and to the point when necessary. As I had a tendency to ramble on if left to my own devices, this would often prove invaluable. On one occasion I was regaling him at some length with the failings of one of my recent exes and he suddenly stopped me in mid-rant and said, 'Barbara, you missed something.'

Certain that I had covered all aspects of this man's unreasonable behaviour, I was taken aback.

'What have I missed?'

'You haven't mentioned that he was a bastard.'

You see, that was my problem; choosing the wrong men.

Going to analysis brought a lot of my life into sharp focus. We children of the baby-boomer generation had been brought up to believe in a better world and to have greater expectations of it than our parents had. We had also been brought up to believe - or at any rate, I had been - that for each of us there was a special person out there who was 'the one'. As soon as you had found your 'one', you would get married, have a family and live happily ever after. I had gone through the 1960s and 1970s searching for this perfect partner, kissing quite a few frogs along the way - and none of them had turned out to be the fabulous, talented, sexy, funny Prince Charming I had been promised. And now here I was, in my mid-thirties, still single, with no children, and extremely pissed off that the expectation of finding my 'one' was no nearer to being fulfilled.

It was around this time that there was some press speculation about my sexuality. A successful woman of thirty-five and no sign of a boyfriend? There could only be one explanation: Barbara Dickson must be gay. With hindsight I must concede that I probably fuelled such whispers with my default answer to the question 'So Barbara, do you have a boyfriend at the moment?' I always replied firmly and succinctly in the negative, even when there was actually a man on the scene, simply because I didn't think my love life, or lack of it, was anybody else's business. I'm sure other people in my situation would have been more worldly-wise in handling the media, or would at least have had the self-assurance to laugh off whatever suspicions were doing the rounds, but as usual my innate seriousness meant that I was never able to see anything even faintly amusing about it. On the contrary, I found it completely infuriating. However, the up side was that I found I had a new lesbian fan base.

Rumours or no rumours, to most people Barbara Dickson was the wholesome girl next door who had occasional hit records and appeared on *The Two Ronnies*. But I didn't really recognise that sanitised image of me any more than I did the constructs of the press. Looking back now, I realise that what I went through was simply a normal part of the process of growing up. You make mistakes and perhaps you go out with someone who is just blatantly wrong for you, but as long as you learn from your experiences, both good and bad, and ultimately remain true to yourself, you will be OK in the long run. The only trouble was, in my case growing up seemed to be an incredibly drawn-out business and the fatalistic side of my personality was already telling me I was never going to meet the right person. In addition, it was looking increasingly unlikely that I would ever have time to have a family.

Nowadays it is far more common for women to leave having children until their late thirties and early forties, but in the 1980s it was still considered unusual and medically risky to have your first pregnancy at the age of thirty-five. If I was not quite past it, my biological clock was, at the very least, ticking loudly. This sense of time running out wasn't going to make it any easier to find a partner but frankly, by the end of 1982, I wasn't even looking any more. If I was destined not to have children, then so be it. I never even considered having a baby out of wedlock.

It was a pretty draining year on all fronts, given the two back-to-back tours I undertook to capitalise on the success of *All For A Song*, and by the time the landmark birthday had come and gone and 1982 was drawing to a close I was exhausted. Time to take a break and put my feet up, you would have thought. But life, as I well knew by now, is full of surprises, and it was this moment Willy Russell chose to transform mine for the second time by offering me the lead role in a major new show he'd been working on.

Willy had gone from strength to strength after *John, Paul, George, Ringo... & Bert*. He had written several more plays, the most famous being *Educating Rita*, which opened in 1980 with Julie Walters as Rita, a role she would reprise, alongside Michael Caine, in the 1985 Academy Award-nominated film version. Willy and I were often in touch so I knew that he was working on a new musical, called *Blood Brothers*; indeed, in 1980 I had offered to sing a new song he had written for it, called 'Easy Terms', on a demo tape. I immediately fell in love with that song and I still think it's the best song in the show. It tells of the heart-breaking moment when the lead character, Mrs Johnstone, has to give up one of her twin baby sons and, like all great songs, it grabs you from the very opening lines.

Willy had first staged *Blood Brothers* on a small scale with the Merseyside Young People's Theatre Company at Fazakerley Comprehensive in Liverpool in November 1981 and had spent the whole of 1982 expanding it into a full-blown musical. As it began to take shape he had come to the conclusion that he wanted Mrs Johnstone's songs to be sung pretty much in the same way as I had performed 'Easy Terms' on that demo. But finding an actress with the right sadness and vulnerability in her voice had apparently proved tricky and now - not long before the show was scheduled to open at the Liverpool Playhouse - he wanted me to play the role.

I'd sung 'Easy Terms' for Willy, being his friend, and purely to help him out as he developed the project and I had not for one moment envisaged any involvement beyond that. The full extent of my acting experience had been my turn as the 'Kelty Clippie' in the Great Fife Roadshow years before and the idea that I could learn to act in under four weeks - let alone take the leading role in a musical – seemed utter madness. Furthermore, I had just done over sixty gigs in less than six months and I was well and truly knackered. Certainly, if anybody other than Willy had approached me at that point with such an offer, I would have said no immediately. But it wasn't anybody who had approached me, it was Willy, and because it was Willy, and against my better judgement, rather than saying 'no', I said 'maybe'. Bernard, of course, thought this was the chance of a lifetime and shouldn't be missed. Yet again, I was always flattered by being asked and had difficulty taking my own opinion into account.

It was arranged that Willy and the director of the production, Chris Bond, would come to see me at my house in Clapham. I was perfectly well aware that before trying to persuade me to take the part they were going to try to establish that I was capable of handling it. I was absolutely terrified by that prospect. Every rational part of my mind was telling me to say, 'No, I just can't do this,' and in the days before the meeting I felt sick and panicky. It was only the knowledge that Willy believed I had it in me, and that he could 'hear' me singing his songs, that made me want to go through with it. There has always been a stubborn part of my personality that hates to admit defeat, and to admit defeat before I had even started was something I just couldn't countenance.

Willy and Chris arrived at the appointed time and handed me a speech from the play to read. The only brief they gave me was: 'Mrs Johnstone is a mother. Her son has just been arrested. She has to stop him going to jail. She is in the police station.'

I read the speech, and then they gave me some more background on the character and asked me to read it again. I had to deliver the same lines several more times, and each time they would tell me a little more about Mrs Johnstone, about her other children and about the situation in which she found herself. They were attempting to gauge whether I was able, on absorbing the information, to use it to convey, with each reading, a slightly deeper sense of' the character's history and emotions through the dialogue.

They must have seen at least some raw material they felt they could work on, because when we had finally finished, Willy and Chris looked at each other and then said to me: 'You can do this.' And that was that. I was offered the role of Mrs Johnstone and heard myself accepting. I didn't want to disappoint them.

For those who don't know the story, *Blood Brothers* is a powerful exploration of the big themes of family, love, superstition, betrayal and class. It tells the tale of two brothers separated at birth. The character I was taking on is an indomitable, if much-put-upon, working-class Mother Courage from Liverpool who already has a brood of five children when she discovers that she is pregnant again, this time with twins. On hearing the news, her wastrel husband does a runner, leaving Mrs Johnstone destitute and struggling to feed her family. Realising that there is nothing else she can do to prevent all of her children, including her unborn twins, from being taken into care, Mrs Johnstone makes a deal with the middle-class Mrs Lyons, for whom she cleans, and who is unable to have children herself. She will hand over one of the twins to her employer, and the child will be brought up in comfort on the condition that it never knows who its real mother and family are, and that the twins never meet one another.

But at the age of seven, the twins - two boys, Mickey and Eddie - do meet, by accident, and become best friends. On discovering that they share the same birthday, they make a pact to become 'blood brothers'. Eddie's well-to-do adoptive mother, Mrs Lyons, is horrified by this development and the family moves away from the city. However, the boys meet again at fourteen and, still completely unaware of their true relationship, become inseparable. They both fall in love with the same girl and, as they grow up, their lives blighted by the inequalities of the class system, the consequences of the decision to sever and deny the bond between them begin to play out.

There were only three weeks of rehearsal before the show opened, and I have to say that those three weeks were probably the grimmest of my life up to that point. This was not my natural milieu and I was like a fish out of water. Here was I, a complete amateur, working alongside experienced actors with the question 'What am I doing here?' constantly reverberating round my head. I had great support from Willy and Chris and was heartened by the fact that the wonderful George Costigan, who had played Bert in *John, Paul, George...*, was in the role of my son Mickey. Even so I felt I was struggling badly. Every day was torture as I went through rehearsals juggling a mop, a bucket and my script. Fear of failure is a very powerful emotion and never had I felt it as keenly as I did then.

My one small consolation was that *Blood Brothers* would be opening in Liverpool, where I'd had a rapport with audiences even before *John, Paul, George, Ringo... & Bert*. So if I was going to fall flat on my face, which seemed quite possible, I felt that at least the good people of Liverpool might be kinder to me than most. Another positive to which I clung desperately was the familiarity I had, through my family connections, with my character. I knew the Liverpool of the 1950s Willy was writing about and where Mrs Johnstone came from. I knew the voice she spoke in. I knew the clothes she would wear, the pinny and the shoes; I knew the life she led and I understood the fears and hopes that made her do what she did.

It has been suggested that my portrayal of Mrs Johnstone was based on my mother. This is categorically not true. I certainly drew on my own childhood memories of Liverpool, on what I had heard from my relatives about their lives, on aspects of the Malley family story and on some of their traits, one or two of which my mother shared, but Mrs Johnstone wasn't my mum.

If I found the rehearsals traumatic, all the cast and crew were lovely to me throughout, patient and supportive, and some have remained great friends - Wendy Murray, who played Mrs Lyons, is godmother to my second son, Gabriel. And amid all the stress of the rehearsals there was the occasional lighter moment. Most of these seemed to revolve around hairdos, for some reason, as we experimented with wigs and costumes to see which ones worked and which didn't. At one stage it was suggested that I should adopt a Marilyn Monroe-style blonde wig, an idea that was quickly given the elbow (can you imagine?), but the prize for most entertaining hairstyle had to go to Wendy for the wig Mrs Lyons originally sported on top of her head. It was less 1950s suburbia and more a cross between an eighteenth-century Duchess of Devonshire and Elsa Lanchester in the *Bride Of Frankenstein*. Time after time, as poor Wendy tried to get through a scene, everybody on the stage would end up collapsing in mirth, until eventually Mrs Lyons turned up with a very nice perm.

The build-up to the first night of Willy's first musical since *John, Paul, George, Ringo... & Bert* was immense. But the pressure I was under was intensified by my conviction that, no matter how talented the other actors in the cast were, its success was going to hinge on my ability to bring the character of Mrs Johnstone to life. Afterwards I realised I need not have worried on that score, at least: *Blood Brothers* is so brilliantly written that the show is virtually indestructible. As we were opening on 8 January 1983, the Christmas and New Year festivities of 1982 were a very restrained affair. In over forty years of performing onstage I have never been as terrified as I was that night in the wings of the Liverpool Playhouse. The play began with the theatre in darkness and me singing offstage the first lines. Then the lights went up and I stepped on to the stage from the downstage right wing in my brown coat, pinny and flat shoes, with my hair rolled up in kirby-grips and no make-up apart from a bit of lippy. In my best Scouse accent (thank you, Mother) I said, 'Once I had a husband, you know the sort of chap...'

At which point, to my eternal gratitude (thank you, people of Liverpool) the whole audience burst into applause. A few minutes later I had a funny line to deliver to Mrs Lyons, a line we had rehearsed so assiduously in the previous weeks that we no longer had any idea if it was actually funny. But on the night it got such a big laugh that I had to pause to allow the mirth to subside before continuing. It was all down to timing and, inexperienced as I was as an actor, timing was a skill I had been using all my life in music, and this was not so very different. I was off!

The final song in *Blood Brothers* is the poignant and heart-rending 'Tell Me It's Not True', the opening two lines of which had introduced the show. It was only when I had sung the very last lines and knew I had finished that I dared to acknowledge that I had survived my ordeal. A huge feeling of relief swept over me, quickly followed by the realisation that yes, I could do this - and I could get better.

I wasn't arrogant enough to think I had miraculously become an actress after just one night. My inexperience was still very apparent, but I had worked so hard learning all the lines and all the songs and, with the expert guidance of Chris Bond, had channelled so much of myself into the character of Mrs Johnstone, that the heart and energy I brought to the role must have been palpable not only to the other actors but to the audience as well. And now that I had managed to emerge from the first night unscathed, I was determined I would improve and become really good.

My parents were there that night and when my mother told me afterwards how she had been so caught up in the show that it was Mrs Johnstone she saw up there on the stage and not me, her daughter, I really felt I had succeeded in making the transition from musician to actress. My father, as shy a man as you could meet, guffawed so loudly during one scene - when Sammy, Mrs Johnstone's ten-year-old son, takes some worms from his pocket and says, 'They was alive and wriggling this morning, but by dinnertime they was dead' - that I could hear him from the stage. The worms, I remember, were exquisitely fashioned, if such a thing can be, by our propmaker, Bill. He made the twin babies, too, and his attention to detail was a great help when it came to handling them authentically. Their heads were heavy, like a real baby's, so you instinctively held them in the way you would a real infant. Much better than the dolls they use now.

We knew that the Liverpool audiences loved *Blood Brothers* and thankfully the reviews, too, were overwhelmingly good, acclaiming it as one of the best and most original British musicals ever. It was fantastic news for Willy and Chris and all the cast and crew for the work they had put into the show. To my immense relief; the reviews of my own performance, as an actress as well as a singer, were also positive. We were on our way. It was about six weeks into the run, just as I felt I was settling into the role and improving with every performance, that I experienced my first-ever bout of stage fright. The incident that set me off was in itself fairly innocuous: somebody came onstage with the wrong prop. Any actor will tell you this is one of the complete no-nos in theatre. It might sound like a minor glitch, but the sight of an unexpected object can completely disarm another actor. I've heard stories about people being utterly thrown by the appearance of the wrong actor, too, when an understudy has had to take over and they haven't been informed of the change beforehand. Anyway, this character was supposed to come on with a radio, but instead he emerged touting a vacuum cleaner. My next line referred to the radio so I was totally knocked off course and everything - other than 'What is that bloody thing doing there?' - went clean out of my head.

Somehow, I instinctively managed to mentally accommodate the absence of the radio, and the actor exited the stage again. But quickly digging myself out of that hole had put me off my stroke, and immediately afterwards I dried totally. I had absolutely no idea what my next line was. It was the most horrible feeling. In truth it was probably only a matter of seconds before somebody else managed to get the dialogue started again and, thankfully, audiences rarely notice these incidents; usually they think everything that happens onstage is deliberate. But for actors it's another matter. For you, and for everyone onstage with you, time stands still and the silence seems to go on forever.

Fortunately, as soon as we got through the scene I had a song to sing and the rest of the performance passed off without a hitch. But I knew, and everybody else in the cast knew, that I had dried and I felt that something had changed.

As I've mentioned, I've always been nervous before concerts but I'm able to keep my anxiety in check once I start to sing. Over the years I've learned to actually channel those nerves into heightening my concentration and helping me to give the very best performance I can. If I didn't have butterflies in my stomach before a gig then something would not be right. Occasionally I have forgotten the words of a song onstage, but the band would still be playing, and I would just muddle through or 'la-la-la' until the lyrics came back to me. It could be a bit scary in the moment, but to be honest it was more embarrassing than anything else. I knew it happened to everybody who performs at one time or another and I never dwelled on it.

But in all the time I'd been singing I couldn't remember experiencing anything remotely like this new, paralysing variety of fear. The theatre was different from the concert stage. Here I had no natural defences. I had no band behind me and no resources or preparation to deal with being out there, alone, in total silence. All my insecurities about my lack of acting experience came flooding back and I was simply terrified of forgetting my lines again.

From that night on, I began to feel dreadful, increasingly ill and increasingly tired. I wasn't sleeping at night, or napping during the day. What I should have done was see a doctor, or get some other form of professional advice, but I've always been stubbornly reluctant to ask for help and instead I just told myself I'd get over it - it would pass.

After our three-month run at the Liverpool Playhouse we would be following in the footsteps of *John, Paul, George, Ringo... & Bert* and transferring to the Lyric Theatre in the West End. Before opening in London, we had a fortnight's break in which I would be able to rest and recuperate, so I soldiered on until the end of March without any further mishaps and with the support of Willy and the rest of the cast, who all knew I was struggling.

The prospect of a long run in the West End was not something that should have worried me - after all, I had performed in *John, Paul, George, Ringo... & Bert* for over a year. But in that show I'd only been the leader of the band, not the leading actress. Still, I was already contracted to do *Blood Brothers* in London, I knew how crucial the transfer was going to be to its success and once again, I hated the thought of letting anybody down. So in our two weeks off I girded my loins, readied myself to give the show my all and we duly opened on 11 April 1983.

At first everything went splendidly. *Blood Brothers* continued to be well received by audiences and critics alike and I was happy with my own performances. I had, it seemed, found a second wind. But the underlying problems, my inexperience and my stage fright, or to be more precise, my fear of stage fright, hadn't gone away and after three months I was feeling more worn out than I had ever felt at the Playhouse. It was at this juncture that the stage fright I so dreaded returned and I dried again - at more or less the same point of the show where it had happened before, and to which I had clearly remained potentially allergic ever since. Again, with the help of the cast, I somehow got through to the end of the performance, but I felt terrible, even worse than I had in Liverpool. I had been playing Mrs Johnstone for over six months and it was as if every one of those performances, plus the sixty gigs I'd done in 1982, not to mention six years' worth of non-stop touring and performing, were all piling in on me, culminating that summer in total mental and physical exhaustion. As well as all this, I didn't have anyone close to turn to; to just talk to about my feelings or the pressure I felt was weighing me down.

One evening I was in my dressing room getting ready for a performance when, without any warning, I suddenly began to weep. I don't know how long I sat there before Rosemary Curr, the company manager, found me crying my eyes out. When she asked me what was wrong, I remember replying, 'I don't know.'

'Can I help at all?' said Rosemary gently.

'I don't think so. I am just so tired I can hardly put one foot in front of the other.'

Obviously it was clear to Rosemary that something was seriously amiss, and to my eternal gratitude, she did not try to rally me into going onstage. Instead she immediately instructed the understudy to get ready and got someone to take me home straight away.

I remained in a terrible state until I was safely home, where I remember pouring myself a glass of wine and then going to bed. It must have been the relief that a decision had been made for me that enabled me to sleep, because I was out for the count right through until the next morning. I hadn't had a good night's sleep in months, and when I finally surfaced I felt fine. But I knew the reason I felt fine was because I didn't have to go back to the theatre that day - I had been signed off *Blood Brothers* for two weeks with exhaustion.

Slowly I began to recuperate and I was feeling a lot better, but I was dithering over addressing the inevitable question: what was I going to do about the show? Would I ever return to it? Willy came to see me and asked me what I wanted to do. All I could tell him was that I didn't know. Of course the truthful answer would have been that I didn't want to go back, but at the same time I didn't want to let people down and I didn't want anyone to think that Barbara Dickson was unprofessional. My analyst told me: 'Barbara, you are a perfectionist, and it is that perfectionism that's driving you on to prove to yourself that you can do this. But you have to realise that nobody is perfect and all you are doing is mentally flagellating yourself and making yourself ill. You could easily have a breakdown if you don't relax.'

Looking back on that summer I can see now that I simply did not have the experience or the acting stamina to perform in a production like *Blood Brothers* eight times a week, month after month after month. My analyst was right: it was in my nature to take the show so seriously that I would be giving 101 per cent to every single performance and it was inevitable that I would wear myself out.

Chris Bond, who had been briefly working in New York when I experienced my first bout of stage fright in Liverpool, had called me then to see how I was. This time he said, 'Barbara, it's only a show.' However, he had a plan he thought might make things easier for me if I did decide to return. He promised that he would stand in the wings and if, at any time, I felt it was all too much, I just had to give him a signal and he would personally take me offstage and bring the curtain down. He also told me that if the worst thing that could happen was Mrs Johnstone fainting and falling into the orchestra pit, the audience would cheer as she climbed back out again. That's how much they loved her. As well as being keen to get his Mrs Johnstone back, Chris also wanted me to be able to end this experience on a high and his suggestion offered me a way of achieving that with the safety net of his constant support. I will always love him for the great help he was to me at that time. He proved himself to be a good friend indeed.

So I went back to *Blood Brothers*, and the wonderful Chris Bond was true to his word: he was there for every minute of my script run-through and every minute of the show. I cried most of the way to the theatre, threw up when I got there and walked on to the stage trembling and shaking with fear. But I did the show. It was by no means my best performance, or anywhere close to it, but I got through it. The cast were absolutely fantastic to me that night, and on all the other nights of the remainder of the run.

Towards the end of my contract, the producer, Bob Swash, and my manager, Bernard Theobald, asked me out for lunch. I've still no idea if this was the brainchild of Bernard or Bob. With *Blood Brothers* drawing ever larger audiences, I should have smelled a rat. When they asked me if I would consider agreeing to an extension of the contract, I bowed my head and began to weep quietly right there at the table. I was so miserable. I just couldn't believe that, after all my suffering, they could possibly expect me to carry on regardless. I don't remember now if I even formally said no, but they had their answer. There wasn't a sum of money, or any other incentive, in the world that could have persuaded me to shake out my pinny and get back on that stage for one minute after my agreed stint was over. I had done my nine months and I had earned a rest.

When our involvement in the show finally ended Wendy Murray and I took a flight to St Lucia in the Caribbean for a three-week holiday. Despite the fact that for the previous six months her character, Mrs Lyons, had tried to stab me onstage every night, we had become great friends. We had a wonderfully relaxing time in St Lucia without a sharp implement in sight. The sunshine, cocktails and reggae were just the treatment I needed.
I don't want to give the impression that *Blood Brothers* was hell on earth for me because, for the most part, it wasn't like that at all. Aside from the bouts of stage fright and subsequent exhaustion, it was a wonderful, life-changing experience, with long periods of feeling fine. I

was immensely proud to have been involved with such a fantastic, groundbreaking production and to have been given the opportunity to play as strong and memorable a character as Mrs Johnstone. I always felt very proprietorial about and protective of her. I remember being interviewed down the line for a radio station in Wales very early on, in the first few weeks of the original run in Liverpool, when the presenter suddenly asked me, 'Barbara, what is it like playing a slut?'

I have been asked all sorts of surprising, and sometimes inane, questions by interviewers in my time but I could not believe what this man had just said. I was absolutely furious. How dare he? There followed a long pause (ideal for the radio) before I calmed down enough to reply, 'Look here! Mrs Johnstone might be poor, but she is not a slut.'

When the Society of West End Theatre awards were announced, Willy deservedly won the award for Best Musical. And as if that wasn't thrilling enough, I was both astonished and delighted to take the award for Best Actress in a Musical. At the time the awards were known by their acronym, SWET (they later became the rather more dignified-sounding Olivier awards), and my God, I certainly felt I had sweated plenty in my time in *Blood Brothers*.

I honestly wouldn't say I have ever been the kind of person who craves recognition or awards, but of course, it is absolutely wonderful when you actually get one. And to win it for my first foray into acting was amazing. It was particularly special since, as far as I was concerned, it was also likely to be the last acting award I was ever going to receive. At the end of the night, after all the thanks and the congratulations and the photographs, once I was safely back in the privacy of my own house, I clutched the trophy to my bosom and burst into tears. Again. Everything was very emotional at that time.

After *Blood Brothers* I was, not surprisingly, in no rush to set foot on a theatre stage again. But if I thought I'd put my stage fright behind me, I was mistaken. When I returned to singing I found that this most unwelcome ghost now haunted me on the concert stage, too. The terror I had of it recurring was now with me constantly. The realisation that in the professional arena where I had always felt most secure, playing for an audience with my band or on my own with my guitar, I now had to contend with crippling nerves and the ever-present fear that I would dry and forget everything, was dreadful. I'd never known this to happen in my world of music.

Many actors do very long runs indeed and never seem to have problems of the kind that troubled me; equally, there are plenty of examples of truly great actors and other performers, from Laurence Olivier down, who suddenly experience that horrible moment when they feel they cannot go on. Some have to fight those demons for years and there are those in the acting profession who are forced to give up the stage altogether and stick to recording film and TV only. These are very fine artistes indeed and it's no indication of their ability, only their sensitivity.

I can't speak for other people, of course, but I think in my case the problem has its roots in the necessity to expose the vulnerable core of myself while performing. My musical or acting skills are harnessing something in my soul, creating an alchemy which, when it is working at its very best, is what moves the observer. Victoria Wood once kindly said to me that I have a 'repose' which has nothing to do with exterior performance. If I do have such a quality, it is coming from somewhere deep within me. Opening myself up in that way, and then adding a dose of unrealistic perfectionism, is bound to be fraught with risk and what had happened to me onstage in *Blood Brothers* had somehow upset the delicate balance between the source of what I was expressing and the expression itself.

Whatever the cause, for someone like me, whose goal in life for as long as I could remember was simply to sing and to sing well, to be suddenly fearful of going onstage was terribly demoralising. I would suffer from this affliction through most of the following decade, sometimes intermittently, sometimes very badly, and I tried all manner of techniques in my efforts to overcome it. For a while I would drink a very large brandy before I went onstage, but that didn't last long: the terror seemed immune to alcohol and all the drink did was take the edge off my sharpness. Fortunately, I didn't decide to go down the route of trying two glasses of brandy. I remember at another stage being offered medication, which back then would have meant some sort of Valium-type drug, but I declined, thinking that if alcohol took the edge off my sharpness, then tranquillisers certainly would, too. Of course, being such a stubborn so-and-so, I didn't do the sensible thing and actively seek help. For some reason I felt that I had brought the fear on myself and it was therefore up to me to find a way of conquering it. And eventually I did. It was, though, a long, dark process involving identifying the triggers but above all the great healer, time.

What I am sure made my insecurities and fear more acute when this problem first surfaced during *Blood Brothers* was that I had nobody to share my worries with. Chris and Willy and Wendy and Rosemary, and the rest of the cast and crew, were fantastically supportive, as were my friends and family, who were always looking out for me, and I was still going to see my analyst, too. But at the end of every show, when everybody had left and I was back in my own house, there was nobody there to talk to me and put their arms around me and tell me it would be OK. I had gone into the production more resolutely single than I had been for years, and as I've said, another relationship was the last thing on my mind. But it was then, just when I was at one of the lowest points in my personal and professional life, that I met the man I would ultimately marry.

In fact I met Oliver Cookson on the very first morning of the rehearsals for *Blood Brothers* in Liverpool. He was Assistant Stage Manager and the first words he ever said to me were: 'Hello, I'm Oliver. Would you like to join the tea club?' Oliver was from London and had been born into a theatrical family: his father was the wonderful character actor Barrie Cookson and his mother, Avril, had trodden the boards as Avril Conquest before her marriage. They had met as the leading actors at the Theatre Royal, Bath. How romantic is that? Oliver had wanted to become an actor, too - he'd caught the bug at youth theatre in Richmond, where several notables had begun their careers - but had been talked out of pursuing such an insecure profession by his mother. Nevertheless, the theatre, it seemed, was in his blood, and after working initially for Lancia and Jaeger (a strange brew) he had ended up doing a course in stage management which had eventually brought him to the Liverpool Playhouse culminating in being 'on the book' in *Blood Brothers*.

I liked Oliver immediately and from the very beginning there was a mutual attraction. Apart from the fact that I wasn't looking to get involved with anybody at that point, I had another serious reservation. While I had just celebrated that watershed thirty-fifth birthday, Oliver was only twenty-four: eleven years my junior. Although the age gap didn't seem to bother him in the slightest, I very much doubted that a relationship between us could ever work, and as a result it developed very slowly at first. It was only when things started to get tough for me with the show, and I found Oliver was always there and always supportive, that it began to dawn on me how genuine he was and how committed he was as a friend, in spite of his relative youth, to demonstrating that he was in there for the long haul. Even so, I was still not convinced.

I remember saying to him once, 'What are you thinking? When you are forty-nine, I will be sixty. Is that really what you want?' Oliver replied, 'I don't care.' It's strange to realise now that we actually passed that milestone a couple of years ago.

It was Oliver's unshakeable confidence, his optimism and his absolute certainty that he wanted to be with me that eventually won me over. He has always been the calmer of the two of us, the one with the more openly positive view of the world, while I am the over-imaginative, emotional, irrational one who panics at the first sign of trouble. Rather like the Chinese symbols of Yin and Yang, we complement each other to form a harmonious whole - most of the time, anyway. Oliver has never found it difficult to cope with my success and, from the very beginning, our relationship has been an equal partnership.

When I felt sure, at long last, that Oliver was right for me, that was that. We were together, and that is the way it has been ever since, I'm glad to say. We have recently celebrated our silver wedding anniversary: it's hard to believe that twenty-five years have passed since those days of doubt and uncertainty.

CHAPTER ELEVEN
I KN⊕W HIℼ S⊕ WELL

There were some further decisions Oliver and I had to take to give our relationship the best possible chance. Although we had met in the theatre, I felt that if either of us remained in that environment on a long-term basis we would have no prospect of any kind of social life or time together. If we were going to have a future as a couple we needed to make some changes and in the summer of 1983, Oliver left the theatre and joined the BBC.

With that obstacle cleared, on my return from my Caribbean holiday with Wendy Murray, Oliver introduced me to his parents. At the end of the year he proposed and I accepted. We arranged our wedding for August 1984 at the Church of St Elizabeth of Portugal in Richmond, Surrey. I had moved to Richmond from Clapham in 1985 and, coincidentally, found I was living only two hundred yards away from my future in-laws. Luckily, we always got on very well.

In the run-up to our wedding I was commissioned to make a television special, part travel guide, part musical guide, for the BBC. For that programme, in the summer of 1984, I journeyed across the picturesque Highland countryside on the West Highland Railway from Inverness to the Kyle of Lochalsh before taking a boat to Skye (the Skye Bridge had not yet been built) where, inevitably, I was obliged to sing 'The Skye Boat Song'. All slightly cheesy, but effective. And I must say that it was somewhat more comfortable than my trip to Skye with Ian McCalman back in the 1960s. I will always have very fond memories of that 1984 visit: I was excited about my wedding and it was lovely to be spending my final days as a single woman in the Scottish Highlands. For the last day of shooting we were on the beautiful Loch Ness, seeing if we could spot the monster, and once the filming was complete, I headed for Inverness Airport, flew down to London and married Oliver that weekend.

Oliver had been brought up a Catholic and I was very willing to marry in church and that is why we chose St Elizabeth of Portugal, a Catholic church, and asked a friend of the Cooksons,

Peter Beasley, from Worth in Sussex, who happened to be a Benedictine monk, to conduct the ceremony. My father, sadly, was in poor health and not well enough to travel down from Lancashire for the wedding, but my mother and many of my family and friends were all present to watch my brother Alastair walk me down the aisle and give me away. Neither Oliver nor I wanted a 'showbiz' wedding, but there were still plenty of actor and musician friends in attendance and the whole day was a wonderful combination of the formal and the informal.

Not that it was all plain sailing: these occasions never are. First of all, at the rehearsal the night before the ceremony, we'd discovered that the church organ was not working properly. Either it was making no sound. at all or it would emit noises that were very unmusical indeed. On being informed of this potentially disastrous setback, Fr Peter decided that further assistance was required. He went over to the troublesome organ, laid his hand on it and said, 'Lord, can you please allow us to sing your praises during the marriage of Oliver and Barbara tomorrow? There are some very good musicians going to be present and we need this organ to work.' Then we all trooped home and the next day the organ sounded absolutely glorious.

I wore a simple straight cream skirt and jacket created for me by the Glaswegian designer Elaine Closs, topped off by a specially made hat with a veil. Ian Adam, an inspirational singing teacher who lived in London but hailed originally from Inverness, sang beautifully during the ceremony and Janet Edwards played the church organ. She was very relieved that it worked!

I may have thought I knew all about stage fright, but I was absolutely terrified as I stood in front of Fr Peter and our forty guests, the most important people in our lives. Here were Oliver and I making all those promises and I was keenly aware that everything I was saying now I would have to live up to. Standing there, listening intently and feeling solemn, I knew with total conviction that this was the only time in my life I would get married. This was not a rehearsal or a sound check and there would be no take two. This was it, and I had to get it right.

When the ceremony was over there was another glitch, fortunately more minor than the business with the organ: the limo booked to take us back to the house, where we and our guests would be spending the afternoon, broke down. But it was a lovely day, so we all just walked across Richmond Bridge in the sunshine, laughing and joking. Later we were all joined by around another hundred friends for an evening party at Maxim's in the West End, where pride of place was taken by a multi-tiered chocolate wedding cake. It was a fabulous night and I can say, without fear or favour, the best wedding I've ever had.

Because of work commitments we had to postpone our honeymoon for three months, but at least we'd been on holiday together earlier that summer to the west of Ireland. Unfortunately it had rained incessantly throughout our trip and when we did manage to venture outdoors we were in constant danger of being blown off the cliffs. One day we got soaked to the skin playing pitch and putt in Kilkee, Co Clare. Despite the lashing rain and being inappropriately dressed in shorts and hiking boots, we were determined to finish the game (I must have been winning). No amount of rain could spoil it for us: we had a whale of a time.

From the moment Oliver and I made that huge commitment to each other the whole question of the age gap simply melted away. It wasn't a problem for us and it wasn't a problem for our family or our friends. All the people who were most important to me adored Oliver. Perhaps it has helped that Oliver has always seemed mature beyond his years while I have, I think, always been the opposite. I have certainly never felt any need to try to seem younger to make our relationship work, and I doubt I'd be capable of doing that anyway. I cannot be anything other than myself and the same applies to Oliver. We hoped and believed that as long as we were true to ourselves and true to each other everything would be fine and, touch wood, so far it has been.

I was happy that, from the outset, Oliver had expressed the wish to have a family and as I was approaching thirty-seven at the time of our wedding I was keen too. But even though Oliver has always been the practical one, when I announced that I wanted a baby, I was little taken aback by his reply: 'I want to have a baby, too, but you're not having a baby until you get your overdraft down.'

It is fair to say that since becoming professionally successful I had enjoyed spending the money I had made. That photo session with Regis for the *Answer Me* album ignited a passion for buying clothes without much thought for the cost, and it is possibly true that over the years I had bought more shoes - and in the early days of my increased earning power I had a particular fondness for shoes from Terry de Havilland's shop on the King's Road - than could be deemed strictly necessary, although I had always managed to justify the need for every pair I purchased. I was therefore more than a little disgruntled that my new husband saw fit to make such pronouncements on my finances, even if at the time I didn't actually have any idea what my bank balance was. A cursory investigation revealed (though I would never have admitted this to Oliver) that my overdraft was perhaps a little on the high side so, through gritted teeth and with much dark muttering, I began to make economies on my spending. Eventually, and with steam still coming out of my ears, I was able to flourish my much-improved bank statement in front of him. 'Now,' Oliver said calmly, 'we can have a baby.'

Amid all this domestic bliss I still had a career to pursue, of course, and in 1984, I went back on the road, stage fright and all. After I finished *Blood Brothers*, Chris Bond agreed to direct my concerts and brought a new theatrical feel to the shows. He would interpret individual songs, using appropriate lighting and props, and also introduced some acting into the format. The reaction to his innovations and ideas were very positive and I was to follow his template for the next fifteen years or so.

I was also being offered more television work. As well as the Scottish Highlands programme I'd filmed just before we married I made various other television specials during the 1980s, for which I travelled to some of the most beautiful parts of Britain and Ireland - among them Lincolnshire, the Isles of Scilly, South Wales and the west of Ireland - and they were all great shows to film and fantastic places to visit. I was also very fortunate to be able to work with my longstanding musical director, Ian Lynn, on those specials. Once I had selected the songs to be featured, he tackled the job of making them work in the context of the programmes.

It was through the director of the Highlands special, Ken Stephinson (with whom I'd worked earlier on a series with Richard Stilgoe), that I was asked to appear in a profile of the famous Rochdale singer Gracie Fields, who had died only five years before, in 1979. Ken, who had been commissioned by the BBC to direct the documentary, saw more than a passing resemblance between Gracie and me – even though vocally we were quite different, as she was a soprano and my voice is no higher than an alto - and was keen for me to sing as Gracie for the programme. I'm still not really sure whether I was up to the job. My voice would naturally break on a B flat and I have never felt comfortable singing an entire song higher than that, so hitting the high notes on Gracie's signature number, 'Sally', was difficult, to say the least. Strangely enough, as I've got older, my voice has become happier singing in the higher register, so nowadays, maybe I would be more confident up there!

On both the Highlands special and the Gracie documentary, as well as fulfilling my singing role, I was given the opportunity to do all the links to camera and I really enjoyed my first attempts at television presenting. I must have made a reasonable fist of it as the BBC then offered me the chance to co-present a weekly programme called *The Afternoon Show*, initially with Penny Junor and latterly with the much-missed Pattie Coldwell.

The Afternoon Show was one of the first to employ the now firmly established format of combining interviews, features, consumer affairs and special guests. I was expected to do no singing whatsoever: maybe that was where I'd been going wrong all those years. I really enjoyed working on that show, which was recorded as live in Glasgow and networked across the UK. The ratings for the first series were good enough for another to be commissioned in 1985. I was disappointed when I heard that Penny Junor wasn't available for the second series, but I needn't have worried: I had a fantastic time working with her replacement, Pattie Coldwell. Pattie, who had made her name as a consumer-rights champion on *Nationwide*, was both uncompromising and great fun. One of the joys of *The Afternoon Show* was that we might be discussing orthopaedic surgery or dementia one minute and interviewing Billy Connolly the next, and Pattie was at home with them all.

As we both used to stay overnight in Glasgow before recordings, we would regularly repair to the Ubiquitous Chip or some other such hostelry in the city's West End, where Pattie would keep me entertained for hours with hilarious stories, libellous gossip and pearls of wisdom, all delivered in her inimitable gravelly Lancashire accent. When Pattie had first appeared on television in the 1970s someone had described her voice as being capable of descaling a kettle but she never tried to modify it in any way, and quite right, too. She was a popular broadcaster and widely mourned when she died of cancer, aged only fifty, in 2002. I couldn't believe I was never going to hear that wonderful voice again or see that wicked smile.

I loved branching out into television, and especially my stint on *The Afternoon Show*, but of course music and singing were still my true passion. My first new album after the *Blood Brothers* soundtrack, which had been released in 1985, was *Heartbeats*, featuring 'Tell Me It's

Not True' from *Blood Brothers* and a version of the great traditional song 'MacCrimmon's Lament' that I had reintroduced in 1978 into my concerts as an acoustic counterpoint to all the pop material. *Heartbeats* came out in 1984 and did moderately well, reaching number twenty-one in the charts, but, with no hit singles, it achieved nowhere near the success of *All For A Song*. *Heartbeats* was my last album for CBS: I then signed with K-Tel, better known for their compilation albums and ebullient television advertising. I was planning my first album for them, a mixture of new material and covers, when Tim Rice re-entered my life.

I had kept in touch with Tim in the years since 'Another Suitcase In Another Hall', and he contacted me to tell me about a new project he was developing with Bjorn Ulvaeus and Benny Andersson, half of the hugely successful group Abba who had recently disbanded. The new project was *Chess*, which would be first of all a concept album and then a musical. It was the story of two grandmasters, one American and one Russian, competing for the World Chess Championship and also involved in a love triangle with the American's manager, Florence, who had fallen in love with the Russian. Elaine Paige, who had played Eva Per6n in *Evita*, would sing the role of Florence on the album, but there was a smaller female role, the Russian's estranged wife, Svetlana. She had two songs on the album and Tim thought they might suit me. He sent me a demo of one of them, a duet for Florence and Svetlana, to see if I would consider singing it. That was when I heard 'I Know Him So Well' for the first time.

I remember listening to it and thinking to myself that it sounded like an Abba song: it had that undercurrent of Scandinavian melancholy that characterised the best Abba ballads. I was an admirer of Bjorn and Benny's songwriting and had met Benny once, in 1980 at a music conference in Bournemouth, where we ended up talking about accordions - it turns out we both have a fondness for them.

I quickly got back to Tim and said yes, I would love to do the song, and two weeks later I was on a plane to Stockholm to record my part. Strange as it seems now, I had never actually met Elaine before we made 'I Know Him So Well' - and I didn't meet her at this point, either, as she had already recorded her vocals. As I'd done with 'Another Suitcase', where I'd recorded the song as part of a whole project, I just sang my two duets, one with Elaine's voice in the headphones and one with Tommy Korberg's, enjoyed working with Tim, Benny and Bjorn, had some schnaps and got on the plane home thinking, job done.

The first single to be released from *Chess* was 'One Night In Bangkok', sung by Murray Head, who played the American. It was a surprisingly big hit and the record label decided to release a second single. 'I Know Him So Well' had already created a buzz among those who had heard it and word was going round that it could do really well in the charts, but I'd had years of people from record companies telling me that this song or that song was going to be a smash hit and I knew it meant nothing. In my experience most of the songs everyone thought were going to be popular never were and it was those you least expected to do anything that caught the public mood. So when 'I Know Him So Well' was selected as the next single I was far more cautious than anybody else about its prospects despite its pedigree.

As part of the promotion for the single we had to make that video, with its big hair, even bigger shoulder pads and enormous amounts of lip gloss - and it was only then that I finally met Elaine. We got on famously from the start. As solo performers, it was a pleasant novelty for us both to be working with somebody else. The single was released in January 1985 and for once all the record label execs were right: it seemed as if every woman and every gay man in Britain went out and bought it.

Elaine and I spent a whole month promoting the record in Britain, Europe and Ireland, going from country to country, television studio to television studio and interview to interview. It was all quite surreal. When we arrived at Dublin, for example, and got into the car taking us from the airport to the RTE studios, we saw this middle-aged, respectably dressed man racing towards us. He banged urgently on the car window and I thought to myself, 'Oh my God, something must have happened,' I rolled down the window to find out what was going on and the man said to me, in a broad Dublin accent, 'I tell you one thing, Barbara, that's a great record.' Absolute madness. Still, I had been around long enough not to get carried away by all the hullabaloo and I just enjoyed the attention for what it was and for as long as it lasted. Having Elaine for company was great: it meant I had somebody to share the ride with me and to talk to over dinner afterwards.

'I Know Him So Well' reached number one in the UK and remained there for four weeks. It was the oddest sensation. I had always been far too much of a musical snob to think that being number one in the charts was important. Even though I had been a 'pop singer' since 1975 I still saw myself as the folk singer I'd been in the 1960s and early seventies, and being 'top of the pops' was all slightly unreal. My idea of a successful musical career was one like James Taylor's or Bob Dylan's, in which you made acclaimed albums and built up a respected body of work, and now here I was with a record that was bought by just shy of one million people in Britain alone, where it ended up being the second-biggest-selling single of the year after 'The Power Of Love' by Jennifer Rush, and a massive hit in numerous other countries into the bargain.

All the same, if it was a bit bewildering, the whole 'I Know Him So Well' period was great fun and I am immensely proud to be associated with Elaine and Tim and Benny and Bjorn. But if I could have my time again and was allowed to change just one thing in my career it would be that bloody video for 'I Know Him So Well'. Whenever I am forced to watch it - which unfortunately is quite often, as television producers seem to find it highly amusing - I still cringe at the sight of myself towering over Elaine like a not especially attractive drag queen. I know that after all these years I should be able to laugh at the ridiculousness of it all, but I can't. Worse still, it lingers in the public memory. In my time I have done so many things as a musician and an actress for which people might know me, but invariably, the second you say the words 'Barbara Dickson', the image everybody has in their minds is that video. I just wish it would disappear and I could expunge it from the collective consciousness. Even today, over twenty-five years later, whenever people meet me for the first time they are nearly always momentarily surprised that I am not taller. I am and have always been of slightly above-average height. It is obviously working with Elaine, who is so petite, that has conveyed the erroneous impression that I am some sort of Amazon - the 'silent friend Cynthia' to Elaine's Hylda Baker, which incidentally Matthew Kelly played for a while. (Younger readers may not remember the great Yorkshire comedienne Hylda Baker and her friend, who was traditionally played by a tall, gaunt young man, but they were very funny.)

Although I loved 'I Know Him So Well', the song would become a double-edged sword for me. It was so well known and well loved that for the next few years it was all anyone seemed to want me to sing. As a musician, once you finish one project you move on to the next, put your heart and soul into it and hope that your audience will join you on your journey. I always want to improve and stretch myself. But in the 1980s and 1990s I realised that there were a lot of people coming to hear me in concert who were only there for one song. Could I ever persuade them to love other songs I chose to sing?

I always sang 'I Know Him So Well' in concert then, but when I began to change my musical direction I didn't know how to tackle it. It really stuck out like a sore thumb, this one 1980s power ballad in the middle of an evening of folk and acoustic material. When I began working with Troy Donockley, my current music partner, we had a long discussion about it and decided to remove most of the original big arrangement, strip the song right back to its essence - while, most importantly, retaining its original sentiment - and perform it as an intimate acoustic guitar ballad. 'I Know Him So Well' now sits happily alongside a traditional Border ballad or a piece of Bertolt Brecht and the response to them all is equally warm and appreciative. It shows that the song is good enough to be rearranged and not suffer.

My involvement with *Chess* was for the album alone and not for the musical. The character of Svetlana had only a minor role in the stage version in any case, and even if there had been a larger part to play there was no way on earth I was going back into a theatre for a long run so soon after *Blood Brothers*. As happened with *Evita*, I think many people assume I was in *Chess* through a combination of the success of 'I Know Him So Well', my connections elsewhere with musical theatre and, again as was the case with *Evita*, a sort of intertwining of Elaine and myself in the minds of the public. For the record, although I have never appeared in *Evita*, I did eventually appear in *Chess* when, in 1997, I agreed to take on the lead role of Florence in Melbourne, Australia. To be honest, it wasn't one of my best career decisions, but as bad decisions go, having to spend a couple of months of the British winter in the Australian sunshine wasn't as bad as some. Plus I loved Australia and long to go back there to sing one day.

Although Elaine and I did sing the song together in a very intimate and regal setting in 2002, it wasn't until the following year that we teamed up again to perform it on television for the first time since 1985, for a BBC special. In my determination to look as far removed as possible from the drag queen in the nineteen-year-old video, I went into the studio wearing what even I would admit was one of my less carefully thought-out outfits: a swirly jacket and crêpe trousers, which I insisted the wardrobe man shortened, even though this made them look as if I was wearing them at half-mast. I became so hysterical about the danger of my hair resembling anything like the style in the video that I agreed to have it pinned up. The overall look I achieved could only be described as Miss Marple in green pedal-pushers. Very nice. Elaine, meanwhile, looked, as she always does, chic and elegant.
Even after all these years, 'I Know Him So Well' still means so much to so many people that it often crops up when you least expect it. I have performed it with the 'Birkenhead Bombsite'

herself, Lily Savage, and it surfaced recently in an episode of *Gavin and Stacey*, with Alison Steadman and Larry Lamb doing the honours. It's a song I am proud to sing and, thanks to the new arrangement, I have, I think, now reclaimed it for the new millennium and finally come to terms with its significance in my career. But will I ever be reconciled with that video? Not bloody likely!

CHAPTER TWELVE
DON'T THINK TWICE,
IT'S ALL RIGHT

If 1985 turned out to be my most successful year as a recording artist, in my family life it was to be my most traumatic. As part of my spring and early-summer UK tour of that year I was playing for the first time in Shetland, the homeland of Aly Bain, and it was while staying in those beautiful islands that I received the news that my father had died. It was an awful moment: although my dad had been in poor health for a long time he was only sixty-nine, and his death seemed so sudden and unexpected. It came as a terrible shock. To make matters worse, I probably couldn't have been anywhere in Britain less accessible than Shetland and I was not going to be able to get to Southport quickly to help my mother.

Eventually I arrived in Southport and Alastair flew over from Canada. We were very fortunate that Rob, cousin Ivy's husband, was a hospital administrator and had been on hand straight away, and he was immensely kind and helpful to my mother in the immediate aftermath. The funeral, indeed the whole time I was in Southport, seemed to pass in a haze. On the outside I seemed calm, collected and organised and when I returned to London I went back to work as normal. But, in retrospect, the loss of my father did not sink in.

Three months later I was pregnant, and while I was appearing for three nights at the New Theatre in Hull, I had a miscarriage. I sort of knew something was happening but not quite what. I was taken to hospital in Hull and then sent home to London to recover after one night. All the staff in the hospital were extremely kind and understanding, although it was also the scene of one of the most surreal moments of my life. Even now I find it difficult to believe this actually happened, but on the day I was leaving after the miscarriage, the consultant handed me a cassette of his daughter's songs and asked if I would listen to them.

When you suffer a miscarriage you are given advice about the physical effects, but psychologically I had no idea of how to feel. I remember thinking, why me?

Will it happen again?

Will I ever be able to have a baby?

What's wrong with me?

Back home, one night shortly afterwards, I began to cry and couldn't stop. Perhaps I was weeping not just for the lost baby, but also for my father. When Oliver asked me what was wrong, I wasn't able to explain. Perhaps my distress over the miscarriage had unlocked all the grief that had built up in the previous three months. I cannot recall crying at my father's funeral, so perhaps it was only now, in the safety of my own house at last, that I was finally able to let go.

I found I was also now able to take a step back and reflect on how complex my father was as a person. I had always considered him to be slightly puritanical - he was, after all, a Presbyterian Scotsman and a former policeman - but I'd discovered over the years that he was far more broad-minded than I ever gave him credit for. I remembered with a smile what he'd said to me that time after first seeing *John, Paul, George, Ringo... & Bert,* which was quite near the knuckle in places. 'For goodness' sake, Barbara. I used to be in the army.' But he was, as I've already said, a man of few words, and if I might have liked to have been a little more intimate with him - to have known him a little better, to have said more to him and for him to have said more to me - in the end it didn't really matter. What mattered was that he had always been a patient, loyal and good father.

After his death my mother received many touching letters of condolence from family members. There were two in particular, from first cousins of mine who had spent time with my dad when they were children, which say so much about the kind of man he was. One read: 'Aunty Ruth, I wanted to say how sad I was to hear of Uncle Alastair's death. I really loved Uncle Alastair and it was Uncle Alastair who taught me to tell the time.' And the other; 'I really miss Uncle Alastair, Aunty Ruth, as it was Uncle Alastair who taught me to tie my shoelaces.' He always loved children and was very patient as those recollections indicate.

Oliver was great throughout those days and soon we decided that the best way to put events behind us was to try again to have a baby. When I found out that I was expecting, I was both elated and terrified I would miscarry a second time. I did have one scare early on in the pregnancy, but thankfully all proved to be well and our son, Colm Alastair Cookson, was born, healthy and happy, two weeks ahead of schedule in August 1986. Nothing in life can prepare you for the moment when you first hold this tiny, helpless person in your arms. It may be the most natural thing in the world, but to me, and to every new mother, it feels surreal. And the knowledge that the baby is totally dependent on you scares you to death. What a responsibility.

We named our son after Colm Cille, the original name of the Irish-born St Columba, who founded the famous monastery on the beautiful Scottish island of Iona, the spiritual centre of Scotland from the sixth century. I have always had a great interest in and admiration for St

Above: Penny Junor and I co-presented *The Afternoon Show*, a weekly magazine programme for BBC Scotland which was networked on a Thursday afternoon at 2 p.m. We did a mixture of things, serious and lighthearted, and I even used my influence to cheekily get Billy Connolly on for an interview.

Right: Although Billy's nearly five years older than me, we did frequently bump into each other on the folk circuit. Here we are much later on with Bob Geldof at the British Photographic Industry awards in 1987.

PHIL CUTTS

PHOTOSTAGE

PHOTOSTAGE

Blood Brothers

Above: The cast, crew and band (plus Pete Filleul, *far left*, the original musical arranger), taken on stage at our daily warm-up. Oliver is lying very casually across the front.

Left: Me in full 'pinny' rig as Mrs Johnstone. The clothes were very hot to wear on stage, especially as I had to keep taking off my coat and putting it back on again throughout the first act.

Bottom: Mrs Johnstone and 'children' – Hazel Ellerby, Peter Christian and George Costigan – off to the new house in the countryside with their belongings. 'Bright New Day' is what we're singing which ends Act One.

Above: Making a speech at the SWET Awards on being awarded the statuette for 'Best Actress in a Musical 1983'. Donald Sinden and Robert Preston are in the background.

Below: At our wedding party on 25 August 1984. We were married in the afternoon in front of family only then re-grouped at Maxim's in the evening with about 100 friends. Oliver wanted a Devil's Food chocolate cake, which we're about to cut – delicious!

Left: Collecting the Gold disc for 'Chess' with some of those involved – *left to right*: Bjorn Ulvaeus, Elaine Paige, Tim Rice and me. But where's Benny Andersson?

REX FEATURES

Right: A production still from Taggart, 1994, when I played Marie McDonald, a hard-bitten, ruthless former pop star. I can't think why they thought of me for the role, can you?

MIRRORPIX.COM

Band of Gold

Top left: When I heard Tony Doyle was to play my boyfriend, George Ferguson, I was really excited as I was a huge fan of his. He sadly died not long afterwards – a great loss.

Top right: This 'accident' was a nightmare to film – I volunteered to do my own stunt and had to roll over the bonnet of a car.

Right: Anita abandoned by George, who was a stinker; but he was HER stinker. This sequence was very powerful stuff and exciting to do – all high octane.

Bottom left: The scene where we've just heard that Gina (played by Ruth Gemmell) has been murdered. Rose (Geraldine James) and Carol (Cathy Tyson) have arrived at my flat to tell me, hence my dressing gown and no make-up.

Bottom right: After my 'accident' – I rather enjoyed my hospital stint, acting in bed. I was hooked up to loads of equipment and the medical advisor told me I was fit as a fiddle from all the (real) readings.

Spend Spend Spend

Left: Me in full flight as Viv Nicholson, rigged for work in the beauty salon.

Below: A wonderfully bawdy microcosm of the show. Me, Rachel Leskovac and Steven Houghton giving V signs to the world at large.

PHOTOSHOT

PA PHOTOS

PHOTOSHOT

Left: Still with my bleached blond hair, four months after we closed. I was picking up my second 'Actress of the Year in a Musical' award. This time it was a bust of Laurence Olivier.

Above: I was appearing in *Spend Spend Spend* at the Piccadilly Theatre when I fulfilled a previous booking at the Banqueting Hall in Whitehall – a charity event organised by the Lady Taverners in the presence of HRH The Princess Royal. I am an honorary Lady Taverner and also Honorary Patron of my local branch in Lincolnshire.

Right: This is me approaching the art of playing piano rather differently. How did I get up there?

Bottom: The family at the palace with my brand new OBE. Oliver very kindly stayed outside as only three guests are permitted and he wanted the boys to see their mother greeted by HM The Queen.

Left: An early 1990s picture of me, Mum and Alastair, taken at my house in Lincolnshire. I can't remember the occasion, but we look pretty happy!

Below: The boys, Gabriel, Archie and Colm, in 1993 before the restoration of our house. Nice hairstyles.

Left: Our Mauritian holiday, November 2008. We had a lovely time, just the two of us, belatedly celebrating Oliver's 50th birthday.

Columba and we thought Colm Cookson had a wonderful ring to it, too. He could become a general or have an allotment, although so far he has shown no inclination to do either. His middle name, Alastair, is, of course, a tribute to both my father and my brother.

Meanwhile, against the backdrop of all these family dramas, and thanks to the success of 'I Know Him So Well', my career had reached unprecedented levels in commercial terms. Confounding all expectations, the album *The Barbara Dickson Songbook*, which had come out at the beginning of 1985 on K-Tel, reached the dizzy heights of number five on the back of the single and became my third gold album, selling over 100,000 copies in the process. The record label was understandably delighted and I began working on a follow-up with top producer Pip Williams behind the studio desk and regular cohorts Ian Lynn and Pete Zorn among the musicians. The new album was to be another combination of covers and new material, which I would be co-writing with my good friend Charlie Dore, a respected singer-songwriter who had had a hit in 1979 with her own song 'Pilot Of The Airwaves' and had created hits for big name artistes like Celine Dion.

The album was released in November 1985, just in time for the Christmas market, and the first song on it was 'I Know Him So Well'. You would have thought by the end of that year, with nearly a million copies of the single sold at the beginning, the public might have begun to tire of it, but this didn't seem to be the case. The record label had optimistically decided to call the album *Gold*, and their confidence was rewarded: not only did *Gold* go gold but, with sales of over 500,000 copies, it went platinum as well - my second album to achieve that status. After the phenomenal success of *The Barbara Dickson Songbook* and *Gold* the record company, not surprisingly, wanted another pop album and *The Right Moment* was released in November 1986. Yet despite the input of Ian Lynn and Pete Zorn, Del Newman doing the production honours and the same mix of covers and new songs co-written by Charlie Dore and me - not to mention having as the title track a beautiful song written by Gerry Rafferty - sales were only so-so and there were no hit singles. There then followed a few years during which a couple of compilations came out, plus a live album with accompanying video called *After Dark*, which Bernard and I released ourselves. It was not until 1989 that I began work on a new pop album, this time for Telstar.

In the meantime, in November 1988, we had another son, Gabriel Rory. I had continued to tour throughout the 1980s playing around thirty dates a year, and audiences remained very supportive and appreciative. With pregnancies and little children to care for itineraries and tour dates had to be juggled with military precision; I was also battling stage fright during much of that period. But I was still a working performer, concerts were my bread and butter and I never for a moment lost my enthusiasm for being on the road. In the wake of the *Blood Brothers* and the 'I Know Him So Well' years, I began to notice a change in my audiences as the younger crowd, who had come to hear the pop material and the hit records, were gradually replaced by a more mature audience. Slowly, I started to adjust my concerts to mirror this shift, broadening the material I sang.

The Telstar album, *Coming Alive Again*, was released in April 1989 and while it made the lower reaches of the charts, I didn't feel it really worked and, like *The Right Moment*, it produced no hit singles despite being a pop album. It was now four years since 'I Know Him So Well' - an eternity for an artist not to have a hit record. What happened with *Coming Alive Again* crystallised for me many of the concerns I had about where my career was heading. By this time I realised that my spell as a 'pop star' had probably come to an end in 1985 and that bringing out still more pop albums, regardless of whether they consisted of covers or of new material, was no longer the way to go. Not that I was complaining: since 1975, when 'Answer Me' had been in the Top 10, I'd had far more success over a much more sustained period than I'd ever expected, and the rewards of that success had transformed my life. But I was in my forties now, a mother of two - and by 1990 there was a third baby on the way - and being a pop star was not my game. I hadn't been all that young at the height of my pop career, of course: even more reason to be faintly embarrassed about sticking with it when I was approaching middle age. And if I was not careful, that was exactly what I was going to be doing.

I wanted to change my musical direction. I felt that I had matured as a person and I wanted my music to reflect this, but I was not sure how to bring about such a change. With Bernard's encouragement, I had been singing 'MacCrimmon's Lament' unaccompanied in concert since 1978, but the rest of the set still consisted of pop material and, although I was now gearing the songs I performed to the increasing maturity of the people who came to see me, I did not want to alienate them by abandoning everything I had been doing for the previous fifteen years. Wherever I was going I wanted to take my audiences there with me.

In October 1990, Archie Frederick Cookson was born. All through the pregnancy and labour I was convinced I was having a girl. Immediately after the birth there was apparently a brief moment of alarm and the paediatrician immediately whisked the baby away to clear out his airways. Thankfully, I was unaware of this drama, but in his haste to deal with my baby the doctor had neglected to mention his gender. So when my healthy and, happily, breathing child was brought back and handed to me I was completely shocked to find I didn't have a girl after all, but another little boy.

Before I had my own children I had always had this simplistic notion that brothers were fairly similar to each other. I only had one brother, of course, but I had sort of assumed that if I'd had others they would have been like Alastair. Now that I had my three boys I soon discovered that they were wonderfully individual characters, different from each other and all completely unique.

As the Cookson family expanded, Oliver and I felt we wanted a change of pace and had decided to move out of London. We had hoped to do so before Gabriel arrived, but the recession of the late 1980s foiled that plan and in the end it was 1992 before we finally found our new home. Both Oliver and I needed to be in England for our respective work commitments - in Oliver's case, somewhere within easy reach of the studios in London, Birmingham and Leeds where most of Britain's television drama was made at that time.

We looked at houses in Kent and Herefordshire and Wiltshire and Oxfordshire and Sussex before eventually finding the perfect place in the rolling hills of the Lincolnshire Wolds. It was an area I knew a little, from when I'd briefly shared the Navenby cottage with Bernard back in 1973 before moving to London, and the moment Oliver and I laid eyes on a Victorian rectory three miles from the town of Louth, complete with ten acres of land and plenty of room for the five of us, we immediately fell in love with both the house and the location.

We quickly settled into rural life and I felt at home in my new surroundings from the start. For the first year or so we were not especially social as we were focused on the new house and the boys and the boys' schooling although, if I'm honest, I probably haven't ever been a particularly social animal. I'm not keen on gatherings unless they involve people I know well and feel comfortable with. I dread those dinner parties where other guests you don't know engage you in conversation about *The Two Ronnies* or Elaine Paige. They might be private functions but I still feel as if I'm on public display and can't relax and enjoy myself.

Many performers who have achieved some level of fame are quite private and shy away from their working environment, and that sense of being constantly 'on duty' in the company of anyone other than close friends probably has a lot to do with it. Certainly I can attest to the fact that, at home in Lincolnshire with her family, Barbara Dickson leads a pretty quiet life.

The musical shift I was so desperate to achieve did not take shape until 1992, when I recorded a new album, *Don't Think Twice, It's All Right*. The title comes from the wonderful and bittersweet song of unrequited love from the 1963 album *The Freewheelin' Bob Dylan*, which also includes 'Blowin' In The Wind' and 'A Hard Rain's A-Gonna Fall.'. This was the record that propelled Bob Dylan to international stardom and turned him into the voice of a generation, and which I first heard as a sixteen-year-old fledgling folk singer.

I sincerely believe that Bob Dylan is the greatest living songwriter and *Don't Think Twice, It's All Right* was to consist solely of Bob Dylan numbers. It was an opportunity not only to record songs that had meant so much to me personally for many years, but also to show that, as an artist, I was still alive and kicking. Even better, I had the chance to co-produce the album alongside Ian Lynn, and I was able to choose my favourite songs. Most of them were from the early Dylan albums, songs I'd spent many happy hours learning as a teenager.

It was a joy to be back in a studio working on such great material with such great musicians and, although if you listen to it now, the production does perhaps sound of its time, I think it still stands up. And I still sing 'Don't Think Twice, It's All Right' in concert today in the same arrangement Ian created and which we used on the record. The album was issued by Columbia Records and it well received on its release. It had good reviews and it didn't sell badly, reaching number thirty-one in the charts. But more important than its chart position was what it represented for me. *Don't Think Twice, It's All Right* was a watershed in my career. Not only was it a genuine and heartfelt tribute to the music of a man who had been such a big influence on my generation but, at a stroke, it seemed to put all the pop years behind me. For the first time in ages people who had forgotten about me began to wonder if there might be something more substantial and interesting to my work after all. And last but by no means least, recording it gave me the confidence to finally stride out on a new, more challenging path. It was a creative project and helped to cancel out the compilation albums which continued to be released of my older work, and still do to this day. They make artistes look as if they've retired. Many have, but not me.

Don't Think Twice, It's All Right couldn't sweep away all the insecurities I had about my career, of course. There was still the conflict between the nervousness and caution I felt about performing and the 100 per cent drive and determination I found within me to overcome that anxiety. It was what had got me on to that stage at the Brucefield in Dunfermline when I was sixteen and what made *Blood Brothers* so exhilarating and so terrifying at the same time. It was as if I sought out the toughest possible challenges, just so I could prove to myself that I could meet them. Sometimes I would overcompensate and that would lead me into making poor decisions. I would be flattered that somebody thought I could do something and find myself saying yes, even when, deep down, I really didn't feel that it was the right thing to do.

I had come to realise that the stage fright that had plagued me since *Blood Brothers* was more likely to occur when I was performing material I was unsure of. So changing my musical direction and ensuring that I was happy with what I was performing really helped with that and, gradually, the bouts became less frequent.

Throughout the 1980s, even after I was married, I continued to see my analyst, though I did so less often. I found that, with time, I was working through a lot of the worries that had come to a head at the start of the decade and which had made me seek help in the first place. Of course, I now had Oliver to share my life with, and when the family came along I had new priorities and new responsibilities to occupy me. Analysis cannot provide you with all the answers, but what it did do for me was give me a better understanding about myself, and what makes me tick, than I could have acquired on my own, and that was the reason why I kept going. It didn't stop me from getting things wrong, but it helped me to recognise why I was getting them wrong. My wise analyst also made me aware that my perfectionism was an integral part of my work as a performer, even though the perfection I desired was, by its very nature, impossible to achieve. By the time our sessions finally came to an end, I was able to acknowledge that my life might not be perfect, but that was perfectly all right.

CHAPTER THIRTEEN
THE GREAT SILKIE

When I was recording *Don't Think Twice, It's All Right* I was able to take Archie with me in his carrycot to the studio, but once we had moved out to Lincolnshire with our three small children Oliver and I had to fit our work commitments around first nursery and then primary-school hours. We would usually alternate, so that when Oliver was at work I would stay at home, and vice-versa. We were better off than many parents in that we were able to afford additional help. We had a lovely local nanny, Sue Wilkinson, who came fresh from working with horses - same theory apparently!

It was easier when the boys were little. I tended to be at home a lot of the time then anyway. The exception was my annual tour, but in the early days I could simply take them with me. I also did private functions, which could be quite lucrative. I would not be playing until around 10.50pm, by which time the baby would be safely asleep, and I'd only be away from him for about forty-five minutes. What could be more straightforward?

But babies, of course, could not care less if Mummy is due on stage in five minutes. Mummy is food, which must be available on demand. There were several occasions when one of them woke up at exactly the wrong moment leaving my poor PA, Penny, or Sue, my Australian nanny in London, literally holding the (screaming) baby for three quarters of an hour until the show was over and I was back for him to latch on to. I soon realised the value of having expressed milk handy for these eventualities. However, I never did it. It seemed comical to me.

And before we knew it the boys were no longer infants, they were walking, talking individuals. And just when we'd got around that marvel, these walking, talking individuals were suddenly old enough to have to go to school and, though we tried to limit our absences as much as possible, separations became unavoidable. I found it very difficult to leave the children when I went on tour, but I just had to get on with it and look forward to big hugs when I returned. We were never in a position where we could just retire and live happily ever after in our country pile. Neither of us would just abandon our careers. Singing and performing were such a fundamental part of my very existence that it would have been impossible for me to give them up. I just wouldn't have been me anymore.

Becoming a parent made me realise that, as with everything, you just have to do what you think is right. It is easy to beat yourself up for not being there at certain times in your children's lives, but that isn't going to solve anything. It is more important that you do the best you can. And of course your children's experience can be enhanced by the interests and passions you bring into their world from outside the four walls of the family home.

As it happens, all three of my boys are musical and all of them have played in bands. Although Archie did not seem all that thrilled when I found an old cassette recently, recorded when he was very young indeed and featuring him singing 'Puff The Magic Dragon', accompanied by me on the piano. I, of course, thought it was fantastic.

Archie was only three when I discovered to my delight that he seemed to have inherited my ability to memorise songs quickly. In the early 1990s one of the pieces I was singing in concert was the witch's song, 'The Last Midnight' from the Stephen Sondheim show *Into The Woods*. At home one evening, I went upstairs to the bathroom, where Archie was in the bath. As I approached the door, I was astonished to hear my tiny son singing, in a lovely, clear voice, the opening lines of the song. And he was note-perfect as well.

Yes, motherhood was proving to be even richer and more rewarding than I had ever imagined.

Encouraged by the positive response to *Don't Think Twice, It's All Right*, in 1994 I began work on a new album. *Parcel Of Rogues* was a return to folk and traditional music and my first folk album since *From The Beggars Mantle* way back in 1972. The title track came from one of Robert Burns's most famous songs, which features the well-known lines on the decision by Scottish MPs to agree to the Act of Union of 1707 between the English and Scottish Parliaments, and the suspicion that the MPs went along with it, against the wishes of the Scottish people, because they were bribed to do so.

We're bought and sold for English gold
Such a parcel of rogues in a nation.

The opportunity to revisit all the folk music I loved was just glorious. Pip Williams was the producer and some wonderful musicians agreed to play on the album. Kevin McAlea was on keyboards, Alistair Anderson played the concertina and the Northumbrian pipes, Tom McConville the fiddle and Troy Donockley the uilleann pipes. And my old compadre, Archie Fisher, came down and sang backing vocals. For the cover, photographer Brian Aris shot me in full Celtic warrior queen garb. It is one of my favourite photos of myself.

Like *Don't Think Twice, It's All Right*, *Parcel Of Rogues* is perhaps slightly overblown for my taste now, but at the time it grabbed people's attention and attracted good reviews. And I was gratified to find that enough of my audience were willing to follow me away from pop to take the record to number thirty in the album charts.

Further emboldened by the response to *Parcel Of Rogues*, I began work on a follow-up, *Dark End Of The Street*, which was released in 1995. Pip Williams again produced most of the songs and many of the musicians from *Parcel Of Rogues*, including Pete Zorn, Tom McConville and Troy Donockley, came back for more. They were joined by Ian Lynn on keyboards and such folk luminaries as Dave Mattacks on drums and Danny Thompson on double bass. *Dark End Of The Street* had a 'darker' feel than *Parcel Of Rogues* and included traditional and folk material as well as more modern songs. It was a thoughtful album and, although in the end not all of it worked as well as I had hoped, I was glad I'd had the courage to push myself artistically. I was determined that from now on I would produce only the very best material. I had found a rich new vein of music in which to immerse myself and I was delighted. Little did I realise then that it would be eight years before I would make another album.

It had been twelve years since I'd played Mrs Johnstone on the West End stage and won my SWET award, and in all that time I had never done any more acting, other than to reprise my *Blood Brothers* role for the musical's tenth anniversary in 1993. I'd been persuaded to pick up my mop again for a fourteen-week run at the Phoenix Theatre in the West End. Not surprisingly I was very scared, fearing that the worst would happen, but I couldn't have been more wrong. It was great to return to the part and, being older and, I hope, wiser, I felt I was able to give a greater depth to my performance. It was still quite nerve-racking to be onstage night after night for quite so long, and I must admit I was glad when it was over. But it enabled me to lay some ghosts to rest and in fact on two further occasions, in 2001 and 2004, I would play the part again, back in Liverpool, where it all began. The 1993 run made me even more proprietorial about Mrs Johnstone. Deep down, I felt I was the only person who could truly portray her. More than that, it reminded me what an extraordinary privilege it had been to have been given the chance to do so in the first place. I had the trust of Willy Russell, too, so that was a huge responsibility.

But apart from Mrs Johnstone, not a single acting job in twelve years. Because of the bruising experience of the initial *Blood Brothers* run I was adamant I wouldn't return to the stage in the foreseeable future, but I was more than open to testing my acting skills on television or in film. In the minds of directors and producers, however, I was firmly cast as a singer who appeared in musical theatre, and every single offer I received was for a musical. Even if I had been prepared to go back into that arena, I had no interest in appearing in anything that wasn't as good as *Blood Brothers*, and musicals as good as *Blood Brothers* only come around two or three times in a lifetime. So that was that.

While I was promoting *Parcel Of Rogues* I was asked several times in interviews what I was planning to do next, and I'd reply that I would like to do some television acting. Someone must have been listening, because suddenly, like the proverbial London buses, two great TV acting parts came along more or less at once. One was a character named Anita Braithwaite in a new ITV drama series called *Band Of Gold*, written by Kay Mellor, and the other was a three-episode story of the long-running Scottish detective show *Taggart*. I immediately said yes to both.

The *Taggart* shoot came up first and off I went to Glasgow. There had been some doubt whether this three-parter would go ahead at all after Mark McManus, who-played the DCI famous for uttering the words 'There's been a murder' with such Glaswegian relish, died unexpectedly in 1994, just as filming began. It was eventually decided that the show, which had been running since 1985, would go on, and this story, 'Legends' - in which the body of a rock 'n' roll guitarist is found in a swimming pool in suspicious circumstances - was one of the first to be made without its eponymous character.

I was to play Marie McDonald, the wealthy, hard-bitten, slightly over-the-hill lead singer of the rock group with more than a few dirty secrets, and the prime suspect for the crime. I wonder why they thought of me for that role?

I had been extremely nervous beforehand about whether I would be able to pull it off, but everyone in the *Taggart* team was fantastic to me and *Taggart* turned out to be a great introduction to television acting. Marie had plenty of facets to her character, most of them unpleasant, for me to get stuck into. And although she was a singer, I didn't have to sing a note, which left me free to concentrate on my acting.

The role of Anita Braithwaite in *Band Of Gold* was to prove much tougher, even before we reached the filming stage. Kay Mellor was a highly respected writer who had made her name on television with *Coronation Street* and *Children's Ward*, and *Band Of Gold* was to be her first major prime-time drama series. She could not have chosen a more challenging subject matter: the series revolved around a group of prostitutes from Bradford, the 'band' of the title. The casting director, Carolyn Bartlett, who had read one of the interviews in which I'd expressed an interest in television acting, had seen me many years before in *John, Paul, George, Ringo... & Bert* and thought I had something that might be ideal for one of the characters. But, given my complete inexperience, and the fact that Anita was one of the main roles, the producers were far from convinced, and I was told I would have to have a 'meeting', whatever that was, to see if I was suitable. I didn't realise that it was a screen test they wanted.

So I did my first screen test and read the scenes that I was given. Afterwards nobody gave me any indication of how it had gone and I had no idea myself. I was thanked for my time and off I went. When I heard nothing more I assumed the producers had decided I wasn't what they were looking for and had picked somebody with more TV experience. But several weeks later I got a call, out of the blue, asking if I would like to go down to London to meet Richard Standeven, the director of the first episode.

I didn't know what to expect when I got to London. I went in to see Richard and after the introductions had been made the first thing he said was, 'Let's do some acting.' And he handed me some scenes to read. They were not the ones I had prepared. I said, 'Richard, I don't know this scene.'

'Oh, it doesn't matter', he replied. 'Just make it up as you go along.' The next thing I knew, he had called in another actor to read the scenes with me. My head was spinning.

The actor turned out to be big Ray Stevenson, who would eventually play the character of Steve Dixon in *Band Of Gold* and later starred as the soldier Titus Pullo in the epic TV series *Rome*. So I began muddling through unfamiliar scenes with this actor I'd never met, while Richard watched, listened and interrupted occasionally to offer snippets of information, just as Willy and Chris had done when I first read for them as Mrs Johnstone for *Blood Brothers*.

'Now, Barbara, your character has just done this and Ray's character has done that, so can you do the scene again?'

When Richard had heard enough, he phoned the producers and said, 'Give her the job.'

With my role as Anita confirmed, I returned to London for a promotional shoot and to meet the rest of the cast. They were an impressive company: the acclaimed stage and screen actress Geraldine James, who had starred in *The Jewel In The Crown*, played Rose, and Cathy Tyson, who shot to fame in the movie *Mona Lisa*, was Carol. Ruth Gemmell took the role of Gina, who gets killed in the first series. Future Golden Globe winner and Oscar nominee Samantha Morton, still a teenager herself at the time, played the young runaway Tracey. And amid all that incredible talent there was me, Barbara Dickson.

From the outset we all got on very well. Up in Bradford, before we started filming, the producers wanted to give us some sense of the world we would be re-creating so they took us to the notorious Lumb Lane red-light district. We also visited a women's drop-in centre and met some 'working women'. From the moment I read the script for the first episode I had realised what an important and groundbreaking series *Band Of Gold* was going to be and seeing Lumb Lane for myself only reinforced that conviction. I had also realised, from the same moment, how hard it was going to be.

I felt I knew the character of Anita Braithwaite, who she was and why she did what she did. Anita was not a prostitute, but a 'kept woman'. Her boyfriend, George Ferguson, was a loan shark and a married man. He would visit her once a week and give her money, but it wasn't enough for her to live on. To make ends meet Anita rented out rooms in her flat to local prostitutes, who would meet their clients there. The wonderful Irish actor Tony Doyle, best known for his roles in *Amongst Women*, *Between the Lines* and *Ballykissangel*, was cast as George. I had been an admirer of Tony's for years and it was a highlight of my career to be able to work with him. When he died suddenly in 2000 it was a terrible shock. He was a great actor.

To bring Anita to life we had to get her appearance just right. I talked to the costume designer and we came up with Anita's style (if style is the right word): appliqué T-shirts, stretch leggings, high heels, more make-up than strictly necessary and hair that looked like it had just been through a wind tunnel. Although the series was set in Yorkshire, Kay agreed that Anita could be Scottish, and I decided to go for an indeterminate gritty accent. I must have been doing something right as I remember Kay Mellor telling me some while later that Anita had been the least well drawn of all the main roles. It was only when she saw me playing Anita, she said, that the character really became a living, breathing woman. Of all the compliments I received for Anita, nothing could beat that from the writer herself.

To me Anita was basically a good person, but with a cold, selfish streak. Because she was not a prostitute herself she often considered herself a cut above the other girls, even though she was as dependent, if not more so, on men than they were. But whatever their squabbles, the underlying friendship between the women was stronger than their differences.

The response to the first series of *Band Of Gold* in 1995 was so positive that another series was commissioned and screened the following year. In total I ended up doing two four-month blocks of filming for each series. It was a gruelling schedule and the hours were far longer than anything I had encountered before. You would wake up at five in the morning, be in make-up at 6.15 and on the set at 7.30, and sometimes you'd stay there all day. There were several night shoots as well. I remember standing in the pouring rain with Geraldine James in some street in Ashton-under-Lyne, both of us clutching black bin-bags, at some ridiculous time of night. We were soaked to the skin and we both knew we'd be stuck there like drowned rats until we had finished the scene, but I just could not stop laughing at the madness of it all. Every time Geraldine said, 'Come on Dickson, pull yourself together,' all it did was start me off again.

At its peak *Band Of Gold* was attracting 15 million viewers a week. Although the writing and the cast were excellent and we all knew it was going to draw a lot of attention, the response far surpassed our expectations. The series resonated with the public because it was truthful and realistic. The main characters may have been working women but, more importantly, they were ordinary women, too - women with families and boyfriends and aspirations and fears, just like the rest of us. And while people might not immediately identify with prostitution as a means of making a living, everyone could identify with the value of friendship and the 'band' that held the women together. The programme also highlighted for millions of people how dangerous prostitution could be and how incredibly young and vulnerable many of the women and girls involved in it are. But the key to the success of *Band Of Gold* was that its stories had style and a mix of humour and darkness, great strong female characters and, above all, a real heart.

As well as acting in the series I was asked to sing the theme song, which was not, as might have been expected, a version of Freda Payne's hit 'Band Of Gold' but the rather more appropriate 'Love Hurts', a song I had first heard sung by the Everly Brothers.

The next acting role I had was in a two-part comedy drama for the BBC called *The Missing Postman*, which was screened in 1997 and won the British Comedy award for Best Comedy Drama that year. *The Missing Postman* had a fantastic cast headed by James Bolam and was filmed partly on the beautiful Scottish island of Arran. The director was Alan Dossor - the same Alan Dossor for whom, all those years before, I'd had to play 'With A Little Help From My Friends' on the piano to convince him that I was the right person to sing the Beatles' songs in *John, Paul, George, Ringo...& Bert*. I played a fisherman's widow, a gentle, almost fey character, and a complete contrast to Anita Braithwaite. My character might have been gentle and sweet, but *The Missing Postman* was to feature my first-ever nude scene - all tastefully done as I was mostly under the bed covers. To date this remains the only nude scene in my acting career, but never say never, as they say.

The characters I played in *Taggart, Band Of Gold* and *The Missing Postman* had all been Scottish, but when I was offered the part of dinner lady Bev in the 1997 radio series *Dinner Ladies*, set in Rochdale, I had to try to learn a Lancashire accent. I had of course used a Liverpool accent as Mrs Johnstone in *Blood Brothers*, but although Rochdale is geographically close to Liverpool, the way people speak there is very different. *Dinner Ladies*, a forerunner of the Victoria Wood TV show, was a six-part series written by Turan Ali. The wonderful cast included Liz Smith and Brigit Forsyth.

I never felt I got Bev's accent quite right. I ended up sounding nothing like Cyril Smith, the larger-than-life former Liberal MP for Rochdale who had a fantastic rich Lancashire voice. I would probably have got away with it if this had been television, but on the radio, of course, the voice is all. Despite my sludgy accent I had a great time making the series, which has recently been repeated on BBC Radio 7, and working with some fantastic actresses, especially Kaye Wragg, who later starred in *No Angels* and *The Bill*. Kaye actually came from Rochdale and, although it must have been painful for her to act alongside my strangled Lancashire vowels, was incredibly helpful, patient and tolerant.

While I was enjoying these new opportunities to spread my acting wings, Chris Bond, who had been artistic director of my concerts since 1985, was developing an idea he'd been working on for some time: a one-woman show that would be performed in theatres rather than concert halls and would combine acting with my music. *Seven Ages Of Woman* followed the life of an ordinary woman from cradle to grave through childhood, adolescence, first love, heartbreak, motherhood, happiness, sadness and old age. It was a very ambitious project: whereas normally I would sing around twenty-three songs in concert, *Seven Ages Of Woman* had thirty-five (although some of these were just fragments) and the music ranged from traditional and folk songs through Jacques Brel and Stephen Sondheim to Randy Newman and the Beatles.

The musicians would be onstage with me and Andrew Schofield, who had played the Narrator in the original production of *Blood Brothers*, would act alongside me and play guitar in the band. There were so many costume changes that to keep the show going I would need to wear a basic outfit of black trousers, black shirt and black jazz shoes and just stick the different costumes on top.

Chris knew my acting and musical strengths and weaknesses as well as anybody and had tailored the show accordingly. Having recently limbered up playing Florence in *Chess* in

Melbourne, I felt that with the right project, and with Chris at the helm, I was ready at last to return to musical theatre. What better chance would I ever have than a production that had been designed especially for me? But I wasn't prepared to commit to doing any longer than six or seven weeks at a stretch. Even at that, it was a mammoth undertaking.

We premiered *Seven Ages Of Woman* at our old stamping-ground, the Liverpool Playhouse, in 1997. The response was very gratifying and I won the *Liverpool Echo*'s award for Best Actress that year (thank you, Liverpool, once again). We then took it on two mini-tours around the UK in 1997 and 1998 and recorded a soundtrack album.

Seven Ages Of Woman was, as I say, an ambitious project and while I was promoting the show I resisted attempts to impose limitations on it by pigeonholing it, though some interviewers seemed set on doing so. Was it musical theatre? They would ask. Was it a concert? The answer to both questions was yes - and much more besides. It was an excellent piece of writing by Chris. I wanted to make it as good as it could possibly be and I was determined to push myself. But I found the schedule hard going. By the sixth week of a run I was becoming very tired and, with the boys all now at school, I was only getting to see them one day a week and missing them terribly. Crucially, however, I never felt anything like the burn-out I had suffered in *Blood Brothers*, and I got through it all without being incapacitated by nerves.

While I was doing the show I turned fifty. As far as the *Seven Ages Of Woman* were concerned, I was over halfway through them and heading towards the home stretch. But it was not a milestone that depressed me. I have always felt younger than my years, I was fit and well and, as the mother of three children aged between six and eleven, I didn't have either the time or the inclination to come over all nostalgic and retrospective. There were too many exciting things happening in my life now, both personally and professionally, and there was so much to look forward to. And if there was one thing I had learned in my fifty years, it was that you must look forward, not back, no matter what age you are.

CHAPTER FOURTEEN
SINGING BIRD

I n the 1990s I had become a more experienced and, I hope, much-improved actress and was far more comfortable on stage. In 1998 I did a short run of a play called *Friends Like Us*, written by Rod Beacham, in which I starred alongside Roy Hudd and Susan Penhaligon. It was the first time I'd performed live without there being any singing involved. And in 1999 I agreed to appear in a new production of the musical comedy *A Slice of Saturday Night* by the Heather Brothers, set in the 'swinging sixties', as club-owner Erica 'Be-Bop' Devine. To be honest, I had doubts about whether this was right for me from the start, and then, in the middle of rehearsals, I got the 'flu. Yes, I know that sounds suspiciously convenient, but I can assure you I genuinely had the 'flu. I was laid up in bed for a week, feeling sorry for myself.

It was during that week, sitting in my bed surrounded by medicine and hot drinks, that I received a tape and a script by Steve Brown and Justin Greene. I have to admit that I was unfamiliar with both Steve and Justin, though I would later learn that Steve used to sing in folk clubs and had worked with Steve Coogan - in fact it was Steve Brown who played the role of Alan Partridge's musical director, Glen Ponder, in *Knowing Me, Knowing You*. But with plenty of time on my hands for once, I started to read the script, which was entitled *Spend Spend Spend*. It was just what the doctor ordered. The writing was wonderfully fresh and original and I found myself laughing out loud, which is always a good sign. When I had finished reading it I put the tape into the cassette-player. It contained the songs that accompanied the script, and although the recorded versions were fine, the songs themselves were fabulous. Very rich and earthy.

Spend Spend Spend was the best musical script I had read since *Blood Brothers* and indeed it shared many of the characteristics that made *Blood Brothers* so great. It was not your typical all-singing, all-dancing standard fare, but a well-written, tough, brave, intelligent work about real people and real life. I immediately wanted to do it. For years I had been turning down musicals because they could not compare with *Blood Brothers* and now I had found one that did.

There was one small problem. I had committed myself *to A Slice Of Saturday Night* and I am not the sort of person who breaks contracts or goes back on her word. So once I had recovered from the 'flu I went back to the show. The next thing that happened was that Gabriel was taken ill and had to be rushed to hospital and I immediately suspended my performances. He was diagnosed with appendicitis that had turned nasty and was very ill, so it was a harrowing week for the whole family. Thankfully, and during the time I was camped at the bottom of his bed, he began to recover and before long he was back to his cheerful self and I returned again to *A Slice of Saturday Night*, determined to see my contract through. With great regret, I had to tell Steve and Justin that although I thought their musical was absolutely wonderful and I wished them every success with it, sadly, I was not in a position to take up any offer to appear in the production.

I have never been a great believer in fate, but it appeared that the relationship between me and *A Slice Of Saturday Night* was destined not to last. My doubts about whether I should be in that show were being borne out: my fans didn't seem to like the show and fans of the show didn't seem to like me and, despite all our best efforts, we were forced to close. Suddenly and unexpectedly, I was available again.

A meeting was arranged with the producer of *Spend Spend Spend*, André Ptaszynski, and we talked through what he wanted from me. What he wanted, it transpired, was for me to take the lead role and to commit to it for nine months. I knew that nine months was way too long for me. I offered to do six months, but André was adamant. I was so keen to do the show that, against my better judgement, I agreed.

The story of *Spend Spend Spend* follows the fortunes and misfortunes of Viv Nicholson, a struggling young working-class Yorkshirewoman from Castleford, married to a miner, who, in 1961, won over £150,000 on the football pools - the equivalent of something like £5 million today. When Viv, a blonde bombshell, received her cheque and was asked what she planned to do with the money, she famously announced to the world that she was going to 'Spend, spend, spend.' Her declaration, and her overnight elevation from rags to riches, captured the imagination of the public and she became a household name. The phrase has also gone down in history.

Over the next few years Viv was as good as her word, and as the money ran out, her life descended into bankruptcy and tragedy. But Viv, who is still around, is above all a survivor. Her story - told first in her outspoken 1977 autobiography, subsequently in a BBC play by Jack Rosenthal and now by Steve and Justin - was primarily a cautionary tale about being careful for what you wish for. It was also an examination of jealousy and class prejudice. Viv found herself despised by her own community for her ostentatious lifestyle, which included driving around Castleford in her pink Cadillac, and despised by the middle class, whose ranks she aspired to join, for her working-class manners and attitudes.

One of Steve and Justin's great skills was to create a stage character who, while constantly doing and saying the wrong things as she hurtles towards self-destruction, still tugs at the heartstrings. I was to play the role of the older and slightly wiser Viv, now working in a beauty salon, who wryly observes the rise and fall of the impulsive and wayward young Viv, portrayed by the very talented Rachel Leskovac. Steven Houghton was to be her husband, Keith.

From the first time I heard the songs for *Spend Speed Spend* in my sickbed in Lincolnshire, I realised what a fantastic writer Steve Brown was. 'Scars of Love', 'Who's Gonna Love Me' and 'Pieces Of Me' were wonderful songs with great lyrics and great music. What had particularly drawn me to the character of Viv were her humanity and vulnerability. I remember talking to Steve about the lyrics of 'Who's Gonna Love Me', which she sings after Keith's funeral. It includes a couple of lines which, when I first read them, I found very moving.

> I search for traces of you on the pillow,
> The smell of you, an eyelash, or a hair

I asked Steve where he had got the inspiration to write such powerful and sensitive lyrics and he told me that these lines came direct from Viv herself, from her autobiography. It was sensational material to sing.

We began rehearsals in August 1999. Our director was the award-winning and distinguished Jeremy Sams and our choreographer was Craig Revel Horwood, a young man from Ballarat, Australia who, within a few years, would become famous as the gloriously acidic judge on *Strictly Come Dancing*. Craig is a really talented guy who knew how to place actors beautifully onstage. It was he who came up with the famous routine involving the mass flashing of 'V' signs, which was a highlight of the show. As I've mentioned, Craig did his best to coax me into performing a tiny set of moves in the show, but when faced with my historic inability to re-create even the simplest of dance steps, even he had to concede defeat. Still, as one of the main characters I was expected to flash plenty of 'V' signs during the show and found I was surprisingly good at that, so clearly his coaching hadn't gone completely to waste. 'V' signs are very liberating, I find.

We opened in September in Plymouth before moving to the Piccadilly theatre in the West End on 12 October. I'd worked terribly hard to get the role of Viv right, so when I stood onstage on the first night at the Piccadilly theatre I made sure I took my time and looked out at the audience, which included Viv herself, before delivering, in my best Yorkshire accent, the opening line:

'I know what you' re thinking.'

A long pause.
'What's it like havin' all that money?'

The reviews for *Spend Spend Spend* were some of the best seen in the West End for years, and they were all totally deserved (she said modestly). Rachel, Steven and I all received positive notices for our individual performances and the response from audiences was fantastic. For the first six months I was feeling great and relishing being part of such a wonderful show but, as I had feared, two thirds of the way through I began to run out of gas. I had already had a week's break four months into the show and I'd been very reluctant to go back after that; by the time I reached month seven I was completely exhausted. I was living in a flat in the Strand, miles away from my family, and although I kept reminding myself that I had only six more weeks to go I was extremely unhappy.

The important difference this time was that, having been down the same road before, I knew what was happening to me, which meant it wasn't quite so frightening. And this time I had the sense to go and see my doctor, too. I was signed off for a week and that rest enabled me to go back and complete the run, although by the end I was well and truly burned out and dreading every performance. It felt like history repeating itself.

The show was due to close at the end of July, but because it was doing so well and still attracting good audiences the producers wanted to extend the run. To his great credit, André Ptaszynski recognised that I had had enough and put no pressure on me to continue. I was grateful to him for acknowledging that I had done as much as I could do and that if I did any more I really would make myself ill. Because I stopped when I did I was able to have a proper break and enjoy some badly needed rest and recreation with the family, and by the time plans were made to tour *Spend* around the country in 2001, I was refreshed, rejuvenated and delighted to agree to return to the show. It was also done in two three-month chunks, with a break in the middle for a holiday.

On that tour, apart from one wobble, which I managed to get through, I was able to see out a full six months with *Spend Spend Spend*, playing to new and enthusiastic audiences across the UK. Both Willy Russell and Chris Bond came to see the show on tour and they both really liked it which, coming from Willy and Chris, was high praise indeed.

Spend Spend Spend was nominated for several Olivier awards in 2000. Cruelly, it did not win the prize for Best Musical, which it richly deserved, but which, inexplicably, went to *Honk! The Ugly Duckling* instead. The fact that it took the *Evening Standard* award for Best Musical, ahead of some stiff competition, including *The Lion King*, was some consolation. I was lucky enough to win the Olivier that year - my second for Best Actress in a Musical - along with the Variety Club award in the same category. I was as thrilled to be honoured for *Spend Spend Spend* as I had been to be honoured for *Blood Brothers*. It is genuinely satisfying to be recognised for roles that you passionately believe in and have worked so hard to create and, though it might sound like a cliché, you *are* representing all the cast and crew of a production, and when you win an award it really does mean a great deal to everyone involved.

Awards are good for the general health of the industry, too. The media coverage they generate spreads the word about a show and brings more people to see it. And for me, whenever I look at the trophies I have won, the memories of the difficult times playing Mrs Johnstone and Viv are just washed away. It's not unlike giving birth, when the euphoria of having a baby cancels out all the pain you suffered getting it there. And it's nice to imagine that, when I'm no longer around and my awards have been passed down to my children, they might glance at them occasionally and think that, actually, their mother must have been quite good.

All three of the acting roles with which I am most closely associated - Mrs Johnstone from *Blood Brothers*, Anita Braithwaite from *Band Of Gold* and Viv Nicholson from *Spend, Spend, Spend* - have a lot of characteristics in common. All three are strong, determined, complex, working-class women who are also vulnerable, loving and very human. All three suffer considerable tragedy in their lives, but they are survivors; they just get on with it, as that is the only way they know. In all three cases I felt I really understood these women and that I was able to give something of' myself to the character.

My friend and *Band Of Gold* co-star Geraldine James once said to me that, as an actress so often seen as upper class, as she was in *The Jewel In The Crown*, she loved having the opportunity to play different and varied roles - and she does it with great success, too. Geraldine, though, is a fine actress; I am a singer and musician who also acts, and I need to have an affinity with a character, to know who she is and where she comes from, to get under her skin. I have to believe, as I did with Mrs Johnstone, Anita and Viv, that I can do her justice. I have always very much doubted, for example, that I could ever play a character in a Noël Coward play, much to my late mother's disappointment. I just don't have the background or right life experience to draw on.

Maybe, with more acting experience or more self-confidence, I would have been able to put myself forward for female characters from a wider variety of social backgrounds. Indeed, perhaps it is that very lack of experience and self-confidence that compelled me to give so much of myself, probably too much sometimes, to the parts I did take on. But, like the strong women I portrayed, I did it in the only way I knew how.

What the West End run of *Spend Spend Spend* did confirm for me was that I was not physically or mentally suited to long runs in the theatre. It took me an awfully long time to come to terms not only with the exhaustion I experienced in both *Spend* and *Blood Brothers* but with the feeling that, when I have had to take a short period off, I have in some way let people down, both cast and audience, not to mention my own perception that being on my knees with tiredness somehow meant I had failed. Only recently have I been able to accept that I did the very best I could, and that that is all you can do. Or, as Pete Zorn, my great friend and musical mainstay of the last thirty-five years, once said sagely: 'Remember, Barbara, nobody's human.'

The tour of *Spend Spend Spend* took up most of 2001. I don't know whether, other than Willy Russell and Chris Bond, many illustrious people came to see the show, but just before Christmas 2001 I received a phone call enquiring whether I might be interested in accepting an OBE for services to music and drama in the 2002 New Year's Honours List. I was completely shocked that I was even under consideration. Nobody had ever mentioned such a possibility to me and the OBE was a very great honour indeed for which to be put forward. I think there may have been a rather long pause at my end of the telephone line. Once I got over my amazement I said, of course, that I would be delighted to accept it.

You have to keep the news to yourself until it is officially announced and when that day finally came, as well as being happy at how thrilled my friends and family were for me, I was really pleased to see that there was a lot of coverage in the media, especially in Scotland. I was especially delighted that I was going to be invested in the Queen's Golden Jubilee year.

The ceremony was to take place at Buckingham Palace in March 2002, and although you are told the date well in advance you do not know until the day itself whether it will be the Queen or Prince Charles who bestows the honour.

While Oliver and the boys were all pleased about going to the Palace I was thrilled to discover that it would be the Queen herself who would be there. It is not, I hasten to add, that I think any less of Prince Charles - I was just very keen to meet the Queen as I had a personal message I wanted to deliver to her.

A good few years earlier I had been introduced to the Princess Royal and her husband, Timothy Laurence, at a dinner in London for the Calcutta Cup rugby international between England and Scotland (the Princess is the patron of the Scottish Rugby Union), where I had been asked to sing 'Flower Of Scotland' unaccompanied. After that I met them occasionally, and when I had a residency at the Green Room of the Café Royal in London's Piccadilly they kindly came to see me sing. It was through this acquaintanceship that Elaine Paige and I were asked if we would perform at a private concert organised by the Princess's family as part of the Jubilee celebrations for the Queen.

Invitations like that do not come along very often. A date was set and arrangements were made, but in February 2002 the Queen's sister, Princess Margaret, died and understandably the party at Windsor had to be cancelled. So it was something of a coincidence that I should be at Buckingham Palace to receive the OBE from Her Majesty only a few weeks after I should have been singing for her, and I wanted to tell her how sorry I was that I hadn't been able to do that.

When I was called forward, I was, of course, nervous, but the Queen is very warm and welcoming and said a few words to put me at my ease. I then expressed my regret that I hadn't been able to sing for her, to which she replied, rather enigmatically, that perhaps I still would.

During this short interlude, I'd had to curtsey. This was the second occasion as I had been invited to lunch at Buckingham Palace in 1986 and had practised curtseying for ages beforehand. Some people don't bother with such formality these days, but I would never let my parents or the people of Dunfermline down and wanted to get it right for them and for me. When the moment arrived and the Queen proffered her hand, I bobbed and almost fell over, I was so nervous. However, she is most polite and never raised an eyebrow.
And as if by magic - well, she is the Queen after all – the concert was rescheduled for the summer of 2002 and not only were Elaine and I invited to Windsor Castle to perform, we were also asked if we would like to stay there overnight. It was absolutely lovely, and all the staff were kind and hospitable to us. We were given a guided tour of the castle which, with my interest in history, I found fascinating - Windsor dates back over 900 years to the reign of

William the Conqueror - and for the rest of our time there we were allowed to wander around the castle as we liked without any restrictions.

I went for a stroll with Bernard, who had accompanied me, and we were both dumbstruck by the number of famous paintings we found in the Royal Collection that we had only ever seen on greetings cards. This room had a Rembrandt, the next a Rubens and along the corridor would be a Gainsborough. There they were, only a few feet away from us, and we were being allowed to appreciate them completely on our own - a rare experience indeed. I don't think we said a word to each other as we tried to absorb all these artistic delights.

As we walked along a little further we came upon some cabinets full of beautiful porcelain. And next to the cabinet, on the floor, was a very nice dog bowl. Bernard and I looked at the dog bowl, looked at each other, and did a double-take, realising at once that we must have wandered into the private apartments and quickly deciding it would probably be best if we got out of there pretty rapidly, we retraced our footsteps without delay.

Elaine and I took a small band of three with us. We each did a solo spot and, of course sang 'I Know Him So Well' together for the royal family. For my spot I had decided to go for traditional Scottish songs which I hoped the Queen, given her love of Scotland, would enjoy. Windsor Castle was the smallest and most intimate concert venue I had played since my days in the folk clubs. There could not have been any more than forty-five people in the audience and I was performing in what was essentially somebody's front room - but what an audience and what a front room. And what an historic moment, finding yourself singing, with the Queen only a few feet away,

> Carry the lad that's born to be king
> Over the sea to Skye.

Funnily enough, for once in my life I was not especially nervous. Everyone was so nice, and took such trouble to put us at our ease, yet I couldn't stop myself, every now and again, stealing a glance at Her Majesty and hoping for the merest hint of royal approval. I recall that HRH Prince Philip always taps his toe. He likes music.

So, in the space of a few months, I had sung for the Queen and had an OBE to my name. I don't think either experience has changed me in any way. I am still the girl from Ochil Terrace in Dunfermline and deep down I always will be, no matter what success or failure comes my way. But if anybody important is reading this: if I were ever to be offered the Order of the Thistle, the highest honour in Scotland … well, that would be very grand indeed.

With my television roles, the *Seven Ages Of Woman* and the two years with *Spend Spend Spend*, since 1995 I had been as busy as at any time in my career, but I hadn't recorded any new material since the *Dark End Of The Street* album. I had made soundtrack albums for both *Seven Ages* and *Spend*, but the momentum I had built up in carving out a new musical direction for myself with the three albums from 1992 to 1995 had stalled. In between my acting commitments I was still faithfully touring, but I was being regularly told that there was simply no market and no audience for a new album. It was very disappointing and frustrating to be given such depressing advice, especially as I had been so excited by the music I'd been making, but I reluctantly accepted it.

By the new millennium, however, I was itching to get back into a recording studio. Not to do obvious covers or remakes of previous hits, but to produce new material I could really get my teeth into. Other people might have decided I had little more to say as a recording artist, but I didn't have to agree with them. I wasn't that kind of musician.

In 2001 I was talking to Rab Noakes about my desire to produce a new album and how dif6cult it was proving to get a decent contract from a good record label, and he suggested that we make one together, which we could put out on his label. So I went up to Glasgow and we began discussing what sort of material we wanted to record. The initial plan was to do a stripped-down, back-to-basics collection of contemporary songs, songs with a dark edge by writers such as Tom Waits and Robbie Robertson. We began to rehearse, but I had a sense that these songs were not quite right for me. My instinct was that I should be looking for material with a more Celtic feel. Rab and I eventually decided not to continue with the proposed album, but all our discussions and rehearsals had only reinforced my determination to make new music. It would still be some time, however, before my hopes would be fulfilled.

I was also becoming increasingly concerned that the promotion of my tours was not what it should be. There didn't seem to be the same buzz when I arrived in a city to play. Was it in fact substandard promotion, or was it me?

Eventually, in 2003, somebody suggested I contact Danny Betesh from Kennedy Street Enterprises in Manchester, a very experienced music promoter whose CV goes back to the 1960s. With Danny and his colleague, Angie Becker, on board I saw an immediate transformation in the response to my live shows. That was the answer to the question, obviously. Where a few years before a Barbara Dickson concert had passed by almost unnoticed, now people were very much aware that I was around and coming to their town and, gratifyingly, they wanted to see me. All I needed now was a new album.

I'd kept in touch with Troy Donockley, who I'd first met when he played the uilleann pipes on *Parcel Of Rogues* – he also appeared on *Dark End Of The Street* - and talked to him about what I wanted to do. Troy comes from Workington in Cumbria and has been immersed in music all his life. He was a member of the Celtic rock band Iona and has also worked with the folk singer Maddy Prior, Midge Ure and the Finnish band Nightwish. A talented musician, composer and arranger, he is renowned throughout the folk scene for his virtuosity on many instruments, but especially the uilleann pipes. We had always had a musical affinity.

Troy came up with a structure of the idea of us working together. With all the new technology available by this time, he reasoned, we didn't need a major record label to make an album. We just needed loads of ideas. He had his own recording studio in Yorkshire, I had a great relationship with Andy Dransfield, who owned Chapel Studios in Lincolnshire: we were ready to go. The quality of the production would be superb and as for the quality of the music - well, that was up to us.

So I successfully raised the finance required to get the project up and running and, for the first time in my life, I was able to start an album totally independently, with nobody to please but myself. I felt completely liberated and as excited as at any time in my career. But in one respect having this wonderful blank canvas was a bit daunting: what on earth were we going to record? After eight years without an album, my insecurities were beginning to resurface. What sort of sound did I want? What sort of songs did I want to sing? What genre should it be? Could I actually do this? Maybe all those gainsayers were right and nobody was going to be that interested.

As we tossed suggestions around, I happened to mention my shirt box to Troy. Remember my shirt box? It was where I'd stored the words and music for my songs since 1965, when I started trying to learn as many traditional and folk songs as I possibly could, and I still had it. Wherever I went, that box had gone with me. I had taken it when I moved to England, first to Lincolnshire and then to my London flats; it had gone to Clapham and to Richmond and, finally, back to Lincolnshire again. Over the years the box had been bashed several times and the lid had long since disappeared, but even though the shirt box collection had expanded rather unmanageably in all that time, never for one second would I have considered transferring it into a new, more practical container.

A question interviewers are fond of asking is: 'What is your most treasured possession?' I usually say it is my guitars, a Martin and a Fylde, but in truth, if there was a fire, and all the family and cat were safe, and I could only rescue one thing, it wouldn't be my awards or my gold discs or even my guitars, it would be the shirt box. When we moved to the vicarage in Lincolnshire there was one horrible moment when the shirt box went missing. I became so concerned that I had to be given a sedative to calm me down. I only fully recovered my equanimity and my sanity when the shirt box magically, and somewhat suspiciously, if you ask me, reappeared in one of the packing cases.

When he heard about the shirt box, Troy said, 'Why don t we select the songs for the album from the shirt box?' And that was what we did. I put the shirt box, and all my books of Scottish and English folk songs, into the back of my car and drove up to Troy's house. I can't remember being as excited about a new album as I was that day. It never crossed my mind that people might not like the songs we would choose when so much love and joy were invested in them all. My confidence was restored and I felt as if I was bursting with creativity. Troy helped me channel my cornucopia of ideas and together we selected traditional songs, contemporary songs, classical songs and one pop song, 'Living Too Close To The Ground' by Phil Everly, which I'd learned from Rab Noakes. I brought to the project desire, ability and material, but it was Troy who had the vision to bring it to life.

We recorded the traditional songs 'Singing Bird', 'Eriskay Love Song' and 'Corpus Christi Carol'. We recorded 'The Sky Above The Roof' by Ralph Vaughan Williams, 'When I Am Laid To Earth' by Henry Purcell and our version of the country-rock 'Faithless Love' by J.D. Souther, which had been popularised by Linda Ronstadt. It was just the two of us in the studio

- the other musicians recorded later at Chapel Studios in Lincolnshire, with the assistance of engineer Ewan Davies.

We called the album, appropriately enough, *Full Circle* (I suppose we could have called it *The Shirt Box Collection*, but that might have been a little puzzling). Although it was dogged with distribution problems, it was well received, the reviews were generally good and when I began playing the new material in concert the audience embraced both the songs and the change in direction. I was delighted with the whole experience of making *Full Circle*. I felt artistically reborn and I truly believed that Troy and I had created something magical. And even if the reviews had been less kind and the album had disappeared without a trace, I wouldn't have felt any less proud of what Troy and I had achieved. By going back nearly forty years to find the songs, I really had gone full circle, but I'd never felt so alive and optimistic about the future of my musical career.

CHAPTER FIFTEEN
THE RIGS Ø' RYE

I was twenty-six years old when, in 1973, I left Dunfermline for the last time and moved to England permanently, which meant - and it shocked me when I realised this - that by 2000 I had lived away from Scotland for longer than I had ever lived there. It just goes to show how quickly time passes. Though I've always had a yearning to return to my native country it hasn't thus far been a practical possibility. When we left London in 1993 moving to Scotland was never a serious consideration. Not only did I need to be nearer to London but Oliver was continuing his career in television. He progressed up the ladder to First Assistant Director (the person in charge of the crew who gets to say, at the start of a scene, 'And... action!') and he has worked on many popular television series over the past twenty years, including *Between the Lines*, *The Bill*, *Judge John Deed* and *Doctors*.

Once we had settled in Lincolnshire and the boys were at school there was no reason to think of going anywhere else, although in 2003, we decided to move out of the vicarage and into the town of Louth itself, three miles away. That was the point at which I finally had to say farewell to my precious Mini Clubman, which had sat in the garage for twelve years, because there was nowhere at the new house to keep it. A sad day indeed.

Louth is an historic market town with a population of around 17,000 people. The main landmark is St James's church, which dates back to the fifteenth century and boasts a sixteenth-century, 295-foot spire, the tallest of any mediaeval parish church in England. Some may consider Lincolnshire a cultural backwater but the town of Louth is proud to claim among its famous inhabitants the singer Robert Wyatt, who was a member of the band Soft Machine and sang a haunting version of the Elvis Costello song 'Shipbuilding' and comic actor and writer Graham Fellows, better known as his alter ego John Shuttleworth, who many, many moons ago had a hit record under the alias Jilted John. Actor Patrick Mower, who plays the debonair Rodney Blackstock in *Emmerdale*, also lives nearby and the Oscar winner Jim Broadbent is a local boy made good.

People are often surprised when they hear that we live in Lincolnshire, not because there is anything odd about us choosing Lincolnshire in particular, but because they assume somebody like me would be based in London or the home counties. It is now over seventeen years since I lived in London and I must admit I don't miss the bright lights at all. The capital city is only a few hours away by train and when I do go back for work, or to see friends, I always have a good time, but I have never cared much about having a high profile, being seen around town or going to an opening. And when people want to get hold of me, Louth never seems that far away after all.

We have been very content in Lincolnshire and Oliver has spent many happy years there attempting to get his golf handicap down. We have made some good friends and, as time goes by, I realise what a great commodity friendship is and I value friends and family, wherever they live, more and more. Occasionally, mostly on birthdays, anniversaries and Hogmanay, we have a little get together. Guests and family members alike will be asked to sing a song, play a tune or recite a poem or a piece of prose. These evenings always remind me of my childhood in Dunfermline when my mother and father, aunts and uncles would drink the odd dram and sing around the piano, and it is good to keep that tradition alive; everyone loves it.

As much as I enjoy living in Lincolnshire, I have always retained an unbreakable bond with the kingdom of Fife, even though in my youth I never really appreciated how lovely it was, and indeed left at the earliest opportunity. I have fond memories of the community spirit in the Fife towns, of the wonderful big sky and open spaces of the East Neuk. The part of Lincolnshire where I live is not dissimilar to Fife in that respect, which is possibly why I have always felt so at home there. Above all I remember the Fife people - warm, generous, strong people who have always been so supportive and kind to me, even though it is over forty years since I lived among them.

As well as being a Fifer and a proud Scot I have always been aware, of course, that, through my mother, I am also a daughter of Liverpool, which has had a profound impact on my life from my childhood holidays onwards. The city and the opportunities and support I have been given there have shaped my career, and for that I will always be grateful. It was no coincidence that it was in Liverpool that I chose to open my *Seven Ages Of Woman* show and it was only because *Blood Brothers* was back where it first began that I briefly returned to play Mrs Johnstone in 2001 and 2004.

But for all my love and affection for Fife and Liverpool, whenever I imagine living somewhere else, it is Edinburgh that I see in my mind's eye. My years there were one of the happiest periods of my life and I always enjoy returning whenever I can. I go back regularly to visit one of my oldest friends, Yvonne Kirkus, and there is nothing we like better than strolling around the shops and Botanic Gardens, near where she lives, or going into town to see an exhibition followed by a bit of lunch or maybe just a tea and a scone. And from Edinburgh you can look across the Forth to Fife, so the kingdom never feels too far away.
In some ways Scotland has become a sort of security blanket for me, somewhere I feel safe and comfortable. I try to get there regularly, to play concerts or visit friends, and now that the boys are at the age where they are spending less time at home, I long to go home for

good, although I still have some way to go before I convince Oliver. Not that he and the boys, who have all been born and brought up in England, don't love Scotland. All of my sons played rugby and they always support Scotland when they are playing an international, as long as it's not against England - they were born in London after all. And, considering the number of weekends I have spent cheering them on from the touchlines of numerous muddy fields in northern England, freezing to death in the process, it is, I think, only fair.

Not long ago somebody wrote to tell me they had worked out that I had sold more records than any other solo Scottish female artist. Now, I have never tried to calculate my record sales over the years, and I'm sure Lulu, Annie Lennox and Sheena Easton must also have sold more than a few million in the course of their careers. But, for all that I truly believe it is the quality rather than the popularity of music that matters, I must admit to feeling more than a little pride that Barbara Dickson from Dunfermline, with the glasses, the wild hair and the sad voice, has done so well and brought a little joy to so many people.

Because I have lived away from Scotland for so long and because, with the advent of the Scottish Parliament, the country is changing so much now, I do sometimes feel I tend to get overlooked back home. Out of sight, out of mind, I suppose. Which is why, when I am touring, I always try to fit in as many concerts in Scotland as possible, and why I am always on the look-out for opportunities to go and work there. One such invitation came along in 2006, when I was asked to appear in a BBC television series called *Scotland's Music*. The presenter was the iconic Phil Cunningham from Edinburgh, who used to be in the folk band Silly Wizard and is now well known for his double act with that other wonderful musician, the Shetland fiddler Aly Bain.

I was delighted to be approached for the series, a history of Scottish music, and even more delighted when I discovered that not only would I be going back to Edinburgh, but the filming was to take place in Sandy Bell's pub on Forrest Road, the centre of the whole Edinburgh folk scene back in the 1960s, a place where I had spent more happy evenings than I can remember.

I had not actually been to Sandy Bell's since around 1970, so it was over thirty-five years since I had set foot in the bar. Walking into the pub was one of the strangest moments of my life: absolutely nothing had changed. Everything – the bar, the tables, the loos - was exactly as I had left it all those years before. And if that made me feel I had fallen into a time warp, who should I find sitting in the bar, as if they had never been away, but Ian McCalman and Aly Bain, neither of whom I was expecting to see.

I'd arrived at Sandy Bell's with Troy, and Aly asked us what we'd like to drink. Given that it was 9.30 on a Sunday morning, Troy said no alcohol for him, please, could he have a glass of lemonade? Aly nodded and headed for the bar, where he bought Troy a pint of Guinness. Well, he was in Sandy Bell's, after all.

With accompaniment from Troy, Aly and Phil, I was filmed for *Scotland's Music* singing the traditional song 'The Rigs O' Rye', but as you might expect we spent most of the session talking about old times and old friends and the many nights we used to spend in Sandy Bell's -

and the Abbotsford, the Waverley, Paddy's Bar and all the rest - back in the day. And the more we talked and laughed and reminisced, the more it became clear that the only thing that was different about today was that slightly less alcohol was involved and nobody bought a carry-oot when we left.

If traditional music has been a thread running through my career as a singer, then another recurrent theme has been the music of the Beatles. With the release of *Full Circle* demonstrating that Barbara Dickson the recording artist was more than capable of making good music, I was approached by Universal Music to see if I would be interested in doing an album of Beatles songs. It was a great offer and, as I'd found with the collection of Bob Dylan songs, *Don' t Think Twice, It's All Right*, spending time recording songs that have had such a deep and long-lasting significance is no hardship.

However, I was feeling so rejuvenated and enthused by the independence Troy and I had enjoyed during the recording of *Full Circle*, and so delighted with the result, that before I agreed, I wanted to make sure Universal understood that Barbara Dickson was no longer the Barbara Dickson who sang 'I Know Him So Well' but was treading a new artistic path along which I was determined to continue. A meeting was arranged with Tony Swain, formerly a top songwriter and producer in his own right, and Max Hole, the boss of Universal and I gave them a copy of *Full Circle* and told them that this was the musical approach I was currently taking and wanted to continue with. Thankfully, they immediately got where I was coming from and were happy to green-light the project to be recorded in the way I wanted, and with Troy collaborating.

Troy and I went down to Bath in 2006, where we worked with Chris Hughes - a talented producer who had been drummer with Adam and the Ants and had gone on to produce albums for Tears For Fears - and Mark Frith, who was the engineer and bass player on the album. We decided not to go down the route of selecting the most familiar Beatles songs, but instead went for those that meant the most to me personally, and particularly those with which we could do something new. We recorded 'Eleanor Rigby', 'Fool On The Hill', 'Here, There and Everywhere' and 'If I Needed Someone' written by George Harrison. I have always felt that, as a songwriter, George was unlucky to have been so overshadowed by John and Paul. We also recorded my favourite Beatles song of all, John Lennon's 'Across The Universe', from the *Let It Be* album, from whose chorus we took the title for our collection.

I had a very happy time recording *Nothing's Gonna Change My World*, and when I heard the end result I felt vindicated in the approach that we had taken. No matter how familiar the songs were, we had managed to produce something original and new. I still use the arrangements we came up with for songs like 'Eleanor Rigby' in concert today. I'm not claiming they are better than the original version, of course, just different.

The release of the album in 2006 would also mark the end of my management relationship with Bernard. After more than thirty years of tours, hit singles, albums, theatre and television roles, good times and occasionally not so good times, the moment had arrived for us to part company and go our separate ways. Bernard is the only manager I have ever had and, in the same way that I am certain I will only have one husband, I knew I didn't want another manager. I had decided that once the partnership with Bernard finished I would take responsibility for my career. I was clear in my mind that the musical journey on which Troy and I had embarked with *Full Circle* was one I should pursue and to that end I set up my own record company, Chariot Music. The name is a reference to years of private correspondence between Troy and me arising from his name for me: Boudicca, after the warrior queen of the Iceni, who would go into battle and inspect her troops from her chariot. So Chariot Music it was.

In 2007 we began work on the follow-up to *Full Circle*, employing the same *modus operandi* we'd used for the previous album. We started out with a blank piece of paper and once again went back to songs that we loved and on which we felt we could put our special stamp. We recorded the traditional 'Rigs O' Rye' I had sung on *Scotland's Music*, 'Lady Franklin's Lament' and 'The Lowlands Of Holland'. I revisited Archie Fisher's 'The Witch Of The Westmerland', which I had first recorded on the *From The Beggar's Mantle* album I had made in three days back in 1972, and Troy gave the song the contemporary arrangement it deserved. From the 1960s I retrieved the Goffin and King song 'Goin' Back', which had been a hit for Dusty Springfield but which I knew sung by the Byrds, and I recorded 'Palm Sunday', a brand-new song written by Troy and me. All these songs have a rare integrity and once Troy and I had made our selections we put our heart and soul into making them come alive.

We called the album *Time And Tide* and it was released in January 2008. I honestly believe that, after all these years, it is the best work I have ever produced. I see *Time And Tide* and *Full Circle* as the beginning of a new phase of my career, one where Troy and I have the freedom to create music that perfectly blends the traditional and the contemporary, classical and Celtic influences, and where I have complete control over what I record. And it is a revelation to me, having always been such a reluctant songwriter, even when working with someone as talented as Charlie Dore, to find myself in a co-writing partnership that makes me feel so enthusiastic. 'Palm Sunday' was the first song I had written for years and the one I have been most proud of. I hope it will be the forerunner of many original compositions and that the best is still to come.

Maybe I don't sell as many albums as I used to in the 1980s and maybe I haven't had a gold record for a while, but when we play the new songs in concert the response reassures me that we are on the right track. I want this year's tour to be better than last year's tour and next year's to top that. I still enjoy performing 'Answer Me', 'Caravan' and 'I Know Him So Well' because we approach them in a contemporary way and 'Answer Me' we wouldn't rearrange anyway: an evening consisting solely of 'greatest hits' is not, however, something I would ever want to do.

I love music today as much as ever. James Taylor is still an inspiration to me and when I finally got to meet the great man, at the Folk Awards in 2009, it was as much of a thrill for me as it would have been forty years ago. It is no coincidence that James, Randy Newman, Bob Dylan, Paul Simon and all the other great singers and songwriters I have admired for so long have continued to produce excellent and diverse work and have never compromised their creativity or their artistic vision. To go on growing as a musician it is vital to keep looking ahead and to keep discovering new music that captures your heart and your imagination.

Having grown-up sons, I have become familiar with all sorts of new bands and new musical trends. In the Cookson household American punk and nu-metal were for a time particularly popular and often painfully loud. As is the case with all music, some of it you could really do without ever hearing again, or, to be truthful, ever having heard in the first place, but you will also come upon some gems. Eminem for example, is to my mind one of the best musical storytellers since Bob Dylan. My tastes in music have always been catholic but if anything they have become even more diverse as I have got older. Where in the 1960s, at the same time as playing the folk clubs I'd be listening to Cream and The Who, today I might find myself sampling the new album by Randy Newman, followed by some twelfth-century church canticles in Latin and then maybe something by Seth Lakeman, and appreciating all three. If I have a musical philosophy it is that in an ideal world music should touch the heart and soul and be completely free of boundaries.

CHAPTER SIXTEEN
PALM SUNDAY

So that's pretty much the story of my life so far. A happy childhood. No drink or drug problems to speak of. No health crises. No big scandal. Only one marriage and no divorce. Just a musician and actress from Fife with a few hit records and a couple of Olivier Awards to her name. Well, I did make it clear that I've never had any truck with the celebrity lifestyle. That's my view of myself, anyway. I am aware that I am somebody the entertainment business finds it hard to pigeonhole. Pop singer? Folk singer? Singer who acts? Actress who sings?

As for the perception of the wider world, I've usually assumed I will be remembered as the girl-next-door pop singer from the 1970s and 1980s who sang 'I Know Him So Well'. Yet whenever I actually talk to some of the individuals who come to my concerts I find that I mean different things to different people. As well as those who associate me with my pop years, there are plenty who know me from my time in musical theatre and others for whom I will always be Anita Braithwaite in *Band Of Gold* - their first question is generally, 'Is there ever going to be another series?' And of course there are some who go all the way back to my early days as a folk singer or who have discovered me since my return to traditional music with *Parcel Of Rogues*.

It does not concern me in the slightest precisely why my audiences come to see me; I am just glad that they do. For quite a while now a majority of them have been people of my own generation who attend my concerts regularly, as eager to hear the new music I am making as they are their old favourites. It is often the women who like to come and say hello afterwards, bringing their CDs and tour brochures for me to sign - you can usually spot their husbands loitering by the exits, too shy to accompany them - and I'm sure part of the reason they return again and again is that they identify with me as somebody who is just like them: an ordinary woman from an ordinary background; a baby-boomer who has matured into a silver surfer, determined to live life to the full. And not somebody attempting to look thirty when she is past sixty. I just try to look my best, to perform to the best of my ability and to put on a good show of great songs and great music in the hope that they will have a great night, buy my albums and come back again the next year. I need their support to make it all work.

I am conscious of how much a woman of my era I am. I was never any sort of activist for women's rights, but I always believed women should be free, independent and perceived by both sexes as the equals of men, and I lived my life according to those principles. I remember in the 1960s avidly reading Germaine Greer and *Nova* magazine and to this day, if there is one woman I admire and look up to, it is Germaine. Brains and courage: what a combination.

And our generation of women did change the world, if not perhaps in the way we'd hoped. We won the right to make choices in all areas of our lives, from our careers and finances to our marriages and other relationships, but sadly I think we have taken the opportunities we have earned and in some instances used them to turn ourselves into second-class men. Today's young women are certainly more vocal than their predecessors in sticking up for themselves, but they have ended up working twice as hard as men to try to compete with them. In the 1960s I saw myself and my contemporaries as forerunners of a generation of bright, educated young women who would have the chances to achieve whatever ambitions they possessed. But now, instead of a rich seam of budding Germaine Greers, we have a sisterhood that loves to emulate reality TV stars. There are no inspirational young women to be seen on the cover of *Heat* magazine.

One of the great joys of growing older is that over the years I have worked out what I like and what I don't like and acquired the confidence to say what I think. I am probably becoming more and more difficult to please, finding more to dislike than like and becoming increasingly outspoken about it. If that makes me sound like a grumpy old woman, I confess to being guilty as charged. And as a true grumpy old woman, naturally I have nothing but disdain for the celebrities who appear on the television show *Grumpy Old Women*. Not only does it seem completely contrived, but the women on it are simply not grumpy enough to be worthy of the name, and certainly not nearly as grumpy as me.

It is liberating finally to have attained the self-assurance to complain. I cannot be doing with bad service or poor manners or lack of respect or vulgar behaviour. Whereas in the past I would have maintained a British stiff upper lip and resolutely refused to make a fuss, I am now more than happy to put my perfectly reasonable point across and to encourage others to do the same. In short, to be 'crabbit', as we Scots would describe it: a wonderful word that encapsulates our own unique strain of stubbornness and cantankerousness. When it comes to being grumpy, the English are amateurs.

There are many, many things that get my goat, as my friends and family will no doubt confirm, but harking endlessly back to the past when there are so many aspects of life today to celebrate particularly infuriates me. One of the drawbacks of getting older is that this tends to happen to me with increasing frequency. When you do promotions and interviews after being in the entertainment business for forty years, it is inevitable that some hapless interviewer is going to ask you, 'What would you consider to be the highlight of your career?' And you know perfectly well that he will have a clip of that bloody video for 'I Know Him So Well' cued up in the expectation that your answer will be, 'Getting to number one.'

'As far as I am concerned,' I always reply, 'the highlight of my career is yet to come.'

What I am actually thinking is 'Bugger off - I'm not past it, you cheeky wee shite.'

But that doesn't mean my stock response is untruthful. When you are as much of a perfectionist as I am, how could it be? I am simply never entirely satisfied with what I have achieved and I always want to do more. I still want to be the perfect wife, the perfect mother and the perfect singer, and this trait of mine shows no sign of ever fading. 'Barbara, attempting to be perfect is just crap,' my analyst told me succinctly in the 1980s, but it hasn't stopped me trying.

In fact, rather than slowing down, my life seems to be speeding up and becoming more hectic than ever, which is perhaps another reason why people's preoccupation with the past irritates me. Though I love working in my garden, I am a long way from sitting back and smelling the roses on a permanent basis, and that suits me just fine. I fervently believe that life is for living, no matter what age I am, and there are always wonderful new songs to record or new projects to excite me along the way.

The more distant past is another matter, of course. I remain as fascinated by history as I have always been, and one of my ambitions is to take an Open University course in the subject. My passion for traditional music is entwined with a deep interest in its origins - the lives of the people in the times and places in which it was written. As much as I love to read and learn and become engrossed in a new topic, I still find that a song can often tell a story as well as any book. I love going to galleries and to the cinema and theatre, too, although that doesn't necessarily mean I am going to love what I see when I get there. I am, as I say, very hard to please and I find it impossible to watch any play or a musical in which I've appeared as I just cannot give up my ownership of 'my' character.

For over twenty-five years now Oliver has been a perfect partner and I never forget how lucky I am. For so long, singing and music were the most important things in my life but then he and the boys came along and enriched my life. Oliver and I are determined to allow our boys, in turn, to discover what enriches their lives; not to push them, but to support them in whatever dreams they have. We haven' t ever tried to influence them to follow the family into music, acting or the theatre - or not to, for that matter.

If luck has a part to play in our lives, it is only in presenting us with opportunities. It is what each of us decides to do with those opportunities that shape our destinies. Such choices are rarely easy and they require courage: far and away the hardest decision I ever had to make was taking that chance to go to Denmark in 1968. It meant sacrificing my job and my security, but I knew in my heart that if I didn't take that risk I would always regret it. I believe that one should be encouraged to follow the heart rather than settle, out of fear and a lack of self-confidence, for the safe and limiting option and be left for ever wondering what might have been. If I can do it, anyone can. A modest view of one's own talent is a good thing, however, and stops a person aiming too high too quickly.

In spite of being brought up in a non-religious family, the Church, in one form or another, has been part of the backdrop to my life ever since the days when the Church of Scotland rounded up all the non-attending Brucefield children and I started going to Sunday school, and as I have grown older faith has become more important to me. After my brief flirtation with the Episcopalians, the affinity with the Catholic Church that I felt able to embrace once I'd left home and moved to Edinburgh remained. When I went to visit my friend Rosemary Clark in Liverpool I would accompany her to St Peter's and St Paul's in Great Crosby, and in London I liked to go to St Patrick's in Soho Square. Whenever I had a meeting at the CBS offices nearby I would leave home early so that I had time to light a candle and sit and reflect awhile in St Patrick's.

I have always cherished the quiet and solitude of churches and their role as a refuge from the relentless activity of the outside world. They provided a place where I could pause and ponder what was happening in my life with no distractions, and it was always Catholic churches that I chose.

When I first met Oliver I had no idea he was a Catholic. Religion was never a factor in any of my relationships and he was not a churchgoer anyway. Although I was not a Catholic, I took the marriage vows we made in front of Fr Peter and our families and friends very seriously. Because we had a Catholic ceremony I agreed that any children would be baptised as Catholics, and Oliver was to make sure that they were taught their catechism; as far as I was concerned, if that was what he had promised, that was what was going to happen.

But since we didn't go to church, when Colm, Gabriel and Archie came along they weren't taught their Hail Marys, and as they began to grow up the knowledge that this promise had also lapsed began to bother me more and more until I decided that it was now incumbent on me, the non-Catholic of the family, to do something about it. I went to see the parish priest at St Mary's in Louth, and Fr Mendel told me it didn't matter that I wasn't a Catholic, I should come along with the family to church. So, amid much wailing and gnashing of teeth about having to get up and dress respectably on a Sunday morning, all five Cooksons started to attend St Mary's.

At no time did anybody put any pressure on me to become a Catholic - I think they were just pleased to see some new faces there and everyone was very kind to me - but I began to realise that deep down I wanted to be a Catholic and had wanted to be a Catholic ever since I was a teenager. And now that I was going to church with my Catholic husband and my Catholic children, what was to stop me becoming a Catholic as well? Of all the major decisions in my life the decision to do so was probably the easiest and most straightforward I ever made. I felt completely comfortable with the liturgy and immediately at peace in my spiritual home. If anything I wondered why it had taken me so long to get there.

When I was younger I would have been embarrassed to call myself a Christian and even now my faith is very personal to me, but it has become the cornerstone of my life. When I am away or touring I take the time to seek out a church where I can sit quietly, read the psalms and say the office of Morning or Evening Prayer. And before walking out onstage I say a Hail Mary and cross myself. It steadies me. I love nothing more than going to a church dating back hundreds of years and reading those wonderful ancient texts. It is at these moments that I can see the thread that connects everything together and my own tiny place in the world begins to make sense.

Pausing to take stock of my situation is something I do a lot, perhaps because my life has never been conducted according to any great master plan. I am just a singer who wants to make music and everything beyond that has been a series of accidents, some happy and some less so. I've never wanted to concentrate purely on television or the theatre: whenever I have accepted an invitation or a role it has been on the basis that I considered it too great an opportunity to turn down or simply because it seemed like a good idea at the time. Sometimes it was, but I ended up putting a lot of pressure on myself. With the benefit of a little more wisdom, I have finally learned how to say no and not feel guilty about it.

I did recently return to acting when I appeared in an episode of the BBC afternoon series *Doctors*. I had great fun on the show, but I have no intention of ever becoming a regular on TV. A few years ago, when a revival of *Crossroads* was being planned, I was asked if I would be interested in playing the lead character. I politely declined, not because I had some amazing ability to see that the revival was not going to last, but because I was not prepared to commit to the two or three years a soap requires or to endure the separation from my family it would have entailed. And because, when it came down to it, and I ran out of excuses, I just didn't want to do it.

When I say yes, it is to shows I want to do and which I think I will enjoy. The TV offers that appeal to me the most are those for programmes in areas where I have a genuine interest. For example, as an aficionado of words and word games, I loved appearing on *Countdown* and it's an experience I would happily repeat if I am ever asked. *Songs Of Praise* is another one that was great to do. Having researched my family tree (and got over the disappointment of finding out that my great-granny was a Wookey rather than a Wolki), I'd relish the chance to delve deeper on *Who Do You Think You Are*? And of course, given my passion for history, projects on that subject are invariably an attractive proposition for me.

Musical programmes, obviously, are a perennial delight. In 2008 I was asked by my old friend Rab Noakes to present a Christmas Day special for BBC Radio Scotland called *Joy To The World*. It was a wonderful opportunity to play some of my favourite music by some of my favourite artists and, even better, I was commissioned to record some new music for the programme. Troy and I decided to steer clear of familiar carols like 'Silent Night' and instead opted for older pieces of music, some in Latin, several dating back to the thirteenth century, that we could sprinkle with our own unique Dickson-Donockley snowflakes. It would be great if that programme were to lead to further special programmes.

I am sixty-two at the time of writing, and that's just fine by me. I have never been overly concerned about ageing. I cleanse and moisturise and after years of battling with my unruly locks I try to make sure my hair looks as good as possible, with the help of visits to my favourite hairdresser. When I am working I put in time and effort, choosing make-up and clothes that show me in my best light, but I haven't the energy or the inclination to do that all the time. If I do need to dress up it's hard to go wrong, I think, with a black velvet outfit, shoes with killer heels and diamond earrings - a girl's best friend. In that combination I always feel fantastic. A sound piece of rational advice.

I go to the gym three times a week, but I don't follow any particular regime. I didn't eat-meat for twenty-three years though I did eventually go back to it, mainly because I got fed up with the lack of variety in restaurants and all those carbs. But I try to buy good-quality produce. Though I've never been teetotal I drink very little alcohol: I always was a lightweight when it came to handling it and now I have no tolerance at all. And I still have that very Scottish reluctance to take pills or see the doctor unless it's absolutely necessary: I'd rather try a herbal remedy, or massage or acupuncture, than reach for the paracetamol. I also swear by lots of sleep and drinking plenty of water.

If you see me onstage or TV or in a press photograph, the one thing you can be assured of is that it's all me. No Botox, no lifts or tucks and no features fixed into place stretching out the wrinkles. I have spent so much of my life feeling insecure about how I look, worrying about what other people think of my appearance, being bombarded with advice about bringing out 'glamour' that simply isn't there to bring out and feeling guilty because of it, that now it's just wonderful to have reached the stage where it doesn't matter. I am who I am, a woman in a smart black outfit with a guitar slung around her neck who knows she can sing. Take it or leave it.

The voice, of course - the gift I've acknowledged since childhood and my constant friend - is what it all revolves around. It might have taken me many years to gain real confidence in myself as a person, but I always had confidence in my voice. I've never done anything to try to protect and preserve it. I even smoked from my teenage years until my early thirties. I think I have always had this optimism and faith that my voice would be fine no matter what. I haven't ever gone in for any kind of singing regime or had a permanent vocal coach. The one precaution I do take is to rest my voice when I am not touring or recording and I have a vocal warm-up on my iPod.

At home I listen mostly to folk, jazz and classical music and if I turn on the radio, it will usually be tuned to Radio 4 rather than any music channel. That might sound odd for someone brought up in a house where there was always a record on or somebody singing on the radio, but I just can't bear music as 'background'. I never listen to music on the radio unless it's Radio 3.

While learning a new song, I take my time and immerse myself in the music and words with the piano and acoustic guitar I have at home, just as I've always done, until playing and singing it becomes second nature and beds into my voice as if it's always been there.
Each singer has to do what is right for his or her own voice, and my personal methods and opinions wouldn't suit everyone. But for me singing is not a question of technique or training or good production in the recording studio, it is purely a matter of the voice I was born with and which remains more or less the same as it was when I was fourteen. If anything I think it

has got better as I've grown older. It has more resonance and richness; my younger voice was tighter, with a faster vibe. With the experience gained through singing professionally for more than forty years I feel I have learned to control the sound it produces and to shape that sound into what I want to hear. To be able to sing and be captivated by the sound you are making is indeed a thrill. I know that eventually the day will come when I am not happy with that sound. When it does, regardless of what anyone else thinks, it will be time to stop. But I hope that day is some way in the future.

The present is what concerns me and the present for me now, working with Troy and my fantastic band, is musically as exciting and exhilarating as it has been at any time in my life. I trust my band and they need to trust me, and the deeper the meaning of what we play, the deeper the relationship goes. We don't use charts to play from. We learn songs by playing the music until it is ours. Without them, and all the musicians with whom I have performed over the years, I could not do what I do. If anyone deserves to be singled out it is Pete Zorn: he has been with me man and boy, for thirty-five years and counting, playing every conceivable instrument with the exception of keyboards and drums.

I still play around forty shows a year and when interviewers ask me how tiring this is I tell them it is very tiring indeed and means I am up well past my bedtime. But for an artist nothing on the planet can match the feeling of creating, with no artifice, an evening of great music with great musicians. It's a privilege to walk out on to the stage and deliver a marvellous show - that's what rock 'n' roll is all about. So, as long as I am fit and well and love music as much as I do, and as long as the audiences come to hear me, I will continue to play that many shows a year. I want to go on songwriting and bringing the results to as many people as are willing to listen to them. The present couldn't be more rewarding and the future will take care of itself. Of that, I am confident.

All I hope for is that Oliver and I will be as happy in the next twenty-five years as we have been for the last quarter of a century and that the boys will find happiness and the independence to make their marks on the world in their own ways. As for me, I just want to continue to be true to myself, to strive for new goals and to have the inspiration to make the most of whatever path I find myself walking. After all, the highlight of my life has yet to happen. And long may that remain the case.

CHAPTER SEVENTEERN
THE MAGICAL WEST

It seems hard to believe, but it is more than seven years since I completed the final manuscript for *A Shirt Box Full of Songs*, and here we are reflecting on the time elapsed since the book was published. Some things remain the same; I still perform lots of shows every year, record new albums with my long-time collaborator and musical soul-mate Troy Donockley, and the anticipation and thrill of performing live is as strong as it has ever been. Yet when I look back, not something I often do, I can also see developments in my professional career since then.

The publication of the book in 2009 was a precursor of much treading new ground. Firstly, I found myself being invited to Book Festivals around the country, such as Wigtown in Dumfries and Galloway, The Borders Book Festival in Melrose and Lennoxlove in East Lothian, where, although I brought my guitar and sang a song or two, I also got to talk about my life and answer questions about the book and my personal philosophy. I loved attending these festivals, for as people who know me can testify to I have no problem talking at length on most subjects; it's shutting me up that's the problem! I also got the opportunity to meet authors and writers. These were more intimate affairs than my normal world and attracted a different sort of audience, and having thoroughly enjoyed my literary sojourn I began to consolidate where my musical career was going. There's some reflection required in making an account of one's life story and the book had made me think.

Ever since I became well known I have played with the backing of a band made up of various superb musicians. It is an infrastructure I love and something that I tried to keep for as long as possible, however the economics of playing festivals and smaller venues with a full band was sometimes difficult. Hence, in 2010 when I was asked to perform at Mayfest Blues and Folk Festival in Staffordshire, I was very keen to do it, as it was a chance to show some new music lovers that there was more to me than 'I Know Him So Well'. I knew that I would not be able to make it work with the full band, so I spoke to Troy and asked him 'what should I do?' and he suggested that I play the festival just with Nick Holland, our keyboard player, the two of us, for in Troy's words, together we 'could make a big noise'. As so often in my life I was not immediately convinced by Troy's suggestion, and for that matter neither was Nick, but I didn't want to miss the opportunity of playing there, so we talked ourselves into giving it a go, knowing that if it was a truly hideous experience we wouldn't do it again. It was the most beautiful day, but I was still terrified by what we had let ourselves in for. Nick had his keyboard and a vocal mic for singing, while although I also had a keyboard, for most of the set I would be out front, singing and playing guitars, very much on my own. I had been worried about the show, but we went down a storm, and as we exited the stage, me to the left, and Nick to the right, we ran round the back and gave each other one almighty hug!

Mayfest set a new template for the years ahead. Every 18 months to two years I get together to perform with Troy and the band on a full-scale tour, but in between Nick and myself will play festivals and smaller gigs wherever people want to hear us. Having the duo has been a liberating experience, with only Oliver and our sound engineer David Goodwin for company, rather than all the paraphernalia previously required and we could now perform in more intimate venues and go to more places where people could hear how good the music is and experience us live. My old folk club education talking to the crowd and being able to communicate with people had not disappeared with the years, I found to my great pleasure, during this process.

I also found confidence to play a string of dates with one of my oldest friends and musical collaborators and fellow Fifer, Rab Noakes. Rab and I may have met the best part of 50 years ago, but when we decided to play some shows together neither of us was interested in revisiting the past purely for the sake of nostalgia. With just our guitars, our voices, and some magnificent songs, we wanted to show how good the class of 1968 still was, and to our great delight the tour was very well received and so was our recording of an EP appropriately called *Reunited* with songs old and new included there.

In 2012 I was asked to return to where it all began and perform solo at a celebration at the Glen Pavilion, marking the 50th anniversary of the Dunfermline Folk Club. It was a bittersweet occasion, as the folk club's founder John Watt was seriously ill and declining in hospital and subsequently died the day after the show. On a positive note, with two of my former singing partners, Archie Fisher, and flying in from America, Jack Beck, both also set to appear, it was a night that I didn't want to miss. As part of the evening I reluctantly agreed to perform a short set with no safety net, band-wise. It was the first time in decades that I walked out on any stage alone carrying two guitars and although the circumstances of the 50th anniversary were unique, it also marked what I could do as a musician. For I realised that I did not need production for an audience to appreciate the music I was performing, although I had become well known for that, and even though I am still nervous playing without the comfort blanket of the band, the fact that I now do it, and do it well, has been a wonderful revelation.

Although we had first worked together a decade before 'Full Circle' in 2004, Troy has remained my musical touchstone. He leads the band when we play our national tours, he arranges the material that we perform live, and our collaboration has continued since the book with three further albums, *Words Unspoken* in 2009, *To Each and Everyone,* an album of Gerry Rafferty songs in 2013, and *Winter* in 2015. Because of Troy's newfound fame as a fulltime member of the hugely popular Finnish rock band Nightwish, who are stars across the world with their unique music, we are not able to get together as often as we like, but our musical relationship has if anything grown even deeper over the years and fundamental to the music that I record and perform. I really want that to continue into the future as we seem to think the same way about songs.

The album 'Winter' came about some time after Troy and I made a Christmas programme for BBC Radio Scotland. It was well received and afterwards it was suggested that we make an album of the songs, but adding to the content and widening our remit to secular songs with a winter theme, including Gerry Rafferty's 'Winter's Come'; I am glad to say that *Winter* has proved popular all year round! The success of that show also indirectly led to my being asked to present two series of programmes of mostly folk material from the BBC in Aberdeen. This was a fascinating and hugely enjoyable experience as it gave me the opportunity to discover new artists and new songs from the same folk wellspring that I had sprung decades before, and allowed me to interview and catch up with old friends such as Rab Noakes, Archie Fisher, Ian McCalman, Aly Bain, Dick Gaughan, and Isla St Clair, which was enjoyable in itself.

One of the new singers I have had the pleasure of meeting in the last seven years is a young Londoner by the name of Sam Lee. Sam has spent a lot of time with the travelling people of Britain and Ireland, collecting songs, and giving the material a lovely World Music feel. I was already a fan of his work when we met at another 50th anniversary show, this time for the TMSA (the Traditional Music and Song Association of Scotland) at Celtic Connections in Glasgow. I had first heard Sam in an extraordinary programme on BBC R4 called *'Singing with the Nightingales'*, echoing the first outside broadcast by the BBC from 1924 when the interaction with the nightingales, yes, real nightingales, was between them and a cello in a Sussex garden. The reaction to his programme prompted Sam to make a 'live' event on certain days throughout the season when the nightingales are 'in residence', a short time-frame. So when he invited me to 'sing with the nightingales', nothing was going to stop me from flying South! The plan for the evening is thus: you join Sam, who is also a wilderness expert, along with an ornithologist, and a group of people who have signed up for the experience, then a lovely campfire meal, songs and talks about wildlife and flora, before around 11pm you walk into the woods in absolute silence and in complete darkness as your eyes adjust to the moonlight. You walk and walk deeper into the woods. However, on this particular night instead of hearing the glorious sound of nightingales, we suddenly came amongst croaking noises that, before we knew it, had turned into a full frog chorus, who accompanied first Sam, then me, as we sang our chosen songs. It was a magical moment and although the birds never did turn up that Saturday, thanks to Sam I got to sing with the most unusual line-up of my career!

Performing new material live and gaining an appreciative response, even from frogs, is hugely satisfying, but I still make sure that, although I no longer sing 'I Know Him So Well' solo, as after all it is a duet, we do include 'Another Suitcase in Another Hall; 'Answer Me' and the great 'Caravans', which 36 years on is still the old song audiences most want to hear. I gained a different perspective on appreciation of my archive work, after having a conversation with someone about a terrific artist who had played a concert where he had sung nothing familiar to the audience, and they left disappointed that he had not acknowledged the songs that had brought them to see him in the first place. Therefore, I feel absolutely no dissatisfaction in singing, alongside the new material, hit records that are 30 to 40 years old. Because I am proud of that material, those songs are part of my history as a performer, and most importantly they are an integral part of the reason that people still want to come and hear me sing all these years later.

As someone who has been performing professionally for, would you believe it, almost 50 years, the longevity of a career can lead to unexpected recognition. I have been extremely fortunate and very humbled to have received awards from several educational institutions, and when I am called upon to make a speech at graduation ceremonies I always say to the young graduates if there is one thing I can pass on, it is don't do anything just for money or fame. If I reflect on my own career I can now see that I was very fortunate not to have more hit records or become an international pop star, but instead I have been able to have a long, fulfilling career where I earn a good living, have the creative freedom to record the music that I want, and have the privilege of performing to thousands of people every year, and if that doesn't feed your soul and make you want to carry on, then I don't know what does.

If I have gained recognition at home, this certainly does not apply to the U.S. After catching up with Jack Beck at the 50th anniversary of the Dunfermline Folk Club, it was Jack who asked me to come over to Virginia to play at a festival he and his wife, Wendy Welch, run at Big Stone Gap in the heart of the Appalachian Mountains, an area with a long and rich heritage of Scottish immigrants and Scottish music. In all my years of performing I had only ever played one show in America, and that was in New York in 1990 to a crowd of ex-pats, so going to Virginia for three weeks in 2014 was an adventure for me. A journey that led me to play a show at the local college campus, to an audience where nobody knew me from a bar of soap. I decided to play some of my normal set, no hits of course as I had none in the US, and so had absolutely no idea if the audience would even like me. You know me, always worried, but at the end of the hour's set, the audience gave me a standing ovation. I thought to myself 'Hell's bells, I am a 66-year old woman on my own, with just voice and guitar and this US audience has given me a fantastic reception. I must have learned something useful in the past 50 years that has rubbed off.'

One thing I have definitely learned in the last seven years, whether it be going to America or singing with Sam Lee and frogs in the middle of the Sussex countryside, is that if you are offered something that interests and intrigues you, you should embrace it. I have been part of Ian McCalman's marvellous, 'Far, Far from Ypres'. I took part, in 2015, in the centenary Radio Ballad to mark the year 1915 in regard to WW1 and sang a lovely Julie Matthews song about the sinking of the RMS *Lusitania* called 'Beautiful Day'. In 2016 I was honoured to be asked to sing 'The Flowers o' the Forest' 'a cappella', at South Queensferry, under the shadow of the iconic Forth Bridge, and in the presence of the Princess Royal and the First Minister of Scotland, to mark the centenary of The Battle of Jutland. I was delighted, at the request of John Leonard, producer of the long-running Folk on 2, to narrate *The Ballads of Child Migration* at Celtic Connections, which tells the story of the policy of enforced emigration of children that continued right up until the 1970s.

Closer to home, in 2013 John O'Hara, who is married to Oliver's sister Sally Cookson, asked me to participate in the historic Three Choirs Festival at Gloucester Cathedral. John plays keyboards for Ian Anderson and Jethro Tull, but in his own right, a marvellous musical director and a classical composer. He co-devised and composed an opera called *The Bargee's Wife* that was to be premiered at the Festival that year. Performing with operatic singers, a huge choir, and chamber orchestra was a magical experience unlike anything I had ever tried before, and since Gloucester, I have performed alongside Aly Bain and Phil Cunningham with the Royal Scottish National Orchestra, which just goes to show the unexpected and hugely rewarding opportunities that can come your way if you just have the chance, say yes and go for it. At some point in my past I would have been advised against these artistic ventures, so I am grateful to be in charge of my own destiny.

Another development that has happened in recent years is my involvement with Nordoff Robbins Scotland. I am delighted to be their Ambassador for Alzheimer's Awareness. Nordoff Robbins Music Therapy works very well for those suffering from Alzheimer's, as it's now accepted that music affects a different part of the brain from speech and language, and the first time I saw the inspiring work they do was with a severely physically disadvantaged, but completely brilliant young man called Matthew, at the Royal Blind School in Edinburgh, whose response to the power of music was startling and deeply moving for me to witness. Working with Nordoff Robbins Scotland and the Fife Society for the Blind, plus my new 2016 patronage of Headway, who help people affected by head injury in Fife, are responsibilities that I hope to take very seriously. I am aware that I am asked to help charities because I am a familiar, and as they say in Scotland, a 'weel-kent' face, and if this familiarity can assist them in their work then I am more than happy. For when I look back at the last seven years I realise that although at heart I am still the same lily-livered woman who always doubts herself, I have become much, much bolder and braver at taking on new projects if they inspire me or I feel I can positively contribute to them.

I would like to think that over my career as a singer, a musician, and an actress, I have produced a body of work worthy of recognition, and yes, it is important to me that, particularly in Scotland, I am recognised as somebody who has earned a place at the top table. I know who I am and what I have done, and when my friend and fellow Fifer Rab Noakes, who is certainly not known for hyperbolic praise, said to me, 'nobody in Scotland sings those traditional songs quite like you, Barbara' it is a wonderful compliment that appreciates the fact that I know this music, I know the people in the music, and my voice has never sung that music better. Which is why, seven years on, I am still loving it as much as I have ever done. For, of all the things that I have come to appreciate it is the joy of performing that makes me truly tick. It is who I am.

CHAPTER EIGHTEEN
WHERE I BELONG

When my mother Ruth died in 2009, Oliver, the boys and me were all living in Louth in Lincolnshire. Ruth was 90 years old when she died, and had become very frail in her final months, but she remained a very powerful personality and a huge character. My brother Alastair had flown over from his home in Canada for Ruth's 90th birthday party in 2008, a celebration that my mother had not been very keen on; by this time my mother was poorly, in a wheelchair, but her mind remained as sharp as ever, and when after the party was over she was asked 'well, that wasn't so bad, was it?', she gave a beatific smile and replied 'yes, and it wasn't so good either'. She didn't think being 90 was the least worth celebrating.

I cannot deny that my relationship with Ruth, as is the case with many mothers and daughters, was not without its ups and downs. I knew that she was inordinately proud of my career but at one time her habit of loudly announcing to fellow members of the audience that 'I'm her mother, you know' was something I found embarrassing. She always thought I didn't proclaim my greatness enough, so she would do it for me. I was my father's daughter too and showing off bothered me. However, considering I was nearly 40 before I had a family of my own, it was a blessing that Ruth was there throughout the boys' childhood, and seven years after her passing we still share Grandma anecdotes of the things she said and did. The Scouse acerbic wit is still very much with us all and her unadulterated pure love for us lives on too.

With the passage of time I have grown to realise that in some ways I am quite like my mother. I have inherited the same powerful personality and a love of music, while my brother Alastair, a talented artist in his own right, is quieter and more observant, much like our father. Compared to my mother I have been more fortunate in the opportunities that have come my way, but above all I have had that little extra energy from an early age to follow my profound desire to sing and play. I have no idea where that drive came from, but I have always been extremely grateful that it did, even though it's mixed up with a cowering wreck, quivering in the corner!

Long before my mother's death, the idea of moving back to Scotland had germinated in my mind but was obviously impossible while she was alive and frail. When I visited my close friend Yvonne Kirkus in Edinburgh, she and I, unbeknownst to Oliver, would sneak around looking at possible properties, and with the boys growing up and finishing education and scattering, the initial seed began to take root. By 2013 we were finally able to move to Edinburgh's historic New Town but only as a 'try-out' for the real thing. We had a lovely but small flat to escape to when we could manage. We also wanted to make sure that the permanent move was right for Oliver. I knew I'd be OK but would he? Things did change rapidly. Oliver became as enthusiastic as me at the prospect of moving to Edinburgh. He had always liked visiting the city, and although we discussed Liverpool, the lovely characterful place where we first met, as a possible alternative, both of our hearts were soon set on Edinburgh, where we knew more people, and unlike Louth, with easy access to trains and airport, and very importantly with glorious vistas of Fife on your doorstep! Why is it always sunny in Fife?

Edinburgh also had a special place in my heart. I had lived here in my formative years when I left home. It was where I heard that most emotive of music when I was beginning my career as a musician. And it was where I fell in love and enjoyed all the highs and made all the mistakes that you do when you were young, of which there were plenty of both. When I told Rab Noakes that I was moving back to Scotland I apologised that it was not to his adopted home town, Glasgow, a city in which I have always loved playing, to which Rab replied that he could never imagine me living in Glasgow as I was 'an Edinburgh girl'. And although I am and will always be a proud Fifer, Rab is right for it is Edinburgh where I feel at home particularly with all of its adornments and facilities.

Moving back to Edinburgh has allowed me to spend time with some of my oldest friends, such as Yvonne, Ian McCalman, Dick Gaughan, Aly Bain, Phil Cunningham, and Dolina Maclennan, many of who were around when I first lived here. It also means I can go to the rugby at Murrayfield more often, and see plays and concerts at the Lyceum, The Traverse, the Queens's Hall and the Usher Hall, which is wonderful. Oliver and I have also become parishioners at St Mary's Cathedral, where we are on the rota for reading, and every Friday I am at home I help to arrange the flowers for the altar, the size of the arrangements being something I have never tackled before. It is most fulfilling when you stand back at Mass on Sundays and look at what you have created.

Moving to Edinburgh also coincided with the Independence Referendum of 2014, which reminded me that the last time I had lived in Edinburgh there was also a strong nationalist movement, particularly amongst young people and very similar to today. Then, just as now, I have always approved of people being passionate about their national identity, but at the same time being passionate about the brotherhood of man, (not the band!) as we saw ourselves linking arms with people from all over the world. I suppose at heart I still hold that internationalist outlook, and I cannot find a national identity in the idea of separation. Yet at the same time I think that Nicola Sturgeon is a terrific First Minister and good woman, who genuinely cares and will do what is best for her fellow Scots, whatever that turns out to be.

The family has also embraced the move to Scotland. My eldest son Colm lives in London where he works in the business of constructing rock festivals and events, plus keenly songwriting, but Gabriel and Archie have both joined us in Edinburgh. Although it is still early days I can see both of them maybe putting down roots here. As for Oliver, we have been married now for 32 years, and it is far and away the best thing I ever did. There is nothing more precious, in my opinion, than waking up next to somebody who knows about you, you know about them, and you can share your life on an open and equal basis. And although we are very different we have always looked out for each other, and have always been able to communicate. I am very thankful and very fortunate that I have Oliver and the boys, for I suspect that if I had stayed single I would have become so neurotic that I would have eventually disappeared up my own backside!

It was Dick Gaughan who said to me 'the older you get, the faster you have to get on with projects, as you don't know how long you have got to do them', and as a woman of a certain age I am very aware not only of the necessity of looking after yourself as best as you can, but also looking out for others to make sure they are alright. A serious illness in 2015 prevented Rab and I from undertaking dates that year, although thankfully he is now fully recovered and once more singing up a storm and back to his old strength and powers. Long may it continue.

Sadly, some of my earliest influences are no longer with us. Both Sandy Saddler, who encouraged my love of music at school, and John Watt, who had given me my first opportunities at the Dunfermline Folk Club, are now gone, with John's death particularly poignant, as it was one day after the 50th anniversary concert of the founding of the Folk Club. Sandy and John were both pivotal figures in my early life, but the great Gerry Rafferty was a contemporary of mine, in fact Gerry, Rab Noakes and I were all born in the same year, and the announcement of Gerry's death in 2011 deeply affected me. Although Gerry could be very difficult and single-minded, and some decisions in his life were poor, particularly surrounding drink, he was a huge personality, an extraordinary talent, and at times, a loving and kind man. When he died I was selfishly upset and angry with him for giving up on his life. I just about managed to hold it together at his funeral in Paisley, but whether it was because it brought back so many memories of when we were both young and just starting out, or of some ridiculous notion that I could somehow have saved him, I just could not believe that he was no longer with us. In his final months I had tried to see him, but had been unable to do so. Somebody, undoubtedly meaning well, said that you would not have wanted to see Gerry as he approached the end, but at Paisley Abbey it was Gerry that I wanted to see and not his coffin. Even now every time I think of him I feel empty, and an inexplicable closeness that I can only compare to the relationship I have with my brother Alastair. The strangeness of relationships, eh?

I have always performed Gerry's songs, for above all he was a great songwriter, and after his death I felt that deep closeness once more. A few fans of his suggested that I record an album of Gerry's songs, but I hated the idea of being seen as somehow cashing in on his memory. I spoke to his daughter Martha, his brother Jim, and his friend and fellow son of Paisley, the artist and playwright John Byrne, all of whom convinced me that rather than cashing in, an album would contribute to keeping his work alive. I recorded *To Each and Everyone* with Troy in 2012, a hugely rewarding experience as Troy was not especially familiar with Gerry's work, and it was fascinating to see him look at Gerry's songs with fresh ears and grow to appreciate how great a songwriter he really was.

Earlier that year, Rab Noakes curated a special set of tribute concerts in Glasgow at Celtic Connections that was broadcast by the BBC. Paul Brady, Ron Sexsmith, Jack Bruce (also sadly no longer with us), and Maria Muldaur, were amongst the artists who came to sing Gerry's songs and with his family involved it was a respectful and moving occasion. I was asked to sing 'Steamboat Row', 'Wise as a Serpent' (a big favourite of Martha's), and 'Family Tree' plus 'The Ark' joining the family. The whole experience of both the concert and the album gave me the opportunity to somehow bring Gerry back to life. For every time I sing one of his songs, either with Nick, Rab, or with the band, I think of him and feel his hand on my shoulder.

My faith is very important to me, and since moving to Edinburgh, going to church has become an even more integral part of our lives. We were not sure about the Cathedral here at the first, as it is quite a dark space, but the music and the hymns are beautiful, for I am firmly of the opinion that the sanctity of the music is part of the spiritual process. Oliver and I now attend the High Mass on a Sunday at midday, and although the timing is much later than we were used to back in Lincolnshire, the Mass is conducted with all the fitting solemnity that you could hope for. We have grown to love being part of the community that surrounds the Cathedral and going to church on a Sunday has become even more of a highlight of our new lives in Edinburgh.

When I look back at the last seven years since the first publication of the book I can see that both professionally and personally it has taken me a long time to shake off the downside of the fame attached to when I was a pop star and a stage actress. For too long I was like a stuck record doing what was 'good' for my career, and doing the same things over and over again made me somehow fearful to do the things that in my heart I really wanted to do. However, in the last seven years, I have moved house, embraced performing without the safety-net of a band behind me, and have gone places and done things that I could never have imagined only a few years before. I have even sung with real frogs!

In 2017, fingers crossed, I will be 70 years old, which even more than turning 60 seems like a milestone, yet I just do not see myself as an old woman. I guess I have to be grown up now. Looking back on my charmed life I don't think there has been anybody luckier than me. The boys are well, Oliver is well, and I have never felt so sure, so confident and a spring in my step to take on whatever new, exciting projects come my way. At heart I will always be the girl from Ochil Terrace in Dunfermline whose destiny was forever changed when she failed the 11-plus and found her voice, and back where she belongs she is doing very well indeed for the present!

DISC⊕GRAPHY

◊ = Number one single
○ = Silver-selling album i.e. sold over 60,000 copies in the UK
* = Gold-selling album i.e. sold over 100,000 copies in the UK
∞ = Platinum-selling album i.e. sold over 300,000 copies in the UK

SINGLES

1974
Here Comes The Sun/The Long And Winding Road
1975
Blue Skies/Fine Feathers
1976
Answer Me/From Now On
People Get Ready/Give Me Space
Out of Love With Love/Boys From The Men
1977
Another Suitcase In Another Hall/Requiem For Evita
Lover's Serenade/High Tide
I Could Fall/He's A Fireman
1978
City To City/Benny Gee
Fallen Angel/Light As A Feather
1979
Come Back With The Same Look In Your Eyes/Sweet Oasis
Caravan Song/Caravans On The Move
1980
January February/Island In The Snow
In The Night/Now I Don't Know

It's Really You/Plane Song
1981
Only Seventeen/You Got Me
My Heart Lies/You Know It's Me
Run Like The Wind/Forgotten Time
1982
Take Good Care/Tonight
I Believe In You/I Know You, You Know Me
Barbara Dickson: 4 Track EP (Tracks: January February/Answer Me/Another Suitcase In
Another Hall/Caravan Song)

Here We Go/Tonight (Live)
Stop In The Name Of Love/Find A Better Way
1983
Tell Me It's Not True/Tonight
1984
Keeping My Love For You/Find A Better Way
Don't Believe In Miracles/You Don't Know What You Want
I Know Him So Well (with Elaine Paige)/Chess◊
1985
Still In The Game/Peter
If You're Right/Rivals
1986
We Were Never Really Out Of Love (with Johnny Mathis) (B-Side to Johnny's UK single
'Simple')
Time After Time/She Moves Thro' The Fair
1987
I Think It's Gonna Rain Today/Another Good Day For Goodbye
1988
Only A Dream In Rio/Same Sky
1989
Coming Alive Again/Dream Of You
All I Ask Of You (with Jose Carreras)/Pie Jesu
1991
Tears Of Rage (Radio Edit)/Say It From The Heart/Tears Of Rage (Album
Mix)
1992
Don't Think Twice It's All Right/Tears Of Rage
Blowin' In The Wind/You Ain't Going Nowhere/When The Ship Comes In
1995
Love Hurts/All The Pretty Little Horses

EP'S

2014
Barbara Dickson & Rab Noakes: Reunited (6 Track EP)
2017
Five Songs (5 Track EP)

ALBUMS

1969
The Fate O' Charlie (with Archie Fisher & John MacKinnon)
1970
Thro' The Recent Years (with Archie Fisher)
Do Right Woman
1972
From The Beggar's Mantle... Fringed With Gold
1976
Answer Me ○
1977
Morning Comes Quickly
1978
Sweet Oasis
1980
The Barbara Dickson Album*
1981
You Know It's Me
1982
All For A Song ∞
Here We Go - Live On Tour
1984
Heartbeats
1985
Gold ∞
1986
The Right Moment *
1987
After Dark
1989
Coming Alive Again
1992
Don't Think Twice It's Alright
1994
Parcel of Rogues
1995

Dark End of The Street
1998
The 7 Ages of Woman
2002
For The Record
2004
Full Circle
2006
Nothing's Gonna Change My World
2008
Time and Tide
2009
Barbara Dickson In Concert
2011
Words Unspoken
2013
B4 Seventy-Four: The Folk Club Tapes
To Each and Everyone – The Songs of Gerry Rafferty
2014
Winter
2016
More Brecht Than Broadway: The Complete Theatre Recordings 1974-2000

SOUNDTRACKS

1974
John, Paul, George, Ringo...& Bert (Original Liverpool Cast Recording)
1976
Evita (Original Studio Cast Recording) ∞
1979
Caravans (Original Motion Picture Score)
1985
Blood Brothers (Original London Cast Recording)
Blood Brothers: Mini Album (4 tracks from the Original
London Cast Recording)
1985
Chess (Original Studio Cast Recording) *
1992
Freddie as F.R.O.7 (Original Motion Picture Soundtrack)
2000
Spend Spend Spend (Original London Cast Recording)
Tom's Midnight Garden (Original Soundtrack)
2003
Radio Shuttleworth 2 (Series 2 of the John Shuttleworth BBC radio comedy series)

2007
The Lee Mack Show 2

BACKING VOCALS

1970
Orfeo (Archie Fisher)
1978
Changing Winds (Maddy Prior)
City To City (Gerry Rafferty)
Restless (Rab Noakes)
1979
Night Owl (Gerry Rafferty)
1980
The Midas Touch (Michael Marra)
2003
Hoovering The Moon (Willy Russell)

STAGE CREDITS

John, Paul, George, Ringo... & Bert (1974/75)
Blood Brothers (1985, 1995, 2000, 2004)
Chess (1997)
The 7 Ages Of Woman (1997, 1998)
Friends Like This (1998)
A Slice of Saturday Night (1999)
Spend Spend Spend (1999 - 2001)
Fame (2005)

TELEVISION

Taggart (1995)
Band of Gold (1995 - 1996)
The Missing Postman (1997)
Doctors (2008)

FILM

Sgt Pepper's Lonely Hearts Club Band (1978)
Redemption Road (2001)

RADIO

Dinner Ladies (1997)
Whenever (2006)

ACTING AWARDS

The Society of West End Theatre Award: Best Actress In A Musical for Mrs Johnstone in Blood Brothers (1985)
Liverpool Echo Award: Best Actress in Theatre for The 7 Ages of Woman (1997)
Variety Club Award: Best Actress in A Musical for Viv Nicholson in Spend Spend Spend (2000)
Olivier Award: Best Actress in a Musical for Viv Nicholson in Spend Spend Spend (2000)

OTHER AWARDS

1985: 'Scot of The Year' (Daily Record)
1999: Honorary Master's Degree (University of Lincoln)
2001: Made an OBE by Her Majesty The Queen in the New Year's Honours List for 'Services To Music And Drama'
2005: Made a Companion of the Liverpool Institute for Performing Arts (LIPA) by Sir Paul McCartney
2005: Honorary Fellowship from Liverpool's John Moores University for Services to Music and the Dramatic Arts
2010: Honorary Doctor of Music (from Aberdeen's Robert Gordon University)
2012: Honorary Doctor of Music (from the Royal Conservatoire of Scotland)
2012: Scottish Tartan Clef Sir Reo Stakis Pride of Scotland Lifetime Achievement Award
2014: Honorary Doctor of Music (from the University of Lincoln)
2016: Scottish Variety Awards 'Outstanding Scottish Achievement Award'
2016: Scots Trad Awards: Lifetime Achievement Award

GONZO Books

There is still such a thing as alternative Publishing

Robert Newton Calvert: Born 9 March 1945, Died 14 August 1988 after suffering a heart attack. Contributed poetry, lyrics and vocals to legendary space rock band Hawkwind intermittently on five of their most critically acclaimed albums, including Space Ritual (1973), Quark, Strangeness & Charm (1977) and Hawklords (1978). He also recorded a number of solo albums in the mid 1970s. CENTIGRADE 232 was Robert Calvert's first collection of poems.

Hype   'And now, for all you speeding street smarties out there, the one you've all been waiting for, the one that'll pierce your laid back ears, decoke your sinuses, cut clean thru the schlock rock, MOR/crossover, techno flash mind mush. It's the new Number One with a bullet … with a bullet … It's Tom, Supernova, Mahler with a pan galactic biggie …' And the Hype goes on. And on. Hype, an amphetamine hit of a story by Hawkwind collaborator Robert Calvert. Who's been there and made it back again. The debriefing session starts here.

Rick Wakeman is the world's most unusual rock star, a genius who has pushed back the barriers of electronic rock. He has had some of the world's top orchestras perform his music, has owned eight Rolls Royces at one time, and has broken all the rules of composing and horrified his tutors at the Royal College of Music. Yet he has delighted his millions of fans. This frank book, authorised by Wakeman himself, tells the moving tale of his larger than life career.

There are nine Henrys, pur ported to be the world's first cloned cartoon charac ter. They live in a strange lo fi domestic surrealist world peopled by talking rock buns and elephants on wobbly stilts.

They mooch around in their minimalist universe suffer ing from an existential crisis with some genetically modified humour thrown in.

Marty Wilde on Terry Dene: "Whatever happened to Terry becomes a great deal more comprehensible as you read of the callous way in which he was treated by people who should have known better many of whom, frankly, will never know better of the sad little shadows of the past who eased themselves into Terry's life, took everything they could get and, when it seemed that all was lost, quietly left him … Dan Wood ing's book tells it all."

Rick Wakeman: "There have always been certain 'careers' that have fascinated the public, newspapers, and the media in general. Such include musicians, actors, sportsmen, police, and not surprisingly, the people who give the police their employ ment: The criminal. For the man in the street, all these careers have one thing in common: they are seemingly beyond both his reach and, in many cases, understanding and as such, his only associ ation can be through the media of newspapers or tele vision. The police, however, will always require the ser vices of the grass, the squealer, the snitch, (call him what you will), in order to assist in their investiga tions and arrests; and amaz ingly, this is the area that seldom gets written about."

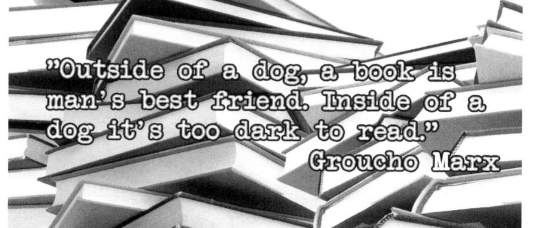

"Outside of a dog, a book is man's best friend. Inside of a dog it's too dark to read."
Groucho Marx

Bill Harkleroad joined Captain Beef heart's Magic Band at a time when they were changing from a straight ahead blues band into something completely dif ferent. Through the vision of Don Van Vliet (Captain Beefheart) they created a new form of music which many at the time considered atonal and difficult, but which over the years has continued to exert a powerful influence. Beefheart re christened Harkleroad as Zoot Horn Rollo, and they embarked on recording one of the classic rock albums of all time Trout Mask Replica - a work of unequalled daring and inventiveness.

Politics, paganism and .... Vlad the Impaler. Selected stories from CJ Stone from 2003 to the present. Meet Ivor Coles, a British Tommy killed in action in September 1915, lost, and then found again. Visit Mothers Club in Erdington, the best psyche delic music club in the UK in the '60s. Celebrate Robin Hood's Day and find out what a huckle duckle is. Travel to Stonehenge at the Summer Solstice and carouse with the hippies. Find out what a Ranter is, and why CJ Stone thinks that he's one. Take LSD with Dr Lilly, the psychedelic scientist. Meet a headless soldier or the ghost of Elvis Presley in Gabalfa, Cardiff. Journey to Whitstable, to New York, to Malta and to Transylvania, and to many other places, real and imagined, polit ical and spiritual, transcendent and mundane. As The Independent says, Chris is "The best guide to the underground since Charon ferried dead souls across the Styx."

This is is the first in the highly acclaimed vampire novels of the late Mick Farren. Victor Renquist, a surprisingly urbane and likable leader of a colony of vampires which has existed for centuries in New York is faced with both admin istrative and emotional prob lems. And when you are a vampire, administration is not a thing which one takes lightly.

"The person, be it gentleman or lady, who has not pleasure in a good novel, must be intolerably stupid."

Jane Austen

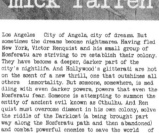

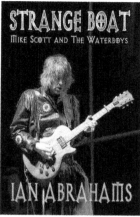

Los Angeles   City of Angels, city of dreams. But sometimes the dreams become nightmares. Having fled New York, Victor Renquist and his small group of Nosferatu are striving to re establish their colony. They have become a deeper, darker part of the city's nightlife. And Hollywood's glitterati are hot on the scent of a new thrill, one that outshines all others   immortality. But someone, somewhere, is med dling with even darker powers, powers that even the Nosferatu fear. Someone is attempting to summon the entity of ancient evil known as Cthulhu. And Ren quist must overcome dissent in his own colony, solve the riddle of the Darklost (a being brought part way along the Nosferatu path and then abandoned) and combat powerful enemies to save the world   of humans!

Canadian born Corky Laing is probably best known as the drummer with Mountain. Corky joined the band shortly after Mountain played at the famous Woodstock Festival, although he did receive a gold disc for sales of the soundtrack album after over dubbing drums on Ten Years After's performance. Whilst with Mountain Corky Laing recorded three studio albums with them before the band split. Follow ing the split Corky, along with Mountain gui tarist Leslie West, formed a rock three piece with former Cream bassist Jack Bruce. West, Bruce and Laing recorded two studio albums and a live album before West and Laing re formed Mountain, along with Felix Pappalardi. Since 1974 Corky and Leslie have led Mountain through various line ups and recordings, and continue to record and perform today at numer ous concerts across the world. In addition to his work with Mountain, Corky Laing has recorded one solo album and formed the band Cork with former Spin Doctors guitarist Eric Shenkman, and recorded a further two studio albums with the band, which has also featured former Jimi Hendrix bassist Noel Redding. The stories are told in an incredibly frank, engaging and amusing manner, and will appeal also to those people who may not necessarily be fans of

To me there's no difference between Mike Scott and The Waterboys; they both mean the same thing. They mean myself and whoever are my current travel ling musical companions." Mike Scott Strange Boat charts the twisting and meandering journey of Mike Scott, describing the literary and spiritual references that inform his songwriting and explor ing the multitude of locations and cultures in which The Waterboys have assembled and reflected in their recordings. From his early forays into the music scene in Scotland at the end of the 1970s, to his creation of a 'Big Music' that peaked with the hit single 'The Whole of the Moon' and onto the Irish adventure which spawned the classic Fisher man's Blues, his constantly restless creativity has led him through a myriad of changes. With his revolving cast of troubadours at his side, he's created some of the most era defining records of the 1980s, reeled and jigged across the Celtic heartlands, reinvented himself as an electric rocker in New York, and sought out personal renewal in the spiritual calm of Findhorn's Scot tish highland retreat. Mike Scott's life has been a tale of continual musical exploration entwined with an ever evolving spirituality. "An intriguing portrait of a modern musician" (Record Collector).

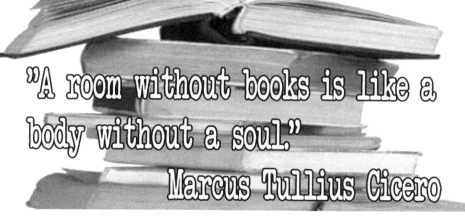

The OZ trial was the longest obscenity trial in history. It was also one of the worst reported. With minor exceptions, the Press chose to rewrite what had occurred, presumably to fit in with what seemed to them the acceptable prejudices of the times. Perhaps this was inevitable. The proceedings dragged on for nearly six weeks in the hot summer of 1971 when there were, no doubt, a great many other events more worthy of attention. Against the background of murder in Ulster, for example, the OZ affair probably fades into its proper insignifi cance. Even so, after the trial, when some newspapers realised that maybe something important had hap pened, it became more and more apparent that what was essential was for anyone who wished to be able to read what had actually been said. Trial and judgment by a badly informed press became the order of the day. This 40th Anniversary edition includes new material by all three of the original defendants, the prosecuting barrister, one of the OZ schoolkids, and even the daughters of the judge. There are also many illustrations including unseen material from Felix Dennis' own collection...

Merrell Fankhauser has led one of the most diverse and interesting careers in music. He was born in Louisville, Kentucky, and moved to California when he was 13 years old. Merrell went on to become one of the innovators of surf music and psychedelic folk rock. His travels from Hollywood to his 15 year jungle experience on the island of Maui have been documented in numerous music books and magazines in the United States and Europe. Merrell has gained legendary international status throughout the field of rock music; his credits include over 250 songs published and released. He is a multi talented singer/songwriter and unique guitar player whose sound has delighted listeners for over 35 years. This extraordi nary book tells a unique story of one of the founding fathers of surf rock, who went on to play in a succession of progressive and psychedelic bands and to meet some of the greatest names in the business, including Captain Beefheart, Randy California, The Beach Boys, Jan and Dean... and there is even a run in with the notorious Manson family.

On September 19, 1985, Frank Zappa testified before the United States Senate Commerce, Technology, and Transportation committee, attacking the Parents Music Resource Center or PMRC, a music organization co founded by Tipper Gore, wife of then senator Al Gore. The PMRC consisted of many wives of politi cians, including the wives of five members of the committee, and was founded to address the issue of song lyrics with sexual or satanic content. Zappa saw their activities as on a path towards censor ship and called their proposal for voluntary labelling of records with explicit content "extor tion" of the music industry. This is what happened.

"Good friends, good books, and a sleepy conscience: this is the ideal life."
Mark Twain

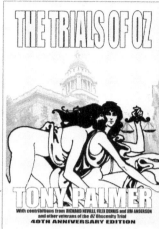

The OZ trial was the longest obscenity trial in history. It was also one of the worst reported. With minor exceptions, the Press chose to rewrite what had occurred, presumably to fit in with what seemed to them the acceptable prejudices of the times. Perhaps this was inevitable. The proceedings dragged on for nearly six weeks in the hot summer of 1971 when there were, no doubt, a great many other events more worthy of attention. Against the background of murder in Ulster, for example, the OZ affair probably fades into its proper insignifi canoe. Even so, after the trial, when some newspapers realised that maybe something important had hap pened, it became more and more apparent that what was essential was for anyone who wished to be able to read what had actually been said. Trial and judgment by a badly informed press became the order of the day. This 40th Anniversary edition includes new material by all three of the original defendants, the prosecuting barrister, one of the OZ schoolkids, and even the daughters of the judge. There are also many illustrations including unseen material from Felix Dennis' own collection...

Merrell Fankhauser has led one of the most diverse and interesting careers in music. He was born in Louisville, Kentucky, and moved to California when he was 13 years old. Merrell went on to become one of the innovators of surf music and psychedelic folk rock. His travels from Hollywood to his 15 year jungle experience on the island of Maui have been documented in numerous music books and magazines in the United States and Europe. Merrell has gained legendary international status throughout the field of rock music; his credits include over 250 songs published and released. He is a multi talented singer/songwriter and unique guitar player whose sound has delighted listeners for over 35 years. This extraordi nary book tells a unique story of one of the founding fathers of surf rock, who went on to play in a succession of progressive and psychedelic bands and to meet some of the greatest names in the business, including Captain Beefheart, Randy California, The Beach Boys, Jan and Dean... and there is even a run in with the notorious Manson family.

On September 19, 1985, Frank Zappa testified before the United States Senate Commerce, Technology, and Transportation committee, attacking the Parents Music Resource Center or PMRC, a music organization co founded by Tipper Gore, wife of then senator Al Gore. The PMRC consisted of many wives of politi cians, including the wives of five members of the committee, and was founded to address the issue of song lyrics with sexual or satanic content. Zappa saw their activities as on a path towards censor shipand called their proposal for voluntary labelling of records with explicit content "extor tion" of the music industry. This is what happened.

"Good friends, good books, and a sleepy conscience: this is the ideal life." Mark Twain

Lightning Source UK Ltd.
Milton Keynes UK
UKOW05f1809260117

292976UK00001B/1/P